A BEAT AROUND THE BUSH

First published in 2003 by

WOODFIELD PUBLISHING
Bognor Regis, West Sussex, England
www.woodfieldpublishing.com

© Alastair Tompkins, 2003

ISBN 1-873203-94-2

A Beat
around the
Bush

MEMOIRS OF A KENYA POLICEMAN 1953-1963

Alastair Tompkins

Woodfield

The Author in the uniform of the Kenya Police.

CONTENTS

~ ~ ~

To my cousin Vic who suggested that I should write this book
and to my wife Pauline without whose dedication
it would never have come to fruition.

~ ~ ~

Jim Duffy, who came to my aid at the American Mission (see page 47).

On patrol. Checking cattle for obliterated brands (see page 91).

FOREWORD

Throughout this book I have used a mixture of pseudonyms and real names and very few places have been identified in order to avoid causing embarrassment or distress to any persons concerned. If they read this book I am sure they will recognise themselves or the other persons involved and I trust that despite the passage of time, the facts contained within this narrative will not be in dispute.

It is important to understand that the Kenya Police, like so many other Colonial Police Forces, was paramilitary. The disciplinary procedures, drill and arms instructions will be instantly recognised by anyone who has served in the armed forces. The major difference was that they were also policemen who went about their everyday duties normally unarmed and, like any Police Force, charged with maintaining order and upholding the law.

In these days of so-called 'political correctness', the term 'colonial' has taken on connotations of oppression and even racism that, to my mind, are wholly unjustified. We upheld one rule of law and it was applied irrespective of race, creed, or colour, as I believe the stories contained in this book will illustrate.

In contrast, the people of many former African colonies have suffered since the departure of the British, corruption has become rife, thousands of innocent people have been slaughtered and no-one has been brought to justice.

Alastair Tompkins
Crowthorne, Berkshire, 2003

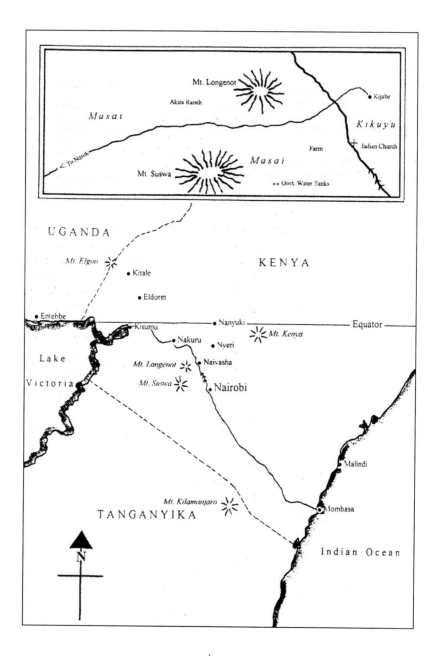

Preface

This book is about Kenya, East Africa, and events long since past, that to the older generation are now distant memories and to the younger generation a period of recent history about which they have no knowledge whatsoever. In order for the reader to understand the full content of this book it is necessary to become acquainted with certain facts. The period covered is from 1953 to 1963 and is based, in the main, on the actual experiences of the author, who served during this period as a Colonial Police Officer. At this time the Crown Colony of Kenya was still young compared to others (for example, West Africa) and had only been in existence for just over sixty years.

In the latter part of the 19th century, British pioneers began to arrive at Mombasa on the Kenya coast. They found a land teeming with game of every description, a climate that varied from high humidity on the coast to pleasant sub-tropical in the hinterland. They encountered savage tribes who were constantly at war with one another, Arab slave traders, malaria and numerous other tropical diseases. Within a short time the Arab slave traders had been crushed and a rule of law established. A single track railway was begun in 1896 and extended from Mombasa to the fledgling city of Nairobi, situated some three hundred miles inland at an altitude of 6,000 feet. Within a period of five years the line had reached the shores of Lake Victoria, a total distance of 582 miles.

From 1914 until 1918 Britain was at war with Germany and the men of the Colony fought a long and bloody campaign in the bush against the Germans who, at that time, controlled Tanganyika (now Tanzania). Following the war the British Government encouraged ex-servicemen to emigrate to this new Colony to assist with its development.

It attracted people with a true pioneering spirit who were prepared to work hard and live rough in order to carve out a future for themselves and their descendants from the virgin bush. Some prospered; some died from tropical diseases and others, due to drought, cattle disease or the 1929 depression, lost everything they had.

As long as man could remember there had existed a 'no-mans land' between the various tribes, and in particular between the Masai and the Kikuyu. The Masai are cattle people, nomadic, tough and skilled in battle. Long before the arrival of the British they had driven the Kikuyu into the hills and, as a result, the Kikuyu had become agriculturist. The only reason for either tribe to enter into this 'no-go-area' was to carry out inter-tribal warfare. These were bloody affairs, the victors (normally the Masai) killing both young and old, and only sparing young girls, who were taken as wives. The only creatures they never, ever killed were the cattle, as these they prized above all else.

In order to prevent this constant bloodshed the British Government established – in what was seen as non-native land – a string of European farms between the various tribes to act as a buffer zone; a move that proved highly effective.

In view of subsequent events it is interesting to note that in 1923 the British Government issued a 'White Paper' that stated:

> "The interests of the native population are paramount and, if ever these interests should clash with those of the immigrant races, the interests of the indigenous population must prevail."

The Kikuyu had a method of land ownership that transcended any logic. Upon the death of a father with two sons, each son inherited half his father's land. When they in turn died, and if they had two sons, each would inherit a quarter of their grandfather's original holding. With a rising population, plus this constant sub-division, within very few years there was extreme pressure within the Kikuyu Reserve for more land, which didn't exist.

Following the second World War and the arrival of more ex-service personnel and others from Britain, plus the development of mechanical farming devices and improved farming methods, the European farms in what was then known as 'The White Highlands' became productive beyond all recognition. Crops such as tea and coffee, together with other foodstuffs, became major exports. Dairy products were put on a proper commercial footing. An efficient railway network connected the coast via Nairobi to Kisumu on the edge of Lake Victoria, to Uganda and Tanganyika. Nairobi had a first-class airport, the Civil Service was efficient, law and order existed. It was a prosperous time and no one of any race, creed, or colour went hungry.

Within the Kikuyu Reserve (for reasons already stated) with the passage of years some plots of land had reached minuscule proportions. A plot some ten feet by thirty feet or less was not unknown. On their boundaries the Kikuyu saw large tracts of land, well farmed, prosperous and European-owned. Many Kikuyu worked on these farms in various capacities, ranging from farm labourers, house servants, cooks, tractor drivers and supervisors. Despite their absence from the Reserve, this did little or nothing to ease the pressure for land. But where could it be found? The answer to some was to annex the European farms. Amongst the Kikuyu tribe a secret society was formed and named 'Mau-Mau'. The intention was to oust the European farmers by force. The instigator was one Jomo Kenyatta, who was later arrested and convicted for his crimes, but nevertheless upon the cessation of British rule in 1963 he became Kenya's first African President.

The Kikuyu had always been a people deeply involved in what we would term 'witchcraft'. There was a common belief that some old women could, at night, transform themselves into hyenas. Tribal ceremonies involving some form of sacrifice, e.g. slaughtering a chicken and drinking its blood, were seen by the participants as having a deep, almost religious significance, and oaths not to reveal the detail of such ceremonies were completely and utterly binding.

The Mau-Mau took advantage of these deeply rooted beliefs and oaths were devised that involved ceremonies quite revolting to Western sensibilities (e.g. the use of menstrual blood) and which were so binding that to reveal any part to an outsider would result in death. One of the more mild initiation oaths was, "If I am asked to bring the little finger of my father or mother I will do so." It was not unknown for a daughter to help to kill her own father on Mau-Mau instructions.

Two 'wings' of Mau-Mau were formed, the 'Passive Wing' and the 'Army Wing'. The job of the Passive Wing was to supply the Army Wing with supplies, food, money and intelligence. The Army Wing started to amass men in the forest in large numbers. Some Mau-Mau gangs contained at least 300 men being made ready to attack the local European population, and in particular the farmers. The oathing of Kikuyu farm workers, who in many instances were trusted employees of the European farmers, began in earnest, as they were able to supply intelligence in respect of the best time to attack their employers, and where the farm rifles and shotguns were stored.

During the latter part of 1951 several small-scale attacks on farms took place, often assisted by trusted Kikuyu employees, resulting in some European farmers and their wives being killed. By 1952 the scale of Mau-Mau activity had reached such proportions that the Governor had to declare a 'State of Emergency'.

During 1952 a Divisional Police Headquarters at Naivasha was attacked, the unprepared police guards killed and a large quantity of arms and ammunition taken. In March 1953, during one attack on a village of their own people who had refused to support them, a Mau-Mau gang slaughtered every inhabitant and hamstrung all the cattle. It became known as the 'Lari Massacre'. This wanton butchering of innocent people revolted even the Kikuyu. As a result, many of them formed themselves into 'Home Guard' units and took an active part, not only in defending their families, but also taking a pro-active role alongside the security forces.

All credit must be given to the European farmers, who often lived on isolated farms many miles from any possible help if they were attacked. They were determined that the farms that they, or their fathers, had created from virgin bush would not be surrendered due to the threat of violence. They had 'guts' and were prepared to stay and fight, often against incredible odds. They stood firm, and sadly, despite their indomitable spirit, some paid with their lives.

The British Government sent British Army units to assist the local police and army, who by now were at 'full stretch'. In addition to this force, they decided that the number of European police officers had to be increased and an advertising campaign in the British press began. Twenty-three thousand applications were received and of these only six hundred were selected. Following a hastily constructed induction programme, most of these officers were engaged on anti-terrorist activities.

With the defeat of Mau-Mau during the latter part of 1956, a large percentage of these officers remained within the Kenya Police and they continued to serve in a force that had managed to cope with an amazing diversity of tasks, that was proud of its heritage, its ability, and standing within the multi-racial society of Kenya.

The author was one such officer....

1   Strange how things can happen

Eighteen-year-olds in post-war Britain had to serve for a period of two years 'National Service' in one of the armed forces, to ensure that, in the event of future hostilities, the nation would have a large reserve of trained service personnel which could quickly be mobilised.

My choice was the Royal Air Force. As a teenager I had joined the Air Cadets, which had given me and many others pre-exposure to Air Force life and weekend flights in aircraft such as Oxfords and Ansons.

Real RAF life was to prove somewhat different. We earned very little and the food, although plentiful, was not 'like mother used to make'. We were often stationed in out-of-the-way places and, if the inhabitants will forgive me, Yatesbury in Wiltshire was one such place.

Some weekends we were free for just forty-eight hours and normally would use this time to hitch-hike home, in many instances a hundred miles or more away; I would normally 'hitch' with my friend Dennis Tuttle, who lived at least thirty miles beyond my destination. Being in uniform it was not difficult to obtain lifts in those days, and we would ride on anything that progressed us towards home. On one occasion we even used the services of the local dustcart to get us through a town to its outskirts, where obtaining a more salubrious lift would be easier. Our best ever lift was in a chauffeur-driven Rolls Royce.

It was during one such weekend that we were given a lift in a brand new Riley motor car, the owner of which was sun-tanned to a much greater degree than could have been acquired during an English Summer. I remarked on this and he said he was from Southern Rhodesia (now Zimbabwe). Naturally, this triggered many questions, such as, "What is it like?" "How long have you lived there?" and finally, "What do you do there?"

He said he was a Police Officer. This triggered yet more questions from both Dennis and myself. It sounded like a fascinating job...

"How old do you have to be to join and what qualifications do you need?"

"The minimum age is 22 and you must have School Certificate,[1] which must include English and Maths."

Apart from age, Dennis and I were both eligible to apply. The thought of being a police officer in Africa stayed with me and, without realising it, this man from Rhodesia had planted a seed in my mind which would take very little to be activated later.

Following my two years with the RAF I returned to my job as a trainee cartographer. I enjoyed the work because it involved, for part of the time, being outside the office and carrying out survey duties before returning to translate these details onto maps. I was the youngest member of staff, the atmosphere was convivial and the head draughtsman congenial – provided you did your job to his satisfaction. The pay was not fantastic, but nevertheless considerably more than my RAF pittance.

Each day I purchased the *Daily Telegraph* and, purely out of curiosity, would scan the 'situations vacant' section. It always contained vacancies for managerial posts with salaries far in excess of my own, but it was really a pointless exercise as I was not well enough qualified or old enough to apply for any of them. Then one day a large boxed advertisement caught my eye. It was for police officers in Kenya. It stipulated the educational qualifications (I qualified), the minimum height requirement (I just qualified) and said that having served in the armed forces would be an advantage. The minimum age was twenty-two (I qualified again, on both counts).

The local library was within walking distance of my office, and that very lunchtime I obtained a book about Kenya. It sounded fascinating and I determined that yes, I would apply! The advertisement stipulated that a *Curriculum Vitae* had to be included with the letter of application and someone at the office very kindly offered to help me with its compilation. With this done, I sent off my letter and waited…

A whole week passed before a reply arrived. It came in a brown envelope from the Crown Agents, Millbank, London. It contained an official application form and requested that I return it as soon as possible, together with two references. Having obtained these I posted it a week later.

---

[1] This was the national 5th year Grammar School examination at the time.

Within days I received a reply. I had been invited for an interview!

I explained to the head draughtsman about my application, he was very understanding and wished me well. My interview was at the Crown Agents in London at 10.00am. The night before I pressed my best suit, gave my shoes an extra shine and chose a sombre business-like tie and white shirt.

I well recall boarding the morning London-bound train and entering a carriage that was full of businessmen. I occupied the only vacant seat, whereupon there was much huffing and shaking of Telegraphs and Times; apparently I was occupying a space always used by a 'regular' commuter. He arrived some moments later, and his cheery morning greeting froze on his lips when he saw I was occupying his seat.

"Oh... mm... oh..." he muttered, seemingly lost for words. Then, "See you chaps at the other end."

It appeared I had stumbled upon some form of businessmen's club and my arrival had disturbed their morning ritual, which, I discovered, consisted initially of an interchange of polite conversation, but once the train had left the platform they became deeply engrossed in their newspapers and daily crossword puzzles. Conversation ceased and I travelled all the way to London feeling like an outcast.

To me, London was always exciting. As a young child I had often been taken there by one of my Aunts and always on the 'Pullman' train. It was very smart with brown and cream livery. Each carriage contained tables with small electric table lamps on them, each table being covered with immaculate white, starched linen. The all-male staff were dressed in black trousers and shoes and short white jackets with blue coloured lapels. They addressed everyone as 'Sir' or 'Madam' and I was always addressed as 'Young Sir'. With the passage of time I cannot recall why, but I always asked for ham sandwiches, which arrived on a plate covered with a paper serviette. The sandwiches were cut into small quarters without crusts on them and adorned with a sprig of parsley. They were always delicious.

At this time in the morning Victoria Station was full of hustle and bustle. Everyone except me appeared to know where they were going. Suddenly I saw the sign for taxis. I realised it would be expensive, but I was unsure which bus to catch and I had never been on the 'Underground'. I joined the queue of businessmen waiting for taxis, most of whom wore bowler hats, and despite the fact it was a bright sunny day, carried rolled umbrellas. I was now at the head of the queue. The taxi stopped and the driver leaned across towards me.

"Where to guv'nor?"

"The Crown Agents, Millbank please."

"Right-o guv'nor."

And I was on my way…

Looking out of the taxi's window it was fascinating to see the red London buses, the number of black taxi cabs, the sheer number of people on the pavements, crossing roads; everyone appeared to be in a hurry.

"Right guv'nor, the Crown Agents. He glanced at the meter. "That'll be three and sixpence."

I included a tip and gave the taxi driver four shillings.

With an enthusiastic "Thanks guv'nor!" he drove off and I was alone outside a grey, imposing building with steps leading up to large swing doors. As I was about to enter, a tall, bronzed man emerged, carrying a crocodile-skin briefcase and wearing suede desert boots. I found it difficult not to stare; he must be a 'colonial'!

Inside the entrance was a pair of huge crossed elephant tusks, marble floors and highly polished woodwork. An elderly man dressed in a smart blue uniform with brass buttons, and wearing a white covered blue-peaked hat with a wide gleaming black leather belt across his chest, interrupted my thoughts.

"Can I help you Sir?"

"Yes, I have come for an interview about the Kenya Police."

"Right Sir, up the stairs to the second landing, take the second door on the right at the top of the stairs. It's clearly marked."

I could feel my heart thumping in my chest and hoped that my nervousness wouldn't show. I opened the door, to be greeted by a secretary and asked to take a seat. One other person was in the room. We smiled at each other as I picked up a magazine, it was the 'Tatler'. I had never read a copy of it before and its cover looked very sophisticated. A young man came out from the office beyond the secretary and my companion was called in. My eyes were blind to the pictures and the words before me. What would they ask? I checked that I still had my 'School Certificate' in an envelope in my inside jacket pocket, together with a reference from my boss.

Some ten minutes later my companion appeared, nodding to me as he left. The telephone on the secretary's desk buzzed. She lifted the receiver, listened, nodded her head, then looked up at me, smiled, and said, "Please go in," then gestured towards the door to the right of her desk.

This was 'it'! Behind a large desk were three middle-aged men. They greeted me, we shook hands and I was invited to sit down. Now should I cross my legs, or have my feet together, and what should I do with my arms? I realised that I should have thought about this when waiting in the anteroom. The questions began.

"Why do you want to join the Kenya Police?"

I mentioned my past encounter with the Rhodesian Police Officer.

"What do you know about Kenya?"

I had always enjoyed history at Grammar School so it was not difficult for me to quote facts and figures from the library book.

"… and how about the Mau-Mau situation? What do you know about that?"

I quoted from some of the reports and articles from the *Daily Telegraph*.

Finally, I was asked if it was my intention to make a career with the Kenya Police.

I hoped I had made suitable replies to all their questions. As requested, I produced my 'School Certificate' and asked if it was in order to show them my additional reference.

Further questions followed regarding my current job and what prompted me to leave a position that I enjoyed.

Did I have any questions?

I cannot recall what they were, but my interviewers seemed satisfied. They looked at each other.

"Well young man, you seem well-informed and have the right credentials. You will now have to pass a medical examination, and, if successful, you will be hearing from us very shortly. The lady outside will direct you where to go."

We shook hands and I exited in a daze – I had been selected!

The doctor occupied a large office. Following the usual examination and eye test he said, "I want you to go behind that curtain in the corner and fill this for me." He handed me a small glass test tube. Behind the curtain and right in the corner was a bucket that already contained liquid from several over enthusiastic suppliers. I returned and handed him my offering.

"I apologise for the crudeness of the facilities, which are no doubt far worse that anything you will encounter in Africa. You can wash your hands over there."

I exited into brilliant sunlight feeling elated and excited and hailed a passing cab. "Victoria Station please."

There and then I decided, to hell with the extra expense, I would return home by Pullman train and order ham sandwiches!

The letter duly arrived. I had been accepted for a two-year probationary period as a Kenya Police Officer! The salary, to my eyes, was huge and I was sure it must exceed the figure earned by my present boss. The letter advised me to contact my doctor to have 'yellow fever', 'smallpox' and TAB injections, also to ensure that my passport was in order. Further details regarding my departure date would follow in due course. I now tendered my resignation and awaited developments.

The first development was my visit to the doctor. Initially I was inoculated against 'yellow fever' and 'smallpox'. A week later I had my first TAB injection, which was into both forearms. The doctor said, "You are to go home and go to bed immediately. The effects of this injection can be very severe."

"I can't do that," I replied. "I'm going out on a survey this afternoon."

The doctor looked very stern.

"You are not going back to work young man, you are going home and going to bed!"

I caught the bus home and arrived at the front door with two forearms that felt very tender and were swelling rapidly by the minute. I felt very hot and had a headache. I spent the next two days in bed, sometimes feeling hot then suddenly shivering. The only thing I felt like was cold fluids, interspersed with hot water bottles. My forearms were like two 'puffballs', and it was agony if I bumped them when turning over in bed. My next T.A.B. injection took place ten days later. This time I did not need any telling. I arrived home as quickly as possible, feeling far worse than before, collapsed into bed and stayed there for another two days.

My final letter arrived. It gave my departure date and contained my air ticket. It also contained a booklet about tropical hygiene and tropical diseases, stressing the need to commence taking the anti-malarial drug Paludrine at least four weeks prior to my departure. The final item was a list of suitable clothing that should be purchased in the

United Kingdom, plus another list of clothing that could be obtained much cheaper in Kenya. As I sat there reading the details over and over again, and despite the fact that this letter confirmed my departure date, it was difficult to imagine that I would soon be in East Africa.

On my final day at work, all the staff from the various offices gathered to wish me farewell. Then following the General Manager's speech, I was handed a leather-bound gentleman's companion set. It contained a hairbrush, comb, razor, soap container, a container for talc, and a small stainless steel mirror. Inside was a card wishing me well from all members of staff. It was an appropriate and not inexpensive gift which I used for many years. I made my speech of thanks saying (which was true) how much I had enjoyed working there. Everyone clapped, the glasses of sherry were issued and my new life was about to begin.

I said goodbye to my family and friends. I recall hugging my young sister and telling her not to cry, as I was not going away for ever, and I would see her again when I returned home on leave. The most poignant farewell was with my Grandmother. She held me close and said, "we will not see each other again."

"Don't be silly Grandma, of course we will," I said, but I had a lump in my throat as I left her room.

She died eighteen months after my departure.

2   Into the unknown

Nowadays, whenever I visit Heathrow Airport to meet an overseas visitor or to go on holiday, I find it difficult to picture it as it was in 1953 when I arrived early in the morning to catch my British Overseas Airways Corporation (BOAC) flight to Nairobi. At that time, most of the buildings consisted of ex-government Nissen huts – prefabricated buildings constructed of curved sheets of corrugated metal to form a long, semi-cylindrical tunnel. Inside the section I entered, the floors were covered in highly polished light brown linoleum and uncomfortable-looking, cloth-covered chairs with wooden arms were the only seats provided for the public. It reminded me of my RAF days, which was not surprising; Heathrow had been used by the RAF during World War II, which had ended just seven years previously.

The aircraft that I and my fellow recruits were to fly in was an 'Argonaut', built by Canadair and powered by four petrol engines, with a tricycle undercarriage. It was then BOAC's major long-distance aircraft. By today's standards it was tiny, having only fifty-six seats, set two and three abreast down each side of the passenger cabin. Partly due to lack of payload and fuel capacity, the aircraft would be landing at Rome, Cairo, Khartoum, Entebbe and finally Nairobi.

Having checked in my baggage and cleared passport control, I made my way to the departure lounge. Even without any introductions, it was not difficult to pick out the Kenya Police recruits. They were all about my age and, like me, had contracted the excitement of our new adventure – and it showed! There were lots of introductions, handshakes, exchanges of names or nicknames and drinks at the bar. We shared a common bond, a common spirit and a common enthusiasm. Within less than seventy-two hours we would be formed into a new recruit-training cadre at a place we had never heard of, Gilgil in the Rift Valley of Kenya. But all of this was yet to unfold.

Soon it was time to board the aircraft and commence our journey towards a land that would be our home for the next three years.

In 1953 the vast volume of tourist traffic encountered today at any airport didn't exist. The cost of flying was prohibitive to the 'man in the street' and here in the UK the standard family holiday was not yet on the Costa Brava but at the English seaside. Places such as Brighton, Bognor, Weymouth, Blackpool, Redcar and all the other seaside towns flourished, so unlike today when most are shadows of their former selves. I, and I am sure the major percentage of my new-found colleagues, had never flown in a civilian airliner. It was all very new and exciting.

Today's civilian jet airliners power down the runway and climb at a steep angle into the sky, but the piston-engined aircraft of the fifties did not possess this degree of thrust. The standard procedure was to position the aircraft at the end of the runway with the brakes fully on, then put all four engines onto maximum power, causing the aircraft to vibrate. Added to this was the almost deafening roar of the engines. Suddenly the captain would release the brakes, the aircraft would roll forward and start to gather speed, going faster and faster down the runway. Just when it seemed it would never take off, there was a soft bump as the wheels left the ground and it would commence a shallow climb over the large reservoir that borders the western end of the main Heathrow runway.

Looking out of the cabin window at the 'shrinking' land below, I was aware that these would be the last glimpses of my homeland. Having gained height, the aircraft turned, causing the sunlight that was streaming through the windows to 'run' down the opposite side of the cabin to where I was seated. I judged from this that we had turned and were now headed in a southerly direction. I settled back in my seat with thoughts of the future, family and friends, wondering what people would be doing at work at this hour? Below the aircraft was thick cloud, causing the ground to be overcast, yet up here above the clouds there was brilliant sunlight.

Some hours later, the Captain having informed us that our flight path had crossed France and the snow-capped Alps, I looked out of my window. The clouds had cleared and there, some nineteen thousand feet below, was Genoa, the surrounding country and coastline looking almost like a page from a school atlas. It was now a completely cloudless sky. As we flew South down the Italian coast, the shallows could be clearly defined by the paler blue colour of the sea. The aircraft turned in towards the coast and commenced to lose height, then with a soft bump and rumble of tyres we arrived at Rome airport where we disembarked for light refreshments while the aircraft was refuelled.

Following this very welcome short break we re-boarded the aircraft, next stop Cairo. When we had landed there and the cabin door was opened the air felt hot and had a strange, musty smell. As we descended the aircraft's steps onto the tarmac the late sunlight was bright and warm and as we made our way to the airport building I noticed the odd palm tree, the arid sandy earth and the sallow complexions of the local people. I was to pass through Cairo airport several times over the years, and to me it always had the same strange smell.

We flew on through the night. The cabin lights were dimmed, blankets and pillows provided. Before settling down and trying to sleep, I looked out of the window into the darkness. I could clearly see the long bright blue flames from the engine exhausts lapping over the wing. It reminded me of the flame produced by a plumber's blowlamp. I slept fitfully and every time I looked out of the cabin window there were those bright blue tongues of flame.

Finally I stirred, removed my blanket and stretched. As I yawned I noticed that to my left in the far distance was the top of a glowing red disc. Sunrise!

Within minutes more of the sun appeared, tingeing the sky with a red/orange hue and very soon I found it far too bright to look at. Down below the aircraft all I could see was arid earth with the rising sun casting long shadows into every depression. Was it possible that thousands of feet below my seat, people would be stirring to greet yet another day of survival within this hot, desolate, and apparently waterless place?

Just after dawn we landed at Khartoum. As we came in to land, all I could see was desert surrounding a city which apparently consisted of hundreds of square sand-coloured flat-roofed houses. My impression was one of utter desolation.

Despite the early hour, as we walked towards the terminal building for breakfast I could feel the hot sun beating through my shirt and onto my back. Recalling late 19th Century history, I wondered how in the past British troops had managed to march and fight in this stifling heat, with the collars of their uniforms buttoned up to the neck.

At the airport terminal, breakfast was served in the open and one of our party needed an extra knife. A Colonial lady returning to Uganda came to his aid.

"If you need anything, you will have to call out 'boy'. He will not understand 'waiter'." We were soon to learn that this was the term used throughout East African hotels if you needed assistance of any kind from an African waiter, regardless of his age.

As we flew on down the length of Africa, all I could see, thousands of feet below us, was brown, arid earth. We flew on over this barren landscape for mile after mile, until at about 1.00pm, the browns started to be mixed with greens, then more greens, and as we circled, shimmering in the sunlight, I could clearly see Africa's vast inland sea, Lake Victoria, its shoreline almost reaching the end of the airport runway.

The aircraft banked, straightened, and we headed towards the runway to land. The airport buildings were white, the green trees looked lush and the ground was deep ochre. How very different to Cairo and Khartoum. There was a soft bump as the wheels touched down; we had landed at Entebbe in Uganda. We vacated the aircraft to have lunch in the airport restaurant. The sun was far hotter than any British summer and the light was so bright that I had to screw up my eyes. I can still recall the smell of the hot earth as we made our way towards the airport terminal. Our next stop would be our destination, Nairobi, Kenya.

Some three hours later we were circling over Nairobi. Looking out of the window it seemed very orderly, and as we descended I could make out traffic and what appeared to be some old-fashioned, single-storey buildings with corrugated-iron roofs that were a faded red colour, intermixed with their modern counterparts. Within minutes the airport buildings were flashing by the wingtips, there was a soft bump and a roar of the aircraft's engines. We had landed and commenced taxiing towards the main airport building. The journey had taken twenty-eight hours.

Prior to leaving England, a near neighbour asked if I could arrange to deliver a small parcel to her daughter, who had recently married a Colonial and who was now living in Nairobi. I had no idea what it contained. We now arrived at Customs.

"Anything to declare Sir?"

Should I mention the parcel?

"I do have a present for someone who lives in Nairobi."

"Do you know what it is Sir?"

I hadn't the foggiest idea and said so.

"In that case Sir, I had better open it."

Had I known what the parcel contained I would never have mentioned it. The Customs Officer carefully opened the parcel and proceeded to produce six pairs of very brief ladies knickers and two sexy nighties! I was surrounded by my new 'band of brothers' who commenced to make applicable, and some unprintable comments! What a start to a new career! It took several days to live this down.

We were booked into the 'Torrs Hotel' for the night, which was directly opposite the world famous 'New Stanley Hotel'. The first novelty I noticed in my room was the mosquito net draped over and around the bed. I looked out of the window, it was just turned seven o'clock in the evening and already dark. The streetlights were on and there was plenty of traffic about. I had a shower and, having changed, went down to the bar to rendezvous with my new colleagues.

We entered the dining room for dinner. An African waiter, dressed in an immaculate long, white, one-piece garment (a *kanzu*) with a red cummerbund, red fez and wearing white gloves, handed out the menus. We could hardly believe our eyes, there was such a wide choice of dishes… and the number of courses! Perhaps at this stage, I should remind the reader that even as late as 1953 in Britain we still had rationing of foodstuffs. Europe had been so ravaged by war, that as a nation we were continuing to send part of our food supplies into Europe, until such time as they could become self-supporting. By contrast, Kenya had a cornucopia of every conceivable food, and the price on the menu was also surprising, only seven Kenya shillings (equal to seven UK shillings or 35p). For this we had soup, fish, a cold meat course, a hot meat course, dessert, fresh fruit and coffee.

Breakfast was to be another 'eye opener'. There was paw-paw served with fresh limes, fresh pineapple, bananas, cereals, toast with lashings of butter, kippers, eggs, bacon and sausages packed with meat (at that time in England sausages were derisively known as 'bread in battle-dress'). At lunchtime we were staggered by the length of the 'cold table'; it must have been at least twenty feet long and was groaning with ham, chicken, turkey, beef, lamb, pates, fish and numerous salads. Then there were the sweets! In addition to all of this, if you wished you could have hot dishes. Coming from a rationed Britain, it was an incredible sight. We were to learn that this mass of food and choices was standard practice throughout all Kenyan hotels.

Having been partly 'kitted out', at Nairobi Police Headquarters, including being issued with a .38 revolver without any ammunition (this was to be issued later) and warned about firearms precautions, we were given a broad overview of the current security situation and were on our way by coach to the temporary Police Training School at Gilgil, roughly equidistant between Nairobi and Nakuru in Kenya's Rift Valley.

As we followed the tarmac road that wound its way down the escarpment, passing a tiny church built by Italian prisoners during the war, I looked left and down towards the floor of the Great Rift Valley, although little did I realise at that moment that in the not-too-distant future this vast area was to be one of my postings.

3   Halt… who goes there?

Our journey to Gilgil had been very interesting – we had seen many different, though fleeting, glimpses of African life. As our coach cruised towards Naivasha, to our left, dominating the skyline, was Mount Longonot. It was here in the far distance that we spotted several groups of giraffe, plus a large herd of zebra, some seventy in number. There was no habitation to be seen, just semi-dry grassland interspersed with thorn bushes as far as the eye could see. This had been the scene ever since we had descended the escarpment, which was now several miles to our rear. We were now on the floor of the Great Rift Valley. Ahead of us we could see some buildings looming in the distance, which evidently was the township of Naivasha. Having crossed an unguarded railway-crossing shaded by some tall trees, the road passed through the centre of the township, dominated by the Naivasha Hotel to our right, then a string of shops. We were told that the T-junction we had passed just before the hotel led to Divisional Police Headquarters. We were also told that it had been attacked by a large gang of Mau-Mau terrorists the previous year, that several police officers had been killed and a large quantity of arms and ammunition taken. It was a sobering thought.

Soon we arrived on the outskirts of the dusty little township of Gilgil. The coach turned right off the tarmac and onto a red dirt road. It was our first experience of being passengers on this type of surface. The coach rattled as it rolled over the numerous corrugations caused by rainwater that ran across the road – a type of surface most of us would experience during our first tour of duty. The coach left a huge cloud of red dust in its wake, which smothered everything on either side of the road, and crept into the coach via every crack. Suddenly we slowed down, turned right off the road and stopped at the guarded gate of our new home.

Those expecting a modern Police Training School were in for a disappointment. In view of the large intake of new recruits and the need to get them 'into the field' as soon as possible, we had been informed that we were not going to the normal Police School at

Kiganjo, but I have to admit that my preconceived mental picture of our destination was not the ex-army camp that now lay before us.

A large area was dotted with single-storey, grey stone buildings with corrugated iron roofs and at the centre was a large, ochre-coloured earth parade ground, the whole camp being surrounded by high wooden posts and barbed wire.

"Welcome to Stalag Luft Six!" said some wag in the rear of the coach. The remark seemed very apt and raised a laugh.

The school was situated within reasonable walking distance of Gilgil, a dusty little township whose main claim to fame was that the Nairobi-Nakuru road passed down its main street. It had a small number of scruffy Asian-owned *dukas* (shops) plus the European-owned and run Gilgil Hotel, at which we were to spend many an evening having dinner.

We were allocated one room per two persons. The accommodation was Spartan and everything was covered in fine ochre dust. One of our first tasks, and something of a novelty, was to engage an African servant who would clean, wash our clothes, press our uniforms and polish our boots. We hadn't a clue what attributes to look for and didn't speak *Kiswahili*, so communication was somewhat limited. We were informed to adhere to the 'going rate' of monthly pay for this type of essential support. That was the easy part. Our 'boy' needed some equipment: a brush to *fagia* (sweep), a *piga pas* (iron), *sabuni* (soap), *rangi ya viatu* (shoe polish) and, last but not least, *makaa* (charcoal). Charcoal? This was for the *piga pas*, which had a lifting lid into which hot charcoal was placed, then by puffing into the air vents near the sole plate of the iron it was kept very hot – as one of my shirts was soon to testify.

With our 'general factotum' in place, the dust disappeared, our boots shone and we commenced to settle into our new abode.

Our Instructor (whom we christened as per his initials 'J.C.') was in his mid-thirties, was a Kenya Police Reserve Officer and, we were to discover, had played small parts in several American films about Kenya. 'JC' oversaw the issue and fitting of our everyday 'uniform', although perhaps the best description of this would be a one-piece, short-sleeved, dark blue 'boiler suit', the ankles of which were secured under our short puttees, with the whole being set off with our shiny black boots. This was topped off with our newly issued police cap, or beret, complete with 'silver' badge showing a rampant lion surmounted with a crown. Next came the Indian tailor to take our measurements for our standard khaki drill jackets, trousers and shorts. Within a few days the garments were ready, fitted almost perfectly and required very little adjustment. We were soon to discover how this dull, matt cotton material could be transformed by careful starching plus vigorous application of the *piga pas*. It was difficult to recognise the original garments from this incredible transformation. Even the texture was different. We now proceeded to affix our 'silver' police buttons and our initial rank, which was one small star on each epaulette.

At 7am every morning except Sundays each intake formed up on the parade ground under the charge of their instructors. There was the usual shouting of orders with much stamping of feet, with which any ex-service person reading this book will be very familiar. To the non-service reader I should explain that orders given on any parade normally consist of the first word of command being very loud and short, with the following word being drawn out, then completed quickly with loud emphasis on the final word. For example, "squad attention" is delivered as "Squad... atten ... SHUN!" "Stand at ease", by the same method, becomes "Stand-at ... EASE!"

Following inspection, we were marched off for lectures on law and *Kiswahili* language training, or to the range for weapon training and firing. Later this was to involve anti-ambush training and how to 'sweep' a river. We were to discover that 'JC' maintained a very good balance between discipline and humour and as a result we enjoyed our stay at Gilgil.

Marching off to the firing range, despite the fact that we were in step, we must have looked like a group that had been dismissed from the 'Salvation Army'. At the front of the squad were the flag bearers carrying the large red (danger) firing range flags. They were followed by almost everyone else carrying full size, flat plywood figure targets plastered with white patches to cover up previously made bullet holes, then, finally, came the tail end of the column, carrying the rifles, with the last two to arrive on parade carrying a very heavy metal box of ammunition.

On arrival the red flags were positioned, the figure targets placed at one hundred yards and the squad divided, one half going into the deep trench well below the figure targets, their job being to point out each bullet hole to the people back at the firing point. Then, under the eagle-eye of JC, the other half of the squad would commence firing at the targets, pausing between each shot to await the marker rising from the 'butts' to point out where the bullet had hit. It was at this juncture that a few of us would fire at the sticks attached to the pointer, with the objective of 'cutting' the stick in two. This was only possible if JC was busily engaged observing at the far end of the firing line.

Being in the 'butts' was another experience, being the first time most of us had been on the receiving end of live ammunition. Unlike the sound effects in cowboy films, when a real bullet passes over your head you hear a sharp 'crack', followed milliseconds later by the sound of the gun being fired. The target was some three feet above our heads, so we were perfectly safe, but I shuddered at the thought of what it must have been like during the First World War to clamber out from the safety of the trench into a crackling hail of bullets and see your comrades fall around you; it must have been a truly terrifying experience. An Uncle of mine had been killed in that war, and for a brief moment my position in the butts gave me an insight into what he and his comrades had faced almost daily.

Upon completion of range practice, the 'Salvation Army' would reassemble and set off back to base singing some song that fitted in with the rhythm of our step. Back at the armoury, the guns were cleaned, the ammunition checked, the numbers stamped on the guns checked, the 'empties' (bullet cases) checked, then everything was handed to the duty armourer. It was then "dismiss" and back to our quarters.

The day arrived when we headed to another part of the range to throw live grenades. We had already practiced with 'dummies', but now it was the real thing. Let me explain what a grenade looks like. It's about four and a half inches long, shaped like a pineapple with deep grooves on its surface, running north, south, east and west, forming a square pattern. At the base of the grenade is a round metal plug about one inch in diameter, which is screwed into the base. Inside the grenade, beyond the metal plug, is a fuse, looking rather like a short length of twisted, smooth string, with one end sealed with a metal cap and the other end sealed into what appears to be a small bullet case. A spring-loaded striker is designed to hit this bullet case, thus activating the fuse. Down the outside of the grenade is a flat metal bar held down by a split pin, which prevents the spring-loaded striker from hitting the fuse case. Until this split pin is removed and the lever released, the grenade is perfectly safe.

The act of throwing involves:

1. grasping the metal bar to ensure that it cannot move.

2. removing the split pin, ensuring that the thrower's fingers securely hold down the metal bar.

The grenade is now ready for throwing and as soon as the bar is released there are just three seconds before it explodes.

Given that a grenade can kill anything within a radius of thirty feet, as I stood in the trench clutching a heavy pineapple-shaped object with the safety pin withdrawn, with JC beside me, I was very conscious that we were in a potentially dangerous situation. Now it was time to throw. The method is to bring the grenade arm to the rear of the body and then lob the grenade over-arm at the target ... and duck! The act of throwing releases the metal bar and the fuse is activated.

I lobbed the grenade, we both ducked, there was a tremendous bang and a 'wheee' as the base plug flew into the air over our heads. JC had to check everyone's ability to handle and throw a live grenade; I sincerely hope that he was well insured!

Our first day off duty saw a mass exodus to the dusty township, visiting what shops there were and having lunch at the hotel. I was fascinated by the skill of the Asian shoemakers who could produce bespoke shoes or suede 'desert boots' within days. First you selected the leather or suede, next you were shown 'dog eared' pictures of various shoe styles that had been removed from an old British 'mail order' catalogue. Having selected the style, a small sheet of brown paper was produced and you were asked to stand on this with feet slightly apart. The *fundi* (shoemaker) would then, with a pencil, draw the outline of each foot. The final measurements were of each ankle and instep. Now all that was required was the type of sole: crepe, rubber or leather?

All these actions were performed by *fundis* squatting outside their premises, from time to time sharpening their small half-circular knives on a whetstone. This knife was used for every shoemaking function. It was rocked onto the leather to cut out the shapes, used to trim off any excess, cut any loose threads, plus every other function where a sharp edge was required during the production process. I couldn't resist it; I ordered a pair of suede desert boots (suede ankle boots) with crepe soles. They were ready in days, fitted perfectly and the quality was excellent. I was still wearing them during my first home leave some three years later.

The local shopkeepers were in their element as they quickly catered for the requirements of each new intake of trainee policemen and the consequent influx of new money. Quality Swiss watches were prominently displayed at less than half the UK price. Most of us, including me, succumbed to this temptation.

The other establishment that absorbed most of our money was the Gilgil Hotel. The food was good, the portions large and the prices by UK standards, ridiculous.

Many intakes had arrived before us and as a result of catering to their every whim, the shoemaking *fundis* of Gilgil, in addition to footwear, sported an assortment of gun belts and holsters that would have enhanced any cowboy film. There were belts with cartridge loops, low slung holsters shaped for 'a quick draw', the height of pretentiousness being the addition of a leather thong for tying to the thigh, which, as we know from watching cowboy films, assists the wearer to make an even faster draw. We soon discovered that 'the tie-down thong brigade' could be spotted at some distance as they all walked with a slight limp. When somewhat closer their narrowed eyes, plus mean look, showed that they had absorbed the true feel of the Wild West. Not wishing to be 'left out', we could hardly wait to join them. My design, consisted of a quick draw holster with six cartridge loops on the side, and, I have to admit, a thong. Now this latter item was somewhat of a disaster. When tied to my thigh it was positioned far too high and was very uncomfortable, as it chafed very close to my 'matrimonial prospects'. I therefore adopted a slightly lower profile, and had the thong whipped round and round, dangling below the holster.

Everyone in our intake soon adopted the narrow-eyed look – not, as we had imagined, to project a mean don't-mess-with-me image but due to continuous exposure to the strong African sunlight. It was almost impossible to look at light colours; anything white was absolutely blinding.

You may recall that prior to my departure from England, the Colonial Office had issued me with a booklet which gave advice on what to buy prior to departure. As a result, I arrived in Kenya with fourteen shirts, I must admit not all new, but all in A1 condition. Following week two of our arrival at Gilgil, our 'boy' arrived looking very dejected and carrying one of my pale cream shirts. I could not understand what he was saying but this was unnecessary as he held it up for my inspection. On the rear panel was a burn hole right through the material the exact shape and size of the *piga pas*. Being somewhat naïve as to the wiles of African servants, by gestures I indicated that he was to throw it away. The following Sunday we were walking towards the Gilgil Hotel for lunch and were overtaken by our 'boy' riding a bicycle. As he passed I noticed that he was wearing a pale cream shirt with a bright blue patch on the back panel in the shape of an iron! This was not the only shirt to suffer. Charcoal, as any barbecue owner will tell you, has a habit of suddenly, and without warning, sending out a shower of tiny sparks. If a shirt is being ironed at the time, its ventilation is immediately increased by at least ten to twenty tiny holes. Upon completion of the induction course, I departed from Gilgil minus three shirts due to such 'accidents'.

The day arrived when we were issued with twelve rounds of live ammunition. This meant that we could now be involved in nightly guard duties to protect the camp from attack. At first it was exciting, but, as the nights went by it became cold and boring. Except for one night...

Dave was patrolling his section of the perimeter when he heard a slight rustling... He stood still, straining to catch the slightest sound. Could he have been mistaken? No, there it was again! With shaking hands he drew his revolver from its police-issue holster. It was dark and at best his visibility was about nine feet. He heard the sound again; it was moving slowly to his left and sounded to be within ten yards of his position.

'Oh my God,' he thought, 'this is for real! It's the Mau-Mau!'

He remembered that he had to challenge in Kiswahili *"Simama, nani wewe?"* (Halt, who are you?) This always struck me as rather odd, as I am sure a terrorist would be hardly likely to reply, "It's me, a Mau-Mau!"

Trying to sound stern and brave, Dave made the challenge. There was no response and the rustling was edging closer, so he opened fire, all six shots...

His fusillade was greeted with a loud 'moo'.

"Oh my God, I've shot a cow!" he shouted. Shining his torch, he could see (on the outside of the perimeter fence) a cow ambling towards him, blinking in the torchlight. It was completely unruffled, despite having been shot at. Dave made several 'psttt' noises to encourage it to come closer in order to make a detailed inspection of its injuries. There wasn't a mark on it, which spoke volumes for the accuracy of his shooting! On hearing shots the camp had meanwhile been 'stood to' and reinforcements rushed to Dave's section of the perimeter, only to find a very red-faced cadet and a contented cow, which was by now happily eating grass.

With the end of our course now only weeks away, we carried out anti-ambush drills and river 'sweeps'. The latter involved one man wading down the centre of the river (subject to depth) carrying a Bren gun. This was a .303 machine gun with a folding tripod under the barrel, a wooden butt, and a curved magazine holding twenty-five bullets clipped onto the top of the gun. The weight, from memory, was circa 20lbs. To his left and right were two men to check under any overhang of the banks, where a terrorist might hide. The remainder of the 'sweep' party were on either side of the bank.

I was selected to carry the Bren gun. The water came up to my chest and to make things even more difficult, the riverbed was uneven. I made my way against the current, thinking not so much of concealed Mau-Mau terrorists, but of the warnings contained in the Colonial Office booklet about water-borne parasites. The exercise completed, we marched back to camp, the water running down my legs to fill my already squelching boots. We halted ready to dismiss for lunch.

JC surprised us by saying "The three men who were in the river are not to change their clothing." – a comment greeted by much muttering in the ranks. "Had you been on a genuine sweep it would be impossible to change. Dismissed!"

We 'fell out' and started to make our way to the dining room. I was soaking wet and would obviously leave a very wet patch on some dining room seat and would not be very popular. To hell with it! I ran back to our room, rapidly changed and ran back to the dining room. However, in the middle of my meal JC entered and noted my pristine condition and as a result I was put on a 'fizzer' which entailed having to report to his quarters at 6:00am for the next seven days in No.1 dress uniform.

Having completed a basic language course, a basic law course, plus small arms, rifle, Bren gun and grenade instruction, we entered the final phase of ambush and anti-ambush drills plus an actual anti-terrorist patrol before being released on active duties.

In the main we were all to be posted to operational areas. However, before leaving we had our 'passing out' party, aptly named, as many did just that! I awoke with a telephone beside my bed with an Addis Ababa telephone number on it! Addis Ababa?

Before we went to our respective postings it was Christmas, so we decided to spend it in Nairobi. I hired an Austin A40 and four of us booked into the New Stanley Hotel. The first thing we ordered from Room Service was four 'John Collins'. This was living it up!

We had arranged to meet JC in the foyer that evening and then, together with his girlfriend, to visit a local night-club. As driver I had to stay sober. This did not apply to the rest of the party and JC seemed determined to 'let his hair down'. By midnight he was well and truly plastered and was singing bawdy songs, supported by a very belligerent demeanour. His girlfriend, who was sober, was not enjoying it one bit. She leaned over and asked me to take her home. She then told her boyfriend she was leaving. This was greeted with a drunken, "Go on then, push off, I'm here for the night!"

She directed me down a dual carriageway and around several roundabouts until we arrived outside her apartment. As the Mau-Mau were active around Nairobi I was armed with my police revolver and escorted her to her door and saw her safe inside. I now had to return to the nightclub. I remembered the last part of the route, but from then on I was lost. More by good luck than judgement I found the city centre. Now all I had to do was find the nightclub. What was it called? It had a French name. Was it the 'Parisien'? I stopped and asked a European passer by. He had never heard of it. I drove around and around. By now at least two hours had passed. I managed to wave down a car being driven by a European.

"Yes, I know of two places with French names. Follow me."

The first one was not what I was looking for, but the second was it, 'Le Son Chique'. I entered the club and walked down the small flight of stairs. On seeing me our instructor rose unsteadily to his feet and shouted, "You bastard, you've been sleeping with my girlfriend!"

The small three-piece band stopped playing and to my acute embarrassment, for a brief moment all eyes turned on me. I attempted to look unconcerned and made my way forward and to my relief the band commenced playing again as I rejoined the party. JC was still swaying on his feet and I was subjected to further abuse until he finally slumped into his chair. We took him home, put him, fully clothed, onto his bed and left. Quite a start to the festive season!

Soon after Christmas, with our initial training completed, we were dispersed to various Police Divisions and our new careers were about to begin.

My initial posting was to a Police Combat Unit. We operated what was basically a 999 system to go to the assistance of any farm under attack by terrorists. Each night a party of eight, consisting of a European Police Officer, an African NCO, five men plus the Land Rover's driver, sat around, dressed and fully armed, ready to instantly respond to any alarm call. Upon receipt of a reported attack, the vehicle would be on its way in minutes, driving over rough dirt roads at speeds in excess of sixty miles an hour, the headlights cutting into the darkness ahead and the VHF radio crackling with HQ calling, "Mike Baker Five, Mike Baker Five" to give us the latest update at our destination.

With no soft top and the windscreen clipped down onto the bonnet of the Land Rover, with the cold night air roaring in our ears and tugging at our berets, adrenalin pumping through our veins, we felt ready for anything.

I recall arriving at one farm where an old African herdsman had been killed. When we arrived we found his body on its back. His throat had been cut so that his windpipe protruded from the cavity onto his chin. He must have been held down in this position before he was killed. His eyes were open and his face had a look of sheer terror. It was a senseless killing of a harmless old man.

It was during this time that we were called upon to assist in trying to find the body of a European Police Officer who had drowned trying to swim in a weed-choked lake. The radio came alive.

"*Mike Baker Five, Mike Baker Five. A small number of terrorists are reported to be within your search area. Acknowledge, over.*"

"*Mike Baker Five, message received and understood. Out.*" was our response.

Within fifteen minutes we were in pursuit and being spread out entered a large plantation of sisal. Slightly ahead and to my right I suddenly heard three shots. Converging on the spot we came across a Mau-Mau terrorist who had been shot twice through the back by one of our men. Although dead he appeared to be still breathing and was making loud gasping noises. One shot had entered the centre of his back, smashing his spinal column, the second was just to the left of this and must have hit his heart. We continued to sweep through the plantation. Returning later that day to collect the body, all we found were lion tracks.

The following day I was detailed to be one of the pallbearers at the funeral of the drowned Police Officer. It was strange to feel the weight of the body within the coffin and as the earth was being shovelled into the grave, to think that just twenty-four hours earlier I had been talking and laughing with him. He would not be returning home to England, and somewhere several thousand miles away, his parents would be grieving for a son they would never see again.

Some months later, having been engaged in anti-terrorist activities, I was sent on a special jungle warfare course (incidentally, Kenya doesn't have any jungles, only bush and forests), conducted by a British Army Officer, Captain Barton. You may recall that we had not been in Kenya for very long and our knowledge of Kiswahili was therefore limited. Captain Barton didn't know a word. This was to be a problem.

Initially we were instructed what to do if ambushed in a vehicle. For this exercise we had an old Canadian Army truck, which had a hole on the passenger side of the roof. This was to be Captain Barton's position for observation and control. For 'ambush ahead' we had to jump out of the rear. For 'ambush right' we had to jump out on the left, etc. I'm sure you get the general picture. The driver's role in this exercise was critical. However, as he didn't understand English, and our Captain didn't understand Kiswahili, it was a disaster in the making as the following incidents demonstrate. Captain Barton crashed his fist on the cab roof.

"Ambush left!" As we tried to jump out on the right-hand side, the driver roared into reverse. Captain Barton went 'potty'! Clinging to the sides of the truck we tried again.

"Ambush right!"

This time the driver slammed on the brakes catapulting us onto the floor of the truck! Before we could recover, the lorry lurched and roared ahead! Our Captain went demented! By this time we could see the funny side of the situation and several of us had tears pouring down our cheeks. It took lots of disjointed words, with the addition of sign language, to secure a semblance of mutual understanding between Captain Barton and his driver.

After lunch the ambush drill was more intensive. Our party was split into two: one section in the truck, the other to hide in the long grass at a position of their choice to carry out the ambush. For this purpose we were armed with 'thunder-flashes', giant fireworks about ten inches long, used to simulate a grenade, but fairly lethal in their own right at close range. We also had rifles and blank ammunition. Being the ambush party we hid in the long grass and waited for the truck. We'd sort them out!

The grass was very dry and tall, making observation difficult. We therefore decided to lob two or three 'thunder-flashes'; this would not disclose our position, then, when they tried to find us in the long grass, we could easily 'pick them off'. A brilliant plan!

As we heard the grinding gearbox of the clapped-out truck approaching, the 'thunder-flash' party was ready...

"O.K lob!" There were three loud bangs, followed by silence.

We waited...

Then we heard Captain Barton shout, "Fire, Fire!"

As we had not yet fired a shot, we assumed this order was directed at us, and despite the fact that we couldn't see a thing, we blazed away. The noise was deafening!

Then we heard Captain Barton's voice shouting again.

"No, no... it's forest fire! You've set the bloody grass alight!"

Our next phase was to be an operational patrol in the forest. For this three-day exercise we had been assigned a special sector to patrol. Prior to setting out, Captain Barton had explained how, by using a prismatic compass then taking a back bearing on, for example, a mountain peak, and then another, where these two vectors crossed would give our actual position. Some of us had already been on anti-terrorist patrols and we knew that due to the denseness of the forestation the chances of taking a bearing on any feature was close to zero. Mention of this was 'pushed to one side'. Our party assembled for the off. It consisted of Captain Barton, our party of ten, plus a little, wizened old African, wearing only a blanket slung over one shoulder and a bright red band around his head. This person, we were informed, was our tracker, and the headband was to ensure that we would not confuse him with the enemy. I have forgotten to add one other item: an empty ex-army 14lb biscuit tin with a wooden handle nailed across its top. This, we were informed, was for brewing tea. This caused some disquiet. We 'operational types', despite our inexperience, knew you never ever made a fire, or smoked, never spoke, and used only sign language. The basic idea was to see, but not be seen.

We set off with the biscuit tin giving off the odd 'bong' sound as it made contact with a tree, and from time to time stopped as Captain Barton studied his map. We had yet to establish our position.

By about 4pm it was obvious all was not well. Due to the denseness of the forest it had not been possible to take any bearings, our party of ten decided we were lost.

The forests of the Aberdare range have numerous watercourses which, over the centuries, have gouged out a series of fairly deep ridges. The easiest way to travel is along the spine of the ridges rather than clamber down into the gully and then claw your way up the opposite side. As the Aberdares tower above twelve thousand feet along the ridge spines, carrying a pack, firearm and ammunition soon has one gasping for breath. You will have gathered from the above brief description that it is impossible to become lost. All one had to do was to follow the flow of a watercourse and it would finally bring you to either African, or European cultivation. Now it was along and down one of the ridge spines that suddenly, and without warning, our tracker sped off like a deer.

"My God he's onto something. Follow me!"

Following the Captain's example, we raced down the ridge in pursuit, jumped over a small watercourse, only to discover our tracker crouched behind a bush, relieving himself! He was now surrounded by eleven armed Europeans, plus a 14lb biscuit tin and I could see from the expression on his face that he was more than a little surprised to discover how much we cared for his welfare and safety!

The patrol continued for the full three days and was completed without encountering any terrorists. The only incident of any note was that on the return journey Captain Barton shot a duck.

It was during this time that we were invited to a farm for a party. The situation was rather unusual as the farm had security forces stationed within its barbed wire perimeter. During the course of the evening, it was noted that young ladies visiting the outside 'powder room' returned rather quickly, looking very flustered, then gathered in small groups for animated conversation. What was going on? Soon all was revealed. Some European members of the Kenya Regiment had removed part of the 'powder room's' rear structure and had then inserted a feather duster, which could be manipulated from the outside!

Having returned to normal duties, and due to a forthcoming 'op' (anti-terrorist sweep), I called at the local Divisional Police HQ for additional stores and came into contact with 'he who guarded the coffers'. The person concerned was a retired army Major who, when the State of Emergency was declared, like so many others had joined the Kenya Police Reserve. Someone, somewhere, considered it imperative to safeguard the Colony's cash flow and in particular the section of the Government coffers set aside for our Division of the Kenya Police. Major Thompson, who must have been about seventy, was placed in charge of our Divisional Stores. His defence of this establishment was such that it was rumoured that he had actually purchased every item with his own money! At this stage I was blissfully unaware of the 'state of play' and, having drawn up a list of requirements, approached the stores like a wide-eyed innocent.

"Morning Major, I have a list of requirements here."

I placed the list on the counter. He didn't look up from his desk and continued to study some papers with differing levels of heavy breathing. Not wishing to distract his attention from such important work, I waited a few more minutes and then repeated my greeting. He still didn't look up. This was ridiculous!

"Major, I need some urgent supplies and I have to leave here in under an hour."

"You damn people are all the same, it's always urgent. These papers are also urgent!" He slammed them onto the desk. "Come back in an hour."

I was determined to stand my ground.

"We have an 'op' coming up and I need these items now. You may be busy, but so are we."

He went very red in the face, said "Give it to me!" and snatched the indent off the counter. "This is ridiculous. What are you people doing with all this stuff? Nine millimetre ammunition, grenades, .303..."

Still muttering, he went into his inner sanctum and returned with the first and third items, thumping them onto the counter. This was followed by a box of grenades accompanied by even more heavy breathing at varying levels of intensity. I opened the box; the tin of grenade fuses was missing.

"Excuse me Major, but we also need the fuses."

With a heavy sigh he left his seat and with lots of additional heavy breathing and mutterings slammed the tin onto the counter with the words, "Next time you'll have to wait!"

Every future visit was slightly up or down on this first encounter.

I was also to meet another retired Major who was perhaps even more bloody-minded than Major Thompson. He was a farmer who employed only Kikuyu (many of this tribe supported Mau-Mau) and objected most strongly to any checks for concealed weapons or signs of Mau-Mau activity within his workforce. He was 'a thorn in the side' of the local security forces to such an extent that (without his knowledge) the Mau-Mau gave him the rank of Honorary Sergeant!

I recall leading my first ever anti-terrorist patrol, which was to last for three days. I was the only European. I had an African Sergeant and seven askaris and we were on patrol in the Aberdare mountain range at a height of about 10,000 feet. During the day the temperature was pleasant, sunlight would stream down through the forest canopy and where it was very thick, shafts of sunlight could still penetrate and light up the undergrowth, but also throwing deep dark shadows. At night it could be bitterly cold, but as stealth was important, there was no question of lighting a fire. The following is what I wrote about it at the time:

'The forest is full of sounds and in the clean atmosphere one's sense of smell is heightened to an incredible degree. Bamboo makes a noise like a pistol shot as part of the stalk splits open in the daytime heat. At night the hyraxes shriek in the forest canopy and a bushbuck's warning cough sounds almost human. There are no footpaths, just game tracks, which from time to time force us to bend very low to avoid being ensnared by the undergrowth. Unlike American films about Africa, we do not carry machetes

(pangas) to slash a path; silence is essential. On the lower slopes, fallen and dead bamboo leaves look almost fluorescent as the light starts to fade, highlighting the game tracks. We move forward with extreme caution, keeping well spread out. The tracker leads and I follow at a distance of some ten feet. We are all on tenterhooks; Mau-Mau gangs in excess of one hundred are not uncommon, but experience has shown that if a contact is made, due to the density of forestation, it is only possible for a patrol leader to control a small number of men, hence our low number on this patrol.

Normally it is dark by 7.00pm, but due to the thick foliage in the forest it is as black as pitch by 6.30pm. If you hold your hand in front of your face you cannot see it. We go down into our first night position. In case we are observed, as a precaution we wait, then move away in the dark, trying not to make the slightest sound. We are deep in the forest and the only help we can hope for is our own. We finally go down in a widely-spaced triangular formation. This minimises the chances of anyone being hit if we are shot at. I take either the first stag (watch) or the last one, the times when an attack are most likely. To combat the cold, underneath my camouflage smock I have put on a police-issue woollen sweater, wound a police puttee around my middle and placed hose tops (like a tube sock with a hole at either end) over the toe caps of my jungle boots.

I sit there, straining my ears for the slightest sound. Nearby a bushbuck coughs; hell, it sounds so human. The rain starts to patter onto my poncho, but this is not good news as it tends to blank out any other sounds. The hyraxes start shrieking again and I can feel the cold seeping into me. Just one more hour and I can wriggle into my lightweight blanket and clip up the sides of my poncho around it like a sleeping bag.

My time is up. I gently shake my relief by the shoulder. He sits up then takes over and I can look forward to a very light sleep. As I wriggle down into my sleeping bag it stops raining. Some hours later, I hear the rain pattering onto the poncho again and before long, rainwater starts to trickle down my neck. I look forward to morning, when the heat of the sun will dry us out. The night ends without incident and we continue our patrol.

From time to time we stop, move off the game track and wait in ambush, just in case some terrorists have spotted our tracks and are following us. Nothing happens, so we move on again, repeating the exercise at regular intervals.

Later our tracker picks up a small stick that is broken in the middle. He breaks it again, compares the newly-broken piece with the colour of the old break and estimates it was trodden on about seven days ago. He conveys this to me by holding up seven fingers, then pointing to a very faint heel-mark almost covered by the fallen bamboo leaves. By holding up all my fingers and thumbs then shrugging my shoulders, I ask "how many men?" He holds up one finger in response. We use this system to communicate as in the forest voices can carry a long way.

We continue deeper into the forest. At day three we exit the forest at dusk and the patrol ends without incident. We have not come across any major signs of Mau-Mau activity, but despite this, every patrol with or without a contact, improves our understanding of the forest environment.

With continual patrolling, plus intelligence obtained from captured terrorists, our understanding of our enemy continues to improve. We learn that, from time to time, in order to confuse us, they walk backwards. We now do the same. We have also learned that in order to disguise their tracks, they sometimes wear chupplies (sandals made from old tyres) with game tracks cut into the soles. It is rumoured that due to the clean air at this height they can smell cigarette smoke at over one hundred yards. As a result no one smokes when on patrol.'

During a visit to Divisional Police Headquarters I bumped into a member of Special Branch. They had been questioning a captured terrorist who had been involved in the theft of European-owned livestock. His speciality was the silent killing of pigs. How was this possible? Entering a pigsty and disturbing the pig generally results in very loud squeals. This is how it was done. Approach very slowly and then commence scratching the pig's back; pigs love it! Then slowly work the palm of the left hand down the pig's flank until you feel the heart beating against your palm. At this point, place the tip of a knife blade between the first and second fingers of the left hand and continue to scratch the area above the pig's heart. Suddenly, using the palm of the right hand, strike the haft of the knife, driving it deep into the pig's heart. The pig dies instantly, without even a grunt.

'Some weeks later Mau-Mau fires can clearly be seen near Fey's Peak. We study the fires through binoculars. They must be some ten miles away and deep in the forest. HQ decides to call in an air strike using the Lincoln bombers of the RAF. We are all briefed to enter the forest to cut off any fleeing terrorists and to ensure that we stay at least three thousand yards from the aiming point. We enter the forest just as dawn is breaking. The RAF will be using 2,000lb bombs, so we find the thickest trees to shelter behind. On time over comes the RAF Harvard and we hear it diving down to drop coloured smoke target markers. The bombers fly in overhead; there is a very loud noise like ripping calico as each front turret opens up with its 0.5-inch machine guns. Then we hear the bombs whistling down onto their target, and feel a tremor in the ground at each explosion. The aircraft having passed over the target area, the rear turrets open up as the bombers head for home. It's all over. We now wait for any fleeing terrorists. No one appears, just the odd terrified bushbuck, so, as ordered, we move forward to the target area and I notice that there is a strange smell in the air. We find numerous craters but no sign of any bodies; this large gang must have moved prior to the air strike. We return to base.'

It was during this period that I met a person who was a legend during the early 1950s, an Australian called 'Davo' Davidson. Davo would broadcast over the African section of the Kenya Radio and challenge a Mau-Mau gang leader to a duel, naming the date, time and place. Davo would be there, but the gang leader invariably failed to appear. Next day Davo would broadcast again, asking why this 'brave' gang leader had failed to show up. It was good psychological warfare.

My first ever meeting with him was within an area known as the South Kinankop. Just outside the Police Station was a bearded man of medium height with very broad shoulders. He was carrying an Italian 'Beretta' machine carbine with a flip bayonet attached. Around his waist was a heavy gun belt with loops containing .45 Special (long) bullets and on each thigh a .45 Special revolver. Also attached to his gun belt was a leather holder containing three 9mm magazines for his machine carbine and, superimposed on the centre section, was a sheath containing a large hunting knife. But this was not all. Also dangling from his belt were two grenades. He didn't have to introduce himself; no one else could look like this, it had to be Davo Davidson! Some months later, during one of his solo challenges, he was ambushed and, in bending forward, some fragments from the gang's bullets went between the plates of his bulletproof vest. Despite being wounded, he killed some of the gang and made his escape.

I was to meet Davo again many years later. With the demise of Mau-Mau he was now building dams in the Reserves. He often had meals with us, and despite his age, which by then must have been over sixty, he played a very good game of tennis.

Davo was an incredible pistol shot. His favourite 'party trick' was to demonstrate what to do if six Mau-Mau were going to kill you. For this, he would line up six figure targets at a distance of about ten paces. Then, flinging himself onto the ground with his head towards the targets, he would draw both his .45 Specials, rapidly roll over and over, with his arms held above his head, and at the same time fire off twelve rapid shots. Every target would have two holes through it!

During my first tour the Mau-Mau were very active, normally attacking 'soft targets' where they had every confidence of achieving success. A Mau-Mau gang about sixty in number raided a European farm that was situated within two hundred yards of the forest edge. It was an ideal 'target'. The proximity of the forest would conceal their presence prior to the attack and, following the raid, it was only a short distance to make good their escape, hours before any possible follow-up by the security forces. The farmer, Phillip Grimwood, shot and killed four terrorists as they tried to break into his house. He and his wife were then saved by a Kenya Police Reserve Officer, Robert Cronchey, who with just four men put the gang to flight. Robert was later awarded the Colonial Police Medal for Gallantry. I later saw some English newspapers with the headlines *The Grimwood Raid*, giving an account of the attack. Without any doubt, both men carried out very brave deeds that night. Soon after this, the Mau-Mau sent a message that they would avenge the death of their comrades. As a result, I was soon to be sent to the farm with a small section to protect Phillip and Nan Grimwood.

About a year after the attack on the Grimwoods I was to meet Robert Cronchey again. This time the Mau-Mau tried to kill him, but more of this later.

Phillip Grimwood was an ex-Ghurkha officer and as such was well versed in the use of firearms, but at the time of the attack his sole firepower was an ex-Italian army rifle with eight rounds of ammunition, a shotgun, plus an automatic pistol. Whilst I was staying with them, Phillip and Nan explained to me what had happened.

It was at night. The gang first attacked the farm labourers' dwellings, blowing bugles and firing guns. As a result they were not taken by surprise and fired off their distress rocket that would have been seen by every Police Post within a radius of twenty miles. It was this rocket that alerted Robert Cronchey. The gang entered into their yard, which was situated at the rear of the house, yelling and firing their weapons. At this point Phillip shot two from the minimum cover provided by their closed-in veranda. The gang, thinking that the shooting had come from the adjacent store, threw in a grenade; had Phillip and Nan Grimwood been in there, it would have killed them.

By now Nan Grimwood was taking cover on the stone flooring of the veranda as the gang fired several bursts of automatic fire, peppering the wall, some four feet above her head. Whilst this was taking place, a series of noises from their lounge alerted Phillip that some members of the gang were trying to force the French window. He crawled along the veranda to the door opening into their lounge and shot two more terrorists through the glass. It was at this stage that Robert Cronchey arrived, driving his Land Rover into the gang, who were milling around in the yard, causing them to flee. You can say it was a very lucky escape, but what really saved their lives were cool heads and basic British guts!

Having been alerted, we arrived at dawn to follow the gang, and as we arrived the CID were fingerprinting the four bodies. We set off in pursuit, initially following a well-defined route caused by some sixty terrorists all heading in the same direction into the denseness of the forest. Later, when their tracks divided, we split our forces, and I was given the task of following the smaller number. We moved forward with caution, as usual well spread out with my position at the front of the patrol directly behind the tracker. We had been moving for several hours when suddenly there was a loud bang.

Ambush! We flung ourselves to the ground, the tracker facing forward, the last man facing to the rear, and everyone else alternately facing left and right. This way we had a complete 360-degree field of fire. There was complete and utter silence. We stayed as we were, looking and listening. Apart from the usual noises one hears in the forest it was quiet. What was going on? The bang had been very close and slightly behind me. Could one of the askaris have discharged his rifle by accident? I turned my head towards the Sergeant and by sign language asked the question. He in turn did the same thing; no one had done so.

By sign language I gave the order to move off the track and crawl into the forest. Some twenty yards off the track and to the right of our line of advance, an askari found an empty 12 bore shotgun cartridge. He held it to his nose; it had recently been discharged. So we had been ambushed! But why by only one man? Was it to cause a diversion? The patrol continued until we lost the tracks and exited the forest at dusk.

Some weeks later I was at Divisional Police Headquarters. There in the custody of two Special Branch Officers was a captured terrorist. To my utter surprise the terrorist greeted me like a long lost brother.

"I don't know you, so how do you know me?" I asked.

His reply surprised me even more.

"A few weeks ago when you were in the forest, I tried to kill you."

He gave me a warm smile. It transpired that his job was to kill the European patrol leader and then flee. It was thought this would cause such uproar that all attempts to chase and catch the gang would be dropped. How he missed me I will never know; he must have shut his eyes when he pulled the trigger. It would have made much more sense to have ambushed the main patrol. This incident illustrated just how easy it was to be ambushed, despite moving with caution and being extremely vigilant.

The authorities considered the Mau-Mau threat to Phillip and Nan Grimwood to be real and as a result I was posted there with ten men to ensure their safety. For the first time ever I was to experience being away from base, on a farm, without barbed wire defences or sand-bagged strongpoints. As ordered, I slept in the house fully dressed and armed, not actually sleeping until after 5a.m. The forest edge was no more than two hundred yards away, and despite the fact our small section was well armed and I had fortified the barn with sandbags and barbed wire as a defensive strongpoint, I have to admit to feeling a degree of unease at being in such an exposed position. Without any doubt, the European farming community had 'guts'.

I stayed with Phillip and Nan Grimwood for several weeks; they were a charming, very unassuming couple. They had no intention whatsoever of giving way to Mau-Mau threats; their determination was typical of the European farming community at that time.

It was also highly likely that the Mau-Mau had plans to kill Robert Cronchey. By this time Robert was working on a farm in a 'semi-safe' area. One evening he went for a stroll and heard a rustle in some nearby bushes. Suddenly he was grabbed from behind and a terrorist thrust a shotgun into his stomach. He managed to knock the gun aside as his would-be killer pulled the trigger. Drawing his revolver and despite being held, he managed to shoot and wound both terrorists. Being only slightly wounded, they made off, leaving Robert shaken but unharmed.

At dawn next morning we arrived to commence the follow-up. Initially the tracks led up rising ground and then onto the nearby railway line. From then on, following their tracks and the occasional spots of blood, we were able to follow at a fast walking pace. After about three miles it was apparent that our quarry had scaled the high bank onto rocky ground. This slowed our pace and by mid-day it was becoming obvious that the chance of making any form of contact was close to zero. However, we continued, despite the fact that by now there were no bloodstains to be seen. We spread out, trying to find even the slightest trace, but it was to no avail. Our quarry had made a successful getaway.

At one stage during Mau-Mau times, the Kenya Government issued an amnesty. Any terrorist carrying a green branch would not be shot at and their safety would be guaranteed.

One day an army Land Rover arrived with a jubilant crew pointing their guns at a little old African man.

"We've picked up a surrendering terrorist!" they shouted.

They held up the green 'branch'. It was a banana leaf that was being used by the old man as his usual 'natural umbrella'! He was looking very frightened, but I assured him that he was safe and told them to drop him off where they had found him.

"Come on granddad, get back in," I translated.

Still looking scared he clambered aboard and off they went.

About a year later we were manning an O.P. (observation post) based on the escarpment above the Italian church on the main Nairobi-Naivasha road. It was the usual three-day 'stint', which was always difficult, because during daylight hours we had to stay hidden in cramped conditions and close proximity to each other; I was glad my companions were not avid curry eaters! Our brief was to watch out for terrorists crossing into the Kedong Valley and onto Mount Longenot. If we spotted any we were to radio in with their co-ordinates. The 'stint' was uneventful and the radio ordered us to stand down.

Below us at a distance of some 150 yards was a very large white sign. In many languages, including all the Asian ones, it stated:

DANGER You are in a terrorist area and picnicking at this spot is forbidden.

Just as we were about to depart, an American car stopped opposite the sign, disgorging about six adult male Asians. From the bags they were starting to remove from the boot it was obvious they were planning a picnic! Had we been a group of terrorists we could have killed them all. I couldn't believe it! How could they be so stupid? This required some action.

I sighted the .303 rifle very carefully and placed a shot into the soft earth about fifteen feet to their right. It had an electrifying effect! Everyone fought to get into the car with their bags – it was every man for himself! The car was moving off with its wheels spinning in the dust with one man clinging to an open door, desperately trying to get inside. He just made it, as the car sped off with blue smoke coming from its spinning tyres. I felt very sure that they would not try to picnic there again and when they spread the word about the 'attack' it would certainly deter any other civilians from breaking the law.

Several miles along the road from the Italian Church and heading in the direction of Naivasha are the Kijabe crossroads. One of the secondary roads leads to Narok, which is the Masai area, the other to the very small township of Kijabe, which consisted of a small number of Indian-owned *dukas* (shops) and a small Police Station. Since dusk we had been manning a roadblock at the crossroads and we had set up two 'hedgehogs' (long wooden planks studded with sharp steel spikes) to ensure that anyone trying to break through the roadblock would have their tyres ripped to shreds. We were armed, having as 'backup' a mounted Bren gun. The night passed without incident and we were looking forward to dawn and the warmth of the sun.

At about 6.30am a black car approached the roadblock. Upon seeing our hand signals, and, no doubt, the 'hedgehog', it stopped. It contained a European who, from his appearance and bearing, was a retired army officer.

"You chaps been here all night? Bet it was bloody cold."

We grunted in agreement. He got out of his car.

"By God it's good to see you chaps out here doing your stuff. Any incidents? See you have the trusty old Bren gun at the ready. Good for you. Can't hang around, must be off!" He returned to his car and started the engine. We moved the 'hedgehog' that was blocking his side of the road onto the grass verge. He set off at speed. What he, and we, had not noticed, was that when he had stopped his front wheels were turned towards the grass verge. There was a rapid series of bangs, pops and loud hisses as his nearside front tyre ran along the full length of the 'hedgehog' and was ripped to shreds. He stopped. The car door opened with a crash!

"What a stupid bloody place to put that thing!"

We had the distinct impression that he was not very happy.

"By God I'll sue every one of you for damaging my tyre. Look at it!"

He gave the shredded tyre a kick. He was definitely very cross.

"With respect Sir, the spikes were off the road and on the grass verge. It wasn't our fault."

"Rubbish, of course it's your fault!"

"Can we help you change your wheel?"

"Not bloody likely, you've done enough damage already!"

He opened the boot of the car with another crash, removed the spare wheel, and muttering constantly about "stupid bloody idiots" plus what he would do, changed the wheel. He got into the car, slammed the door and set off again at speed. True to his word, he lodged a complaint and I had therefore to give a very detailed account of the incident. Fortunately, we never heard another word, and our bank balances remained intact.

From time to time we would attend 'O' Groups (short for operation group meetings) when areas of operation and tactics would be discussed. The Divisional Superintendent was referring to a recent minor 'cock up', when a certain Inspector Brown was heard to say (in jest) "We'll have to sack him." The Superintendent overheard the remark and said rather sarcastically, "Thank you Supol Brown for those words of wisdom." (Supol was the telegraphic name for a Superintendent of Police).

From that day on John Brown's nickname became 'Supol' and as a result the barman in the Mess constantly overheard John referred to as 'Supol', which was to have repercussions. Let me explain why...

Drinks at the Mess bar were not paid for by cash; the barman made out a 'chit' for the amount and the person paying for the round signed it. At the end of the month the bar chits were totalled and then settled with the Mess Secretary. At the end of the month the Superintendent, who was married and hardly ever entered the Mess, queried why he had been sent a bill for several hundred shillings.

Upon investigation the reason was revealed. The barman had written 'Supol' on John's bar chits.

The real Superintendent was not amused. John was based at an operational Police Post and he called him on the radio to say: one, he was to come at once and settle his bar account, and two, to cease immediately using the name 'Supol'!

John apologised, saying that as the Land Rover was causing trouble there would be some delay.

"Listen very carefully Inspector Brown. I don't give a damn if you ride in here on a donkey. You will be here tomorrow without fail!"

John could not resist the opportunity. He called the local District Officer, requesting him to trace a docile donkey and asked if he could use his 'three-tonner' lorry as transport. All was arranged.

Next morning, John dressed in his No.1 uniform and one of his askaris (African police) dressed in a similar manner were dropped off around the corner from Divisional Headquarters. With John now astride the donkey and being led by the askari, they entered the gates of Divisional Police Headquarters, receiving on entry a butt salute from the sentry on duty. Stopping outside the Superintendent's office, John alighted and informed the secretary that, as requested, he had come to report to her boss. She didn't have to inform her boss. A voice roared, "Inspector Brown come in here! What the hell do you think you're playing at?"

John entered the office and saluted.

"I am not playing Sir, merely obeying your orders, and if I might say so Sir, with respect, the order, considering the security situation was unwarranted."

The Superintendent nearly 'exploded'.

"Inspector Brown get out of here!" and with a voice full of menace, "In a few weeks time I am going on home leave, and when I return, I do not want to see you in this Division! Is that clear?"

"Yes Sir, but I was only obeying orders."

"Inspector Brown out, out, get out of my office!"

As expected, John was soon posted.

John's operational area ran alongside part of my boundary and prior to his departure for 'pastures new', I had cause to work with him on a minor anti-terrorist operation. It was completed without incident and we were standing very close to the main Nairobi-Naivasha road, when John suddenly shouted in jest, "I've been shot!" and jumped into the arms of his African Sergeant, who was about six feet six tall and built like a barn door. This must have happened before, as there was no hesitation by the Sergeant in catching him in his arms. John lay back in his Sergeant's arms with his eyes closed, head, legs and arms dangling limply at his side. At this moment a car drew up containing a middle-aged European couple. The lady got out of the car and came over.

"Oh my goodness, has he been shot? Can we do anything to help?"

John opened one eye and smiling said, "Don't worry Madam, I'll be all right in the morning!"

The lady said, "You poor thing, I do hope you recover soon." Then returned to the car. I could see that she was talking animatedly to her husband and kept gesticulating in John's direction as they drove away.

I decided that it was not only his Superintendent who needed home leave, and that John's name should be changed to 'Harpic'!

4   Transferred to 'America'

Having completed the police induction course and experienced some anti-terrorist operations, I was transferred to take charge of security at an American Mission Station. The Mission, which covered quite a large area, was very close to the forest edge – not an ideal location as far as day-to-day security was concerned.

At the Mission was a school catering for the children of American Missionaries who were based across the whole of East Africa, with the ages of the children ranging from about seven to seventeen and totalling close to a hundred in number.

Prior to my arrival, the school building and the attendant outbuildings had been surrounded by a fence of barbed wire about eight feet high and equipped with security lights, the power being supplied by an electrical generator housed within the perimeter. On the periphery of the barbed wire were *pungees* (thick bamboo split in half lengthways, both ends made into very sharp points and then driven deeply into the ground). Each pungee was about three feet long, which, when driven into the ground, left some two feet exposed. Against the external side of the barbed wire the pungees were inserted vertically, the angle decreasing from ninety degrees to about ten degrees within a distance of about four feet. The visual effect was that the external perimeter was surrounded by a long snake-like hedgehog, four feet wide and two feet high. This was now standard practice for all Police Posts, as experience had shown that a large Mau-Mau gang could not rush the barbed wire.

Encompassed within the perimeter were sandbagged 'strongpoints', with low-angled corrugated iron roofs, the lower edge facing onto the wire perimeter.

Scattered around outside this perimeter at varying distances were a score of stone-built bungalows, which housed the American families. The ground fell steeply away from the school in an easterly direction, and at the bottom of this slope about a quarter of a mile away were more buildings which housed the African school, plus again stone housing for the staff.

In order to picture the situation, think of the American School building being a large oblong, double storied with the two longest sides facing North and South. To the North, the ground sloped upwards towards the forest, interspersed with several missionary bungalows. To the South, the ground sloped gently down with just two bungalows within visual distance, then beyond these dwellings light forestation. To the East was the African School; to the West a large open and flat playing field that the children used for games and the police for drill and parades and beyond this, more forestation. There was plenty of lush green grass interspersed with trees, and the earth, where exposed by roads or footpaths, was the colour of ochre. In bright sunlight, as the large 'cotton wool' clouds passed lazily overhead set against an incredibly blue sky, it presented an orderly and tranquil scene.

I was housed in a single-storey building within the school's perimeter, situated in the north-western corner, adjacent to one of the 'strongpoints'. The main school building had a large under-floor above ground area, which housed my twenty 'troops'. There were two gate entrances through the perimeter, one on the northern side, the other on the western side, the latter facing onto the playing field.

My main responsibility was the security of the children. In the event of an attack they had to be defended at all costs. If, and only if, they were not at risk, then if needs be I could release part of my strength to go to the assistance of those outside the wire.

Having arrived and completed the usual taking over of files, equipment, firearms and ammunition, I said goodbye to the previous incumbent and he wished me well for the future. Now that he had finally departed, accompanied by the Sergeant Major I checked the security of the perimeter. Walking through the perimeter wire was an African carrying some vegetables. How was this possible? A missionary informed me that this short-cut led to the vegetable plot and saved the gardener having to walk around to the western gate. So much for security! I had it blocked off.

The next discovery was a drainage ditch on the eastern boundary. I realised that all a terrorist had to do was crouch down low and duck under the wire, which was above the ditch, to gain entry inside our defences. I had this blocked off.

The next two items to be checked were the main gates. The northern gate was left open throughout the day. As the forest edge was only some one hundred or so yards away, on my orders it was closed. The western gate was also closed and I had a barbed wire zig-zag lane (one man width) installed beside it, which was always blocked off and secured before sundown.

There appeared to be a general feeling of 'the Lord will protect us' and I sincerely hoped that he would. However, as I was far from satisfied with security in general, I asked to address everyone following their Sunday afternoon church service.

My address to the congregation was based on (quickly swotted up from the Old Testament) quotes from the Bible, based on 'the Bible in one hand and the sword in the other'. I told the members of the congregation what each household must do to improve individual security which currently was far too lax, plus what to do in the event of an attack. I also briefed them on my duties and responsibilities for the children. It was well received and I stepped down to polite applause.

The next morning I briefed the children on general security; for example not straying beyond the perimeter, what to do if we were attacked, plus what not to do – like looking out of the windows in the school building (if we were attacked). I told them they were to position themselves away from the windows and against the outer stone walls in a prone position. I also ensured that in addition to the live-in tutors, the older pupils were delegated to look after the younger children. I now felt more confident that we had a much better chance of withstanding an attack than I had during my initial inspection.

Every member of the Mission staff was very friendly (as only Americans can be) and until I found a 'cook/house boy' I was invited to eat with the children and their tutors. It was all very pleasant. I was welcomed into their midst, made to feel at home, and soon after this invitations to meals started to arrive.

On the Mission Station was a Doc Proust who, despite being medically qualified, spent the majority of his time away on various projects, such as sinking wells and advising on the construction of dams. In so doing he had to leave his wife and young family at home in an exposed position. In the event of a Mau-Mau attack, and in order for them to have the maximum chance of survival, he had fireproofed his bungalow, fitted very substantial doors and window locks, and in addition, in the centre of the dwelling, he had built a room that could only be entered via a solid steel door. Cut into the door was a firing slot that could only be operated from inside this 'strong room'. He also ensured that his wife knew how to handle a firearm. To my mind he was the only person at the Mission who did not 'have his head in the sand'.

Having listened to the Sergeant Major regarding guard duties and rotas I decided that changes had to be made. When on guard duty at night a two hour 'stint' is about the maximum that anyone can stay really alert. I also informed him that I would be checking the guards throughout the night. Anyone found dozing, or asleep, would be doing 'pack drill' with their rifle held above their head. I then had him introduce me to each of the men in turn, asking them questions about how long they had served in the K.P.R. (Kenya Police Reserve), what made them join, where they came from and about their families. During this session, due to their demeanour and dress, I spotted two potential 'idle lumps'.

Following the introduction session we held an alarm exercise. It was a shambles! Some 'strongpoints' were packed out with bodies whilst others held just one man. This situation was also corrected.

Within a few days of my arrival the two 'idle lumps' were found asleep on guard duty. The Sergeant Major found one and on the same night I found the other. At night sound carries a long way. Hearing snoring, it came as no surprise to find 'idle lump' number one fast asleep. Beside his slumped figure was his rifle. I removed it, then shook him violently. He nearly died of fright!

The following morning both were to come before me on 'maktab' (a charge). At this stage I was an unknown quantity to the 'troops', therefore it was important that the outcome made its mark. The first man was marched in by the Sergeant Major who was resplendent dressed in his uniform with immaculate starched shorts, gleaming boots, with his red sash across his chest and 'swagger cane' held under his left arm.

"Left, right, left, right. Halt! Right turn! Salute! Hat off!"

The crashing of the boots onto the wooden floor caused the papers and pens on my table to jump and quiver.

"Effendi, Constable Ndibo, charged with being asleep on duty Effendi!"

This final 'Effendi' coupled with a very smart salute and more crashing of feet, caused the accused to jump and mirror the effects on my desktop!

"Right Sergeant Major, let me have your report."

The Sergeant Major was also out to impress. With more stamping on the wooden floor, plus another ear shattering "Effendi!" he intoned as, no doubt, many a Sergeant Major before him:

"On the night of the tenth at about 2am, as instructed, I commenced checking the night sentries. On arriving at the post of the accused I found him to be fast asleep. I awoke him and informed him that I was placing him on a charge."

This was followed by another ear shattering, "Effendi!"

"Thank you Sergeant Major, stand at ease."

More crashing of boots.

I only hoped that the wooden floor could stand it! I looked at Constable Ndibo, who had a very similar expression on his face as that seen in a dentist's waiting room.

"Well, what have you got to say?"

"I didn't mean to go to sleep Effendi; I just nodded off."

"Nodded off!" I crashed my fist onto the desk. "How dare you stand there and tell me you just 'nodded off'!"

Had the accused been European he would have turned white, as this was not the case he just became a paler black. I could see he was shaking.

"Anything to add Sergeant Major?"

As expected, more crashing of boots as the Sergeant Major came to attention.

"Effendi, I have had cause to warn the accused in the past, but he has never been found asleep on duty before Effendi."

More crashing of boots. I was beginning to be thankful that we didn't have five more accused as neither my ears or the floor would have survived the physical and auditory onslaught.

"Right, five days pack drill. Dismissed."

I leave it to your imagination as to the sound the Sergeant Major and the accused made as they marched out.

In came another accused. Yes, you're right, more crashing of boots onto my wooden floor and ear shattering "Effendi's."

Constable Kipchunga looked very uneasy as during the first 'maktab' he was standing just outside the door, no doubt listening to every word.

"You were fast asleep and I removed your rifle. Had I been a terrorist you would be dead."

"Ndiyo Effendi." (Yes Sir).

"What have you got to say for yourself?"

"I'm sorry Effendi."

"Sorry!" I crashed my fist onto the desk!

"By God, you could have been murdered, your rifle stolen, we could have been killed in our beds, and all you can say is Sorry!" I crashed my fist onto the desk again. "You should be shot!"

With these words, he wet himself.

"Sergeant Major, seven days pack drill plus an extra day for peeing on my floor. March him out, and when he's cleaned up, bring him back here to wash my floor."

Later that day the Sergeant Major, with a slight grin on his face, reported that word had spread, "whatever you do, never ever appear before the Bwana Inspector on a charge."

We never had another *askari* charged with being asleep on duty!

Some weeks later I learned from my cook Wainaina that the 'troops' had given me an African nickname – *Bwana Kelele* (Mr Noisy)!

As my quarters were very close to the wire perimeter, every night as a personal security measure I always placed a chair against the door, thus hopefully giving me sufficient reaction time to shoot any terrorists who had managed to infiltrate our defences intent on killing the officer in charge. My 'troops' were warned not to enter after dark without knocking and identifying themselves. Each night I was always fully dressed, awake, and if on my bed, my machine carbine was beside me cocked ready for instant action. One night the security chair crashed to the floor and the door started to be pushed open! I was off the bed in a trice and about to open fire, when, as the light was switched on, I saw the hand of a European on the light switch. It was Dave, one of my colleagues.

"Dave you bloody idiot! I could have killed you!"

I explained my personal security system. He seemed quite nonchalant about it, but it had been a very close thing; I could easily have killed him.

My nightly routine consisted of ensuring that the perimeter was secure. Just before sundown I would carry out a quick tour inside the perimeter to ensure that all the security lights were functioning. Then throughout the night, fully dressed and fully armed with machine carbine, grenades and sidearm as backup, I made irregular checks on the guards until about 4.30am. I then slept until about 10.30am when I had morning coffee with the tutors. Later I had lunch with the children and joined them again for dinner around 6pm. Dining with the children allowed both them and me to get to know each other.

Everyone called me by my nickname – 'Chips' – which generated a warm relaxed atmosphere. The origin of this name was an Australian film, screened several years before, in which an actor called 'Chips' Rafferty played the lead role. Evidently, I looked something like him. Considering that he was in his forties and I in my twenties, I was not sure the comparison was complimentary!

During the day, some of the younger children would come and hold my hand as I went about my daily duties. They would ask me questions about England: where I lived, what was school like in England, adding that I had a 'cute' accent. In turn I learned something about the American way of life.

Now you will recall that some of the children were aged around sixteen or seventeen. At this stage of my life I was twenty-two. Imagine my surprise when at first one of my men arrived, gave me a very smart salute then handed me a sealed envelope.

"Where has this come from?"

"A memsahib (woman) Effendi."

"Which memsahib?"

"Sijui jina yake Effendi. (I don't know her name, Sir.)"

With another smart salute he left.

I opened the letter. It read:

> Dear Chips,
> It's just great to have you around and we are very pleased that you have been sent here to look after us.
> We hope that you will be with us for a very long time.
> Signed:
> The Girls
> XXX

Similar notes would arrive from time to time, one even delivered by the Sergeant Major! It was never difficult to identify the senders as during my rounds I would be engaged in polite conversation with young ladies who blushed very easily. It was all very innocent.

I learnt American expressions such as: 'John' (toilet), 'over easy' (eggs flipped over and fried on both sides but retaining soft yolks), 'sunny side up' (eggs fried on one side only), 'Jelly' (jam), 'Vacation' (holiday), 'The Fall' (Autumn) to name but a few. I also experienced for the first time 'hamburgers' (made with beef not ham), 'mutton roasts' (yes, it's lamb), 'chilli con carne' (hot and spicy minced beef), and to appreciate the delights of eating crispy streaky bacon on toast with marmalade, cheese with apple pie, pumpkin pie, pineapple upside down cake (pineapple rings at the base of the cake), and perhaps my favourite, American pancakes spread with butter and served with maple syrup. Delicious!

Having been *in situ* for nearly a month without my own cook/houseboy, it was suggested that I might like to meet Wainaina (pronounced Why-ny-na) who was alleged to be an excellent cook, trained at the Mission. He turned out to be a 'jewel'. All the food was American style and you name it, he could produce it. I had American style pancakes for breakfast, excellent lunches, hot rolls, cakes, cookies (biscuits) and if I shot a game bird, an excellent fricassee of Franklin.

From time to time I would be visited by Jim Duffy, my nearby colleague. Following his first visit, and just before he was leaving, Wainaina handed Jim a paper parcel saying he hoped he would enjoy it. I later asked Wainaina what was in the parcel? His eyes were downcast and he shuffled his feet.

"Effendi, Bwana Duffy has a terrible cook, so I baked him a cake. As he is your friend, I was sure you wouldn't mind." He looked up.

"It's OK Wainaina," I reassured him, "I'm not angry."

He gave a shy grin and from then on Jim's visits normally terminated with a parcel.

During long vacation times the children went home. I would escort each group whilst my position would be manned by a relief until my return. It was hard going. I would brief each group about security, what to do if we were attacked, and to stay within the train's compartments until I said they could descend onto the platform. This final point normally only applied at their destination, which by then was well within a safe area. For these trips I was dressed in standard police uniform which was short sleeved starched jacket, shorts, khaki stockings with navy fold-over tops, black shoes, 'Sam Browne' belt with holster and sidearm and my blue peaked cap. Tucked into my left breast pocket a whistle attached around my left shoulder with a smart blue lanyard. My main firearm was a 'Sten gun' with two full magazines of 9mm ammunition taped together (this way an empty magazine could be removed, rapidly turned through 180 degrees and the replacement inserted into the gun).

Each trip could take up to nearly eighteen hours. During this time (until we were in non Mau-Mau area) I had to stay awake and alert, particularly when arriving at the various stations. The children were always very well behaved and a pleasure to be with.

At each journey's end we would be greeted by their parents, who never failed to invite me to one of their homes until it was time to catch my returning train. It was during this brief break that I could have a shave, shower, change into a fresh uniform and try to catch up on some sleep. I well recall arriving at Kisumu Railway Station just as dawn was breaking. One American family took me down to the lakeside (Lake Victoria) for an alfresco breakfast. At this time of the morning the breeze coming off the lake was cool, the water was tinged with pink from the early morning sun and ripples flashed like beaten gold. Big winged birds flew low over the water, casting black shadows onto the surface. Then coming down to water's edge to drink, not more than fifty yards away, some Impala (like large deer with lyre-shaped horns).

I lay back on the picnic blanket looking up at the now powder blue sky. There was hardly a cloud to be seen and at this time of the morning the only sounds were those caused by the wavelets lapping onto the shoreline. The smell of fresh brewing coffee and the aroma of hot bread rolls reminded me that breakfast was almost ready. It was a perfect morning that I have never forgotten. Some nights when I close my eyes, I can still recall that tranquil scene and the smell of the hot coffee and hot bread rolls; a memory to be savoured.

The return journeys were not so easy. I would normally share a sleeper compartment with another European. Perhaps I was fortunate as everyone proved to be an agreeable travelling companion and until the train entered the terrorist area I could relax. However, once into the area I was an ideal target for any small gang wishing to kill a member of the security forces to increase their weaponry, so once again it was imperative to 'be on ones toes'. It was always good to be 'home'.

It was during one of the school's vacations that I applied for two weeks leave. As everyone was at full stretch, it was to be my only long leave during my initial three years of service. A relief was found and, as luck would have it, Jim Duffy my nearby colleague was granted leave at the same time. We decided to go to Malindi, situated on the coast some forty miles north of Mombasa.

I telephoned the Blue Marlin Hotel and made the booking. We travelled in style, first by train to Nairobi, then by air to Mombasa in an East African Airways Dakota.[2]

When we vacated the aircraft at Mombasa the heat was far greater than Nairobi. As we made our way across the hot tarmac to the small airport terminal, the swaying palms and brilliant blue sky swept away all thoughts of anti-Mau-Mau operations, guard duties or night ambushes. We were several hundred miles within a safe area and free of all these things, and now on leave for two whole weeks!

We took a taxi and headed north for Malindi. It was like paradise with swaying palms, a brilliant blue sea and mile after mile of white sandy beaches that were almost blinding to look at. The road was of the same material, and very corrugated, which gave us a very bumpy dusty ride. Then came our first surprise. We had to cross a river on a hand-pulled ferry. The African ferry staff, numbering about ten, knew how to exploit their unique situation. Blowing on conch shells, stamping on the ferry's deck in perfect rhythm, and at the same time pulling on the chain that ran on pulley wheels connected to either bank, they started to sing in perfect harmony.

"Bwana mbili, wana kwenda safari.
Bwana mbtli wana kwenda Malindi.
(two Bwanas are going on a journey,
two Bwanas are going to Malindi).

I captured this scene with my 35mm camera, although what was really needed to capture the colour, sounds and movement of their dance was a movie camera. We dipped deep into our pockets and awarded them a handsome tip for this wonderful start to our holiday.

On route we passed the deserted town of Geddi, which had been abandoned hundreds of years before. The reason? To this day it has never been established. On the way we passed many bare-breasted African women wearing grass skirts, carrying baskets on their heads, a sight totally unknown 'up-country'. Since our arrival at Mombasa

---

[2] A twin-engined low-wing monoplane, designed and built in America. This 'workhorse' aircraft had been used extensively during the war and when hostilities ended many were sold off at bargain prices, which no doubt was how this one was acquired.

airport, everything was totally different to the Kenya that we knew. The tropical scene continued all the way to Malindi, even one of the hotels that we passed had Arabian architecture. Then within a few hundred yards there was The Blue Marlin. All the buildings were single-storey, painted white, thatched and almost right on the edge of the beach. It was just as I imagined it. We were introduced to Danny the manager, and his wife. They were a charming couple who made our stay very memorable. Nothing was too much trouble.

Being tired after our long journey we collapsed onto our beds and we must have dozed off. We were awoken by one of the African waiters armed with an alarm clock plus the dinner menu. Dinner was from 8pm and would we care to choose from the menu? Without any hesitation we both chose lobster for the main course. Living 'up-country' the only fish available were talarpia, fresh water fish caught in Lake Victoria, which, compared to sea fish, were fairly tasteless. Here on the coast, sea fish was in abundance; one night we even had turtle steaks! The food was always well presented, beautifully cooked and quite delicious.

With the beach only yards away, swimming just after sunrise was a fantastic experience. Beyond the surf and the reef, the sun was just on the edge of the horizon, making the sea flash with red and gold, and the seawater, unlike the UK, was warm and inviting. A quick 'dip' followed by a shower to wash off the salt and it was time to think about breakfast on the terrace, following which we visited a local shop to purchase swimming flippers, facemask, snorkel and spear-gun apiece. Thus equipped we were ready for action.

I was to make a very serious mistake. Even by Kenya standards I was quite brown, but I had overlooked the effect of strong sunlight on seawater. We spent a wonderful day swimming around the coral, face down in the water and breathing through our snorkels, seeing and sometimes joining, scores of brilliantly coloured fish, trying without success to 'bag' the bigger ones for dinner. It had been a very memorable day. Walking up the beach towards the hotel I suddenly noticed that my back felt sore. An hour later I was in agony and at the local hospital having some thick yellow fluid applied to my burning skin. What I had not realised was that to go snorkelling and spear fishing (which involved swimming mainly face down) it was very wise to wear a t-shirt as protection against the effects of the sun. If only I had known!

Within a few days I had recovered and in order to see more of the fish and coral within the reef we hired an Arab 'ngalau', a narrow fishing boat no more than two feet wide by eighteen feet long, made from a hollowed out tree trunk, with a lanteen sail and two outriggers. The anchor was a large rock secured with a rattan rope. This type of local craft could take us into deeper water but still inside the reef. This time, complete with t-shirt, I was determined to shoot a fish with my spear-gun, but I was finding diving down into twenty odd feet of water more difficult than I had imagined. The water was crystal clear and my underwater visibility must have been close to thirty yards.

Breaking the surface I heard the Kiswahili word *papa* (shark)! I have never covered ten yards so fast before or since, and I was quickly pulled into the ngalau by one of the Arab fishermen. He pointed. Just inside the reef, about a hundred yards away on the other side of the ngalau, cutting through the water were two dorsal fins. The fishermen pulled up their stone anchor, hoisted the lanteen sail and made for the beach.

That was the end of our 'fishing' trip.

That evening after dinner we told Danny about our experience. He said it was very, very unusual for shark to be inside the reef, as they did not like to be trapped in shallow water, so they must have come through a gap in the reef at high tide. A European local even doubted our story until I asked him what *papa* meant.

"It means shark in Kiswahili."

"Well, that's the word the Arab fishermen used and that's why we came back to the beach!"

We visited the local fish market. On display with numerous types of smaller fish were two large hammerhead sharks, plus what is best described as an ordinary shark. Seeing its large jaws and razor sharp teeth I was very glad that I had been ten and not fifty yards away from the ngalau!

One day Danny and his wife asked if we would like to join them at their favourite beach. It was a few miles South of Malindi. When we arrived the tide had receded, leaving a fissure in the coral some thirty feet long by six feet wide and some nine feet deep on the seaward side. It was a natural swimming pool, teeming with small, brilliantly-coloured tropical fish. To complete nature's construction, the base of the pool was covered with fine white sand. In my mind's eye I can still picture the pool, the brilliant white sand on the beach, the swaying palm trees that shaded their parked car, with Danny and his wife lounging on the rug and the delicious picnic lunch.

Our idyllic holiday continued... We bathed by the beach, went spear fishing, drank delicious cool milk from coconuts cut from high palm trees, their tops lopped off with a *panga* (machete), we ate well, slept well and forgot about the Mau-Mau terrorists hundreds of miles away.

From time to time we would visit nearby hotels for a pre-dinner 'snifter'. One evening at one of the hotel bars we met a slight, blonde lady with a dachshund. The dog was in a very playful mood.

"Oh, he wants something to chew on," she said, and with that dipped her hand inside the front of her dress, pulled out a 'falsie' and threw it to the dog to play with. I knew people in Kenya were relaxed, but this took top prize!

Suddenly it was our last day; it had finished all too quickly. Following an excellent dinner, we packed ready for our early morning departure. We said goodbye to Danny and his wife and thanked them for an excellent two weeks – without any doubt their hospitality had 'made' our holiday – then into our taxi, passing miles of shimmering white sand and swaying palm trees, trying to absorb into our memories the sights and sounds of this beautiful coastline, then via the hand-operated ferry on to Mombasa airport. It had been a memorable and relaxing two weeks. I could have stayed there forever.

In just a few hours we were circling over Nairobi airport. As the train drew out of Nairobi railway station, it seemed strange to be back into Mau-Mau territory. At the coast it had all seemed so far away, as if in another land. Now it was back to reality.

Once the school's vacation time was over, the parents normally travelled with their children when returning them to school and then it was back to the usual routine. It was during one such vacation period that I was asked by a member of staff if I could look after someone's dog, a pedigree golden coated bitch named 'Pixie'. It was to be for a period of about six months. Having a dog would provide some welcome companionship, so I readily agreed.

'Pixie' was duly delivered from Nairobi by her lady owner, together with her box, lead and feeding instructions. She soon settled in and proved to be a good companion. Obviously it was important that she was inside at night, but during the day roamed at will both inside and just outside the perimeter. Although I had not been charged with guarding her virginity, you can imagine my surprise when one morning I awoke to find Pixie with six black pups in her box! They proved to be an absolute delight, due to their antics of gambolling over each other, playfully biting each other's tails and ears, and generally having a great time, as only young puppies can. They provided a constant daily diversion to my routine. My favourite I named Tumbo, which means 'stomach' in Kiswahili. He was the greediest of the bunch and always the most playful. I decided to keep him. When the litter was old enough they all went to good and caring homes.

A few weeks later the lady arrived from Nairobi to collect her prize bitch and was not very amused to find Tumbo romping over his wayward mother. Tumbo proved to be an excellent guard dog and later in his life sometimes accompanied me on patrol.

When I had first arrived at the Mission Station, during my 'sermon', I had offered to teach the American ladies how to handle their personal firearms and this was enthusiastically accepted. They arrived with an assortment of weapons ranging from an ex-American army Colt 45 automatic, a German chrome-plated 9mm Walther P.38 automatic, plus an assortment of revolvers that would have left Wyatt Earp and Buffalo Bill spoiled for choice! I went to great lengths to explain to the American ladies the vital differences between an automatic pistol and a revolver, stressing the need for safety when handling any firearm. When questioned, very few of the ladies had fired their weapons before and some looked decidedly apprehensive. I took them to the 'firing line' one at a time and told them that they were to face the front and not turn around until I said it was safe to do so.

The first lady was the one with the Colt 45 automatic. I asked her if she knew how the pistol was operated and fired. She answered all my questions correctly. I then asked her to load two bullets into the 'clip' and to ensure that the safety catch was on. I was standing right beside her to ensure that we avoided any accidents. I now asked her to prepare the pistol for firing and to keep her finger away from the trigger. At first she had forgotten to take off the safety catch. Having done this, she correctly 'cocked' the pistol. I now asked her if she knew what would happen when she fired and immediately following the first shot? Again she correctly answered my questions.

"You are now ready to fire. Point the pistol at the target and gently squeeze the trigger."

It fired. She exclaimed "Oh my goodness!" and before I could say anything, immediately fired the second shot, which struck the ground just ten feet in front of us! Thank goodness she had only loaded two bullets! She had turned very pale and was shaking.

"Oh my goodness, what a loud bang, then it went off again on its own!" I tried to reassure her, but it was to no avail, she did not want to try again.

The lady with the Walther P38 automatic was cool, calm and collected. Having fired off the two practice bullets, she had no problem loading a full 'clip' and hitting the target.

I re-explained the differences between the two systems to the 'revolver ladies' and, apart from some finding it hard to pull the trigger, the shoot was completed without further incident.

About 1.30am was my time to check on the sentries. As my quarters were very close to the wire I never had my electric light on, using if needs be, a torch. I opened my door to commence my rounds. As I did so I heard the sentry stationed by the top Northerly gate challenge, followed by a terrible scream! I cocked my machine carbine and ran to where the sentry was. When I found him he was quivering like a jelly.

"Effendi, they tried to kill me!"

About two feet from his side was a spear stuck in the ground.

"Where are they?"

He pointed. Despite the fact that it was semi-moonlight, I fired an 'illuminating flare' into the air and loosed off half a magazine of ammunition in the general direction in which the sentry had pointed. By now, the 'troops', having heard the firing, were running to take up their positions. Together with the Corporal, I went outside the perimeter, shouting to the sentry to warn everyone where we were.

My thoughts were: "If there is a gang about to strike, then let's surprise them and scatter them!" I felt almost detached and 'ice cool'; it was a strange feeling. By this time the alarm system had been activated and the mission bell was tolling, followed by the bell at the African School below. I hoped that this would more than deter the terrorists. I was positive I had seen someone entering into the forest.

We approached cautiously, keeping within every shadow and making no noise. We now entered into the forest edge, moving slowly, ready to react to any sound. I motioned to the Corporal to stop and 'go down' and listen. He was about five yards to my right. In the distance I could hear a vehicle approaching. This would be Jim Duffy, my colleague from the local Police Station about four miles away. I recalled the earth road was very twisty with quite a steep climb and I hoped that this attack was not a diversion to ambush his vehicle.

We continued to wait and listen. We heard the vehicle stop, then the sound of vehicle doors slamming, shouted orders and the sound of running feet. Jim had arrived! By his voice I could tell that he was now close to the forest edge.

"Chips, Chips, where are you?"

As we were exposed, we stayed silent. Jim called again.

"Chips where are you, answer me!" Now this was becoming very 'dodgy'. If there were any Mau-Mau ahead of us our reply would identify our exact position and they would either shoot at us, or rush us. However, Jim's next shout 'clinched the deal'.

"We are about to rake the forest with automatic and rifle fire!"

I motioned to the Corporal to get behind a tree. Once we had done this I shouted. "We are about twenty five yards ahead of you. We are positive there is someone ahead of us. I will now open fire, then we will withdraw from this position. Take no action until we are with you."

I loosed off one magazine in an arc and we quickly made our way back to the rescue party. They then 'blazed away' to scatter any gang hiding in the forest, together with the support of an armoured car unit who had also been called to assist.

About an hour later, all was calm and I questioned the sentry. Evidently he had seen a person standing just on the edge of the illumination given by the security lights and had challenged (which is what I had heard). A second person had crawled undetected in the shadow of 'pungees' cast by the security lighting. Having identified the position of the sentry, the terrorist had stood up and thrown the spear. The obvious intention was to silently eliminate the sentry on the northern gate and then attack. Two things thwarted their plans. One, they failed to kill the sentry, and two, my timely arrival. The other aspect that I found heartening was that the alarm and 'stand to' system had worked. Our training had not been in vain. Following this incident I decided to adopt a more pro-active role with the idea of perhaps surprising a Mau-Mau scouting party probing our defences. Having warned the sentries we were patrolling outside the wire, the security lights would be very briefly switched off to cover our exit. From then we would keep to the shadows and move very slowly. Sometimes it took almost ten minutes to cover as many yards. The patrols consisted of myself and three of the 'troops'. The briefing was always the same.

"Stay together, stay spaced apart, point your loaded and cocked weapon to your left and never ahead, never become separated from the patrol, keep the man ahead of you within visual distance and only use sign language."

On one particular night we were close to the African School; there was no moon, only starlight. We were making our way back to the American School when suddenly there was shouting, followed by a scream and footsteps pounding in our direction. We 'hit the deck' immediately! By being at ground level anyone standing is silhouetted and becomes an easy target. By the shape of the person running towards our position I realised it could be one of our party. I took aim and challenged. It was a member of our patrol!

"Effendi, Effendi don't shoot, its me, the Mau-Mau have taken my gun!" He threw himself down beside me. My first thoughts were "thank God he's safe!" quickly followed by "oh my God, the Mau-Mau have his rifle."

The Mission bell started to toll and this was then taken up by the one based at the African section of the Mission. There were bugle calls (a typical Mau-Mau method of attack), about five shots and lots of shouting. This was it! We were outside our perimeter and in the middle of a Mau-Mau attack! I told my patrol to form a loose triangle and to shoot anyone who was armed and running towards our defences. Now I could hear in the distance one of the American Missionaries shouting and there were lots of other shouts and the odd scream. I felt that we were about to emulate 'Custer's Last Stand'! The only thing in our favour was that the gang did not know that we were outside the wire, therefore, we had the element of surprise. However, the 'downside' was that as it was dark we could come under fire from our own 'troops'. Suddenly there was silence, then again the voice of a male American Missionary, but much closer now. We held our prone position. Now came the sound of several African male voices and an American's voice joining in, which I recognised as the Reverend Devitt. By now they were no more than 25 yards away.

Staying prone I shouted, "It's Chips here, what's going on?"

He shouted in response, "It's all right."

We saw torchlight approaching. I told my men not to fire. At a distance of about ten yards I took aim and challenged. It was the Reverend Devitt, surrounded by about fifteen African schoolboys.

All was now revealed. It wasn't a Mau-Mau attack. The schoolboys had seen one of our patrol passing by their sleeping quarters and thinking he was a Mau-Mau terrorist, they had pounced on him and seized his rifle. It had been a very brave thing to do. The askari at the end of our patrol line had, against orders, detached himself from the patrol to investigate a noise near one of the African School buildings. Being unaware of this, we had continued making our way back to 'base'. Hearing all the shouting and the scream (one of which was made by our askari) the Reverend Devitt had also assumed it was an attack and had blown his ex-army bugle then, to hopefully deter any terrorists, had fired off his Colt 45 automatic pistol.

It just shows how easily there could have been innocent blood shed.

Regarding the bugle calls. The Mau-Mau normally 'hyped themselves up' by smoking *bhang* (hashish), then to give themselves even more 'Dutch courage' and put the 'fear of God' into the defenders, as the gang rushed forward they would blow bugles, shout and fire off their weapons. From this you can easily understand how we thought we were in the middle of one such attack.

The following day, and for seven days thereafter, a certain askari could be seen doing pack drill under the 'eagle eye' of the Sergeant Major, with his (recovered) rifle held high above his head as he doubled up and down the sports field…

By this time I had been at the mission for nearly fifteen months. Everything was in good order; it was time to move on. I was posted to the edge of the Masai Reserve. My brief was to provide security to the farmers and ranchers, prevent thefts of European-owned cattle and to counter any attempts by Mau-Mau terrorists to cross the plains onto Mount Longenot.

This was to be another new experience and Tumbo would be there to share it with me…

5   Masai mischief

If you ever visit Nairobi and have cause to travel by road to Naivasha or journey on to Nakuru, after a score or so miles the tarmac road will start to descend down a steep winding escarpment. By looking to your left where the land falls away you will see the floor of the Great Rift Valley. In the hazy distance is a mountain named Suswa. Ahead, due to distance, the road first becomes a thin line and then disappears into the haze, and as you continue towards Naivasha, also to your left is another mountain named Longenot. Both of these are extinct volcanoes. This whole area that you can now see as you proceed on your way was a part of East Africa where I worked and which I grew to love. At the base of the escarpment (as you are now aware), there is a tiny Italian Church (built with scrap materials by Italian prisoners of war during WW2) and almost opposite off to the left there is a dirt road. If you have the chance take this road it will lead you into a unique area known as the Kedong Valley.

As you descended the escarpment, and had you looked very closely across the Rift, you would have noticed that at first there is cultivation giving a mixture of various greens, fading through browns to yellow, caused by crops of ripening maize and tobacco, almost ready for harvesting. During my time in Kenya these crops were grown by a string of European-owned farms that hugged the edge of this Great Rift Valley. Beyond the farms the whole area is covered with acacia trees, thorn bushes, wild castor oil plants and scrub. The land is arid during the dry season; the grass withers in the heat, wild flowers no longer add their colours to the land, and water is scarce. Beyond the cultivation was a strip of European-owned cattle country where only native-bred 'Boran' cattle could survive the rigours of the climate, and with the paucity of forage during the dry season, the numbers were kept down to no more than two head per acre of grazing. Within days of 'the rains' arriving, dry stream beds would be in flood, green grass shoots and wild flowers would appear as if by magic, and the cattle would visibly fatten as nature continued with its annual cycle.

The European cattle country formed a boundary with the Masai Reserve. The Masai were, and still are, cattle people, and due to the nature of the land, nomadic. A tough, resilient people who, based on their past victories, had a reputation as fearless unbeatable warriors when long before the Europeans came they had driven the Kikuyu from part of this vast plain into the hills above the escarpment. Straddling the European boundaries and as far as the eye can see, is an area teeming with game. Giraffe, zebra, ostrich, Thompson's gazelle, Grant's gazelle, dik-dik , wildebeest, lion, cheetah, leopard, hyena, wild dog, warthog, giant porcupine, and wild birds of nearly every description. On the slopes of Suswa there are rhino, whilst the slopes of Longenot are a favourite haunt of buffalo. The list is almost endless. The only species that we did not have was elephant. To me this hot lowland with its diversity of flora, fauna, climate and fascinating wildlife was, and is, East Africa. I embraced it, revelled in it, and when the time came I didn't want to leave it. As I write these words, the memories come flooding back, and in my mind's eye I can picture it all so clearly. Part of me will remain there forever.

My Police Post was based at a European cattle ranch and some hundred yards away from the farmhouse where I rented a room on a full board basis. The farmer, Arthur Stevens, also agreed that my dog Tumbo could be with me and he soon settled in with the other four dogs and, no doubt based on their tuition, became an excellent guard dog.

Due to the size of my patrol area I had a Land Rover and driver, and 'troops' totalling twenty in number consisting of a Sergeant Major, a Corporal and eighteen men, all KPR (Kenya Police Reserve) volunteers. The post always looked smart with its circle of white painted stones around the flagpole, which was surmounted by the blue Kenya Police flag. The Post was surrounded by barbed wire with the usual sand-bagged 'strong points' and almost in its centre was a large acacia tree, which provided year-round shade for the quarters below its branches. Set off to one side was the radio mast for our VHF transmitter/receiver. It all looked very orderly.

The main farmhouse was of typical Colonial construction; single storied, with stone walls, corrugated roof painted with red-lead (now faded with the sun), spacious airy rooms, with the whole surrounded by a wide cool veranda which was an extension of the shallow angled roof and supported on stone pillars. On the kitchen side of the house, and jutting beyond the veranda, was a cool store made from charcoal contained by a wooden frame and wire netting with its door facing onto the veranda. This store was hosed with water every day by the 'shamba-boy' (gardener) which, owing to constant evaporation, kept its contents surprisingly cool.

Electricity was supplied by an ancient diesel engine and water was pumped by a 'ram method' from the nearby river. On each corner of the building was a stone built water butt some four feet wide and about eight feet high. This was the emergency water supply and would only normally be used during the dry season. The whole building was surrounded by large, neatly trimmed lawns and flowerbeds, interspersed with bushes of frangipani (with flowers similar in shape to a crocus, looking almost like white wax with pale yellow centres and very heavily scented) and bougainvillaea, (which has a mass of deep red flowers). Also within the garden were several jacaranda trees, their pale mauve flowers and leaves providing areas of deep cool shade. It was almost like an oasis in a desert. Beyond the garden boundary in every direction was Africa as it had always been and always will be.

The farmhouse had a small 'shamba' (garden) that provided some vegetables, paw-paw, limes, bananas and other species of tropical fruit. Meat, both farm bred and wild, was available 'on the hoof', as were game birds like guinea fowl and franklin. It was an ideal existence that had been created during the late twenties from virgin bush by vision, determination, hard work and that vital ingredient, British grit.

The farm's owner, Mrs Stephens, was a widow now in her early seventies; she had arrived at the farm as a young bride, having completed the final few miles to her new home on horseback. It was here that she adapted to her new life in the Kenyan bush and raised her four children. Only one, Arthur, now remained at home to run the farm, the boundary of which bordered onto the Masai Reserve.

Having taken over command of the Post, as the next day was quiet, I visited all but one of the farms covered by my area, one of which was owned by a retired army major who lived in a beautiful bungalow tucked right up against the escarpment. The garden was large and a riot of colour containing a large natural swimming pool fed by a series of springs, some very hot and the others cold, the mix providing an ideal temperature. One edge of the pool provided a home for a host of water-loving cannas, their bright deep orange flowers glowing in the bright sunlight. Some sequences for the film *Where No Vultures Fly* had been shot at this location.

The area was not without its history. On a small hillock within the Kedong Valley is Colville's grave. He was revered by the Masai as, in their eyes, his hunting of game on horseback ensured that they had more grazing for their cattle. His part in Kenya's past was featured in the film *'White Mischief'*.

A very capable, no-nonsense widow, supported by a European farm manager and his wife, ran the next farm. A European farm manager who was married and had several children ran the closest farm to the Police Post. I was well received at all these locations and during this 'whirlwind' tour I gained some insight into the different problems that I could face in providing security for this part of my area.

The cattle ranch furthest away was close to an area known as 'Hell's Mouth', so named because of the weird shrieks and howls made by steam escaping from the base of the extinct Longenot volcano. This ranch was vast in size and was managed by a German and his English wife and was some twenty miles away from the Police Post 'as the crow flies'.

I well recall my first visit. When leaving the dirt road that heads in a Westerly direction to Narok and heading off to the right, we drove through hundreds and hundreds of wildebeest, Thompson and Grants gazelle, several stately giraffe making their way across the plain and small herds of zebra. About a year later it was at this ranch that I was to meet Herr Von Opel, who owned the German Opel car company and was also the man responsible for transporting the first panda to London Zoo.

Having roughly grasped the boundaries of my area, and as it was still quiet, now seemed the time to 'lead from the front' to gain the respect of my new team. The first thing I organised was firing practice. I placed ten empty tin cans at a range of thirty yards and in the main most of the men proved to be hopeless shots. Now it was my turn. I could use a .303 rifle and with rapid fire sent all ten cans 'flying in the air'. This was greeted with shouts of "Ah la!" – a typical African expression of surprise.

Thank goodness I had hit all ten tins! Now it was the driver's turn. Being a driver he was armed with a .45 Webley revolver. The tins were placed at just ten yards. He didn't hit one!

I could also use a .38 revolver, with which I sent six cans flying, reloaded and 'finished off' the remaining four. To the accompaniment of more "Ah la's".

That night walking round the 'lines' with the Sergeant Major we could hear the men discussing the range practice.

"Did you see how quickly he fired at those tins! You were hopeless!" This comment was followed by loud laughter.

I had something else organised for the following day.

"Sergeant Major, tomorrow morning at dawn I want the Land Rover with an escort, and you are to select six men. They will be armed, carry one day's rations and must have a full water bottle."

I was about to see if they could walk.

At dawn next morning I arrived at the post, everyone was ready and obviously unsure what was going on. I told them.

"Some of you have been involved in trying to catch cattle thieves and I understand that to date no recoveries have been made. We need to change this. Tracking cattle thieves means walking at an above average pace. So today the driver will drop us off twenty miles from here within the Masai Reserve. We will then walk back here at a fast pace in as straight a line as possible, stopping only every hour for a brief rest. Any questions?"

Their expressions told me that either they thought that I was mad, or it was going to be a waste of time. They were in for a shock! Having patrolled in the Aberdares, sometimes at a height of eleven and twelve thousand feet, I had stayed super fit. Now, being at a much lower altitude, I was sure that I could (with effort) 'walk them off their feet'.

Having dropped us off, the driver and his escort headed back to base leaving a faint cloud of dust in their wake. Despite the early hour the sun was already hot in a cloudless sky and in the far distance I could see a small herd of Thompson's Gazelle grazing. To our north the peak of Mount Longonot stood out proud and clear against the distant skyline.

It was time to move off...

I led the group and we set off at a cracking pace, which took them by surprise. I did not look back and, as we were still going at the original pace after the first thirty minutes, I could sense that at least one of them was finding it difficult to keep up. They were Africans, how was this possible? Not every African 'lives in the bush', some are 'townies' and as a result are not that fit. We stopped after the first hour for a break and a drink. I noted that two of the men sat down somewhat heavier than the others. We set off again at the same cracking pace. At our second stop we had two laggards, but I was determined not to ease the pace. Now, I had been told that there were lions in the area and this group must have been aware of this which would no doubt act as an incentive to keep up. At the third stop three were 'dragging their feet' and arrived several minutes after we had sat down. From now on only four of us kept together and the other three were stumbling along behind.

On arrival at the Post I told 'my' three "Well done!"

As I walked across to the farmhouse, about two hundred yards away I could see the remaining three staggering towards the Post, however I must admit that I was glad that I had not stipulated twenty-one miles! Having consumed several pints of water I collapsed onto my bed and fell asleep.

That evening I again joined the Sergeant Major and we walked around the 'lines', catching snippets of conversation about the day's exercise. From these I gathered that I had definitely 'made my point'. When time permitted, everyone was subjected to the same exercise with the exception of the driver, and, due to his age, the Sergeant Major. Each time the men back at base would be there to cheer those that 'made it' and poke fun as the laggards came stumbling in. From time to time some of the 'troops' would be posted elsewhere and when walking around the lines at night I would hear 'the old hands' telling the new arrivals that tomorrow, if there wasn't any trouble, they were going for a walk with 'Bwana Msharubu'. (I was, by now, sporting a moustache, so my new African nickname was 'Bwana Moustache'.)

"A walk, what's it all about?" This would be greeted with laughter and the words, "You'll find out tomorrow!" More laughter; this told me that morale was good.

Following this first walk, and within less than eight hours, I was about to experience my first stock theft...

Tumbo's growling at my French window woke me up. It was almost dawn and through the glass I could see that the sky was just slightly tinged with pink. Tumbo erupted into a frenzy of barking. Outside was the Corporal. I ordered Tumbo to "stay". He stopped barking but still had a growl deep in his throat. I opened the French window and the early morning air felt chill and I shivered in my pyjamas.

"Effendi, there has been a stock theft from Akira Ranch."

"How many cattle?"

"The report says fifteen, Effendi."

"Right, I need the Land Rover and escort and tell the driver to carry extra petrol. In addition I want six men, fully armed with three days rations and two water bottles each, and one of the men must be a tracker."

"Ndiyo Effendi." The Corporal saluted and hurried off. I hurried to the bathroom, quickly washed and shaved, and within ten minutes I was ready. I had on 'jungle greens' and hat, plus my camouflage smock. Normal police uniform would be useless. I carried a small pack with a medical kit and a small bag of salt to combat heat exhaustion, sterilising tablets, three tins of corned beef and biscuits, plus two one litre army-type water bottles attached to my waist belt, with just a pinch of salt in each bottle. I also packed a woollen police sweater, the same type as issued to the men. I carried my Patchett machine carbine with two full magazines of 9mm ammunition and my sidearm. There was no time for breakfast; I grabbed some bananas, had a quick drink of milk from the cool store and we were off.

It was, as usual, a beautiful morning, with the heavy dew holding down the dust trail made by our vehicle. I must admit that I felt a tinge of excitement and various thoughts ran through my mind. What would we find; would we have a recovery; how many days would it take? A pack of wild dogs ran off to our left, no doubt startled by the noise and size of the Land Rover. We cleared the cattle boundary and skirting along the edge of the Masai Reserve headed north towards the dirt road that leads to Narok.

Until we arrived at the road we were driving across bush country, being bounced and thrown around; the driver adding to our discomfort by swerving to avoid the almost hidden large ant-bear holes; the vehicle leaving a faint dust trail in our wake. We passed herds of Thompson's gazelle, the black stripe on their sides contrasting strongly with their vivid brown topcoat and white under-belly. Apart from raising their heads they seemed unperturbed by our passing and I could not help noticing how their small tails twitched as they raised their heads. In the distance and off to our left was a huge herd of zebra, there must have been at least five hundred of them. Just before 'hitting' the Narok road, two giraffe were walking along in a very stately fashion but as we drew near, moved off at speed running with their usual ungainly loping stride.

We were now on the Narok road, its dirt surface bone dry and the Land Rover leaving a dust trail in its wake. About two miles further on we turned off to the right, taking the track to Akira Ranch and startling the abundance of wildlife that was grazing on the dew-soaked grass. At the ranch we met with the manager and his head herdsman.

"We've lost fifteen head and we reckon that they were taken about 1.00am."

"How was it done?"

"The usual method, cutting the fence. Follow me and I'll show you."

The wires had been cut where they were secured onto the fence posts with staples. The thieves wouldn't have had wire cutters but would simply use their 'simis' (short swords) hitting where the wire was taut against the solid posts.

"Do the cattle have any identifying marks?"

"Yes, they are all branded like this." He pointed to a brand on a nearby cow.

"OK, my men will obtain descriptions of the cattle and we'll be off."

Where you and I would see just a brown cow with white patches, this is not so with cattle people. My tracker Kipkoske was a Kipsigi and not so far removed from the Masai. As a result, he went into great detail with the head herdsman regarding each and every cow's description. As the Land Rover was needed to respond to any emergency, I told our driver to return to base and we set off in pursuit of the cattle thieves on foot.

Initially, tracks were very evident, and the men pointed out that one of the thieves had an abnormally long big toe on his right foot. As and when we might catch up with the stolen stock and the thieves, this would assist us in identifying at least one of the party.

At this juncture it is worth pausing to explain how the Masai stock thieves drive the stolen cattle. They run the cattle at a jogging pace of about five miles an hour, which any Masai can keep up all night or all day and, being cattle people, they handle the stolen stock with ease. As the cattle are being driven in the cool of the night the need to keep stopping for them to drink is averted, which is also in the thieves favour. After some simple arithmetic, you will start to understand how difficult it was going to be for us, not just to catch up with the cattle but to find and arrest the thieves. The cattle were stolen at about 1.00am. It was now 6.30am, so they had a five and a half hour advantage. Multiply this by five miles per hour and by now they were some twenty seven to twenty eight miles away and still running. Initially the ground was dry and soft and, even to my inexperienced eye, the route taken by the thieves was not difficult to follow. However, the Masai are not stupid, and they will do everything possible to cover up their tracks. We were on foot, travelling at an average pace of three miles an hour – they were travelling at five. All we could hope to do was keep following their tracks until (as they had to stop somewhere) we finally traced the stolen cattle and arrested the thieves.

We were heading roughly in the direction of Mount Suswa and were now climbing a ridge of hard ground and I was finding it difficult to see any tracks, but not Kipkoske, he was a skilled tracker and used the barrel of his rifle to point where the tracks were. The sun was now climbing into the sky and it was going to be the usual hot day and where we were heading I was not aware of any water being available. Would this prove to be a major problem? We came across some cattle 'droppings'. To my surprise Kipkoske put a finger into it. We clustered around and he announced that it was still slightly warm; about six hours old. How simple! The hot dung loses its heat at a roughly constant rate and Kipkoske had added into his 'calculations' that is was dropped at night. We continued, with Kipkoske leading the way, using his rifle as a pointer. Now we were onto a patch of dry soft earth. Kipkoske called me to examine some hoof prints.

"Look here Effendi, this cow has a slightly damaged rear hoof."

I looked very closely. I could clearly see the hoof print, but nothing that would indicate to me that it was damaged.

"I saw this track back at the ranch and it fits the description given by the herdsman."

"Is it lame?"

"No Effendi, there isn't a sign of lameness and by the length of each animals track they were still being run when they passed through here." We continued to follow at a fast walking pace.

By mid-day with the sun beating down we paused under a small acacia tree. It didn't give much shade but was better than nothing. Due to the bright sunlight I screwed up my eyes, looking ahead in the direction taken by the stock thieves. The ground was already shimmering in the heat and the beads of sweat trickled down my face and the back of my shirt was soaked with perspiration. I removed my jungle hat, using it to mop my face and then took a deep draught from one of my water bottles. The water was warm and the small amount of salt I had added would help to combat the salt lost in my sweat. I felt like another drink, but caution stopped me. I was carrying water sterilising tablets, but what if we could find no water?

We set off again and despite the shade from the brim of my jungle hat I had to screw up my eyes against the harsh sunlight. About an hour later we came across an old Masai man. Kipkoske could understand Masai, which was just as well, as very few Masai speak Kiswahili.

[To illustrate just how different the two languages are, the Masai greeting is "*Soba*." In Kiswahili it's "*Hujambo*".]

No he hadn't seen anyone with fifteen cattle (and we suspected, if he had he wouldn't tell us anyway). The track we were following suddenly mixed in with other cattle tracks. Now what? Kipkoske told me that our cattle had been deliberately mixed with the others, but all was not lost. We now switched direction and followed this new route, which had been pounded into dust by many herds of cattle.

After about five miles Kipkoske paused to examine some tracks that led off in roughly the same direction as our original route. We all gathered round.

"Effendi look here." He knelt and pointed with his finger.

"It's that cow again… and these Masai footprints are the same as those we have been following all this time." The imprint in the dusty earth of the thief with the long big toe was visible even to my inexperienced eyes. After a few hundred yards I called a halt; we needed to eat and here there was ample shade. We all squatted down under an acacia tree; even in the shade the slight breeze was still warm. I opened my tin of corned beef and spread some onto a biscuit. Due to the heat the meat was soft and the 'hard tack' biscuit, despite the soft corned beef, was difficult to masticate. I washed it down with a mouthful of my precious water. This was so different to the Aberdare forests, where there was an abundance of water and the forest canopy and the altitude kept the daily temperature to a reasonable level. I ate just half a tin of meat; I would need the remainder when we stopped for the night.

The men discussed amongst themselves how far ahead of us the stock thieves might be by now and where they were really heading, adding how clever the Masai are at trying to lose their tracks. Constable Kipchumba asked for my opinion.

"*Effendi, unafikili tuta washika?*" (Sir, do you think we will arrest them?)

"*Tuta jaribu Kipchumba, tuta jaribu.*" (We will try Kipchumba, we will try) was my reply.

We picked up our packs and firearms and once again set off in pursuit.

It was now almost 3pm and I calculated that we must have covered way in excess of twenty miles. We continued tracking and from time to time were diverted and delayed by the stock thieves' tactics of mixing their tracks with other cattle, yet despite these constant halts to check for tracks, thanks to Kipkoske and some of his keen eyed colleagues we were still on their trail!

By now it had turned 6pm and it would be dark within less that an hour. The sun was very low in the sky, starting to tinge the clouds with pink and orange and the very welcome early evening breeze felt cool as it passed over my face and bare forearms. Kipkoske stopped and knelt down, paused, took a few steps, and knelt down again.

"Effendi, they split up here. We have been following five men all day and two of them have gone off in that direction with five head of cattle." He gestured towards the West.

"Is one of them the thief with the big toe?"

"No Effendi, he's still heading in this direction." Kipkoske gestured towards the south. Should I divide my small force? We hadn't any radio, there weren't any Mau-Mau within the Reserve but, if we split up, there was a possibility of the thieves and their friends attacking just three men, despite the fact they were each armed with a .303 rifle. I decided the risk was too great. We would continue to follow the main track and if we caught up with the thieves, they might lead us to the others.

About two miles further on with dusk rapidly descending, tracking became impossible; as a result we halted for the night and I arranged the guard duties. I would take first 'stag' and, based on my Aberdares experience, I instructed the men to sleep in a triangular formation. We were travelling light without ponchos or blankets but the night air, now that the breeze had dropped, felt warm – which would no doubt change before dawn. We ate the balance of our day's ration, consumed some more water, and settled down for the night.

We were in a good position. The ground all around us was devoid of bushes and therefore anyone approaching under the cover of darkness would be spotted (I hoped). The other plus was that the grass was short and not suitable (again I hoped) for lions. The men settled down and I put on my sweater and camouflage smock, tightening the cord on the bottom to keep my body heat in. I cocked my 'Patchett' machine carbine and sat by the apex of our triangle. In this position, anything approaching would be silhouetted.

I was all ears and strained my eyes to penetrate our surroundings. At a distance that I estimated to be no more than four to five hundred yards, I could hear cattle lowing and the soft tinkling of their cowbells. I made a mental note to check there in the morning.

There wasn't a moon, but due to the altitude and the lack of any form of pollution the stars were more brilliant than I had ever seen them before. The heavens were packed with a dazzling array of stars of differing sizes and brightness and I could easily identify 'the Plough'. I recalled seeing star-studded skies back home in England, but never like this. My thoughts returned to the day's events. I couldn't see our water lasting for three days and we must have enough to get us back to 'Akira'. I was sure it was the correct decision not to divide our small force. I glanced at my luminous wrist watch. Was it possible I had already been on guard duty for nearly fifty minutes? The air temperature was falling and in reaction to the cold I automatically shrugged my shoulders inside my smock.

My 'stag' was uneventful and I handed over to my relief. Removing my camouflage smock I lay down, put my knees into the inside of the hood and covered my hunched body with the remainder. Within minutes I was fast asleep.

The cold penetrates my subconscious mind. I stir still semi-asleep, but the cold persists and I wake up and look at my watch – almost 6am. I sit up and look at the man on 'stag'; he grins and makes signs of being cold. The others are still fast asleep underneath their smocks and I put mine on and tighten the draw cords on the bottom and around my neck. In this chilly morning air it is difficult to imagine that it will be another very hot day. In the distance I can hear the cattle lowing and the unusual, almost mono note of their cowbells. Strangely enough it's a pleasant and almost relaxing sound on this, clear, chilly morning. I can also hear voices and whistles as the Masai herdsmen coax the cattle out of their overnight *bomas* (fenced areas made of thorn bush).

What's for breakfast? The person who decided that corned beef and biscuits provide the ideal safari rations should be here with us this morning. Not only is it very boring, but the biscuits could be used to make bullet proof waistcoats! In the Aberdares we had army 'K' ration packs. I open another tin of corned beef; this time the contents are hard and I eat some with two biscuits washed down with water. As the water bottle was exposed overnight the water is ice cold. It tastes delicious but there is less than a quarter of a bottle left. I still have one full bottle, but will it be sufficient?

With everyone 'fed and watered' before seven we set off again and I am enjoying this crisp clear morning. We surprise some Masai leading a small herd of cattle. We stop and Kipkoske speaks to them in their own tongue. There is much head shaking and with Kipkoske we check over the cattle, checking not only for 'ours' but also checking their rumps for brands that would indicate other stolen European stock, but the herd is all clear.

Our track takes us within two hundred yards of a Masai *manyatta* (a small number of huts made from cow dung). The *manyatta* is surrounded by cut thorn bushes about four feet high. The huts are built so low that an adult would need to bend and crawl inside, and they do not have any windows. The construction is a series of vertical sticks, which are bent over to form an arched roof. Other sticks are then woven in horizontally and situated on one corner is a small entrance that juts out at ninety degrees to the main oblong shape. The overall effect is a fat 'L' shape with the entrance section forming the short foot of the 'L'. The whole is then plastered with cow dung softened with cow's urine and allowed to dry. The rough overall dimensions are eight feet long, five feet wide and four feet six inches high. The entrance is the same height and about two feet wide. We decide to check at this manyatta regarding the stolen cattle.

As soon as we draw near, the smell of cow dung and urine is very strong. As expected, no one knows anything. As Kipkoske speaks to them they have flies crawling around their mouths and eyes but they make no attempt to brush them off. Now the flies 'attack' us, no doubt to lick the sweat salt from our faces. I constantly swat at the flies and am very glad when we move on.

"Effendi, these people must have seen the thieves with the cattle. They are lying to us." I can see that Kipkoske would like to do something to get at the truth, but all we can do is to continue to follow the tracks.

Before mid-day the tracks now divide into three, so it would appear that our thieves have obtained local assistance. Here we go again! On balance I decide that we stay together and follow the clearest set of tracks, which includes the man with the extra long toe. With the sun almost directly overhead and only the low growing castor oil bushes as cover there is hardly an inch of shade, and as we pass some rocks I can feel the heat radiating off their surface; once again sweat trickles down my face and the back of my shirt is soaked in perspiration.

By 3pm the tracks have split up yet again and now we are onto rocky ground and by 4pm we are circling round trying to pick up at least something that we can follow. By 5pm I reluctantly decide that we have been out-manoeuvred. These people know what they're are doing when it comes to stealing cattle! We head back to 'Akira Ranch' and, as darkness approaches, we again settle down to sleep in the open.

This second night I take the last 'stag' and before going to sleep after my boring 'dinner', I lie on my back and look again at the night sky and the myriad of brilliant stars. The air is now cool and I can feel a slight breeze on my face. We haven't made an arrest or recovered the stolen cattle, but what keeps pushing these thoughts to one side is this vast open space so far from civilisation. We are out here alone, surrounded by miles and miles of Africa in every direction. This is Africa as I have always imagined it. As I close my eyes I am suddenly very conscious how tired I am and it seems only minutes later that it is my turn to be on guard duty.

Early in the evening of day three we arrive back at 'Akira' hot and thirsty. I drink two whole saucepans of water! It must be at least six pints in one go! I discuss the 'chase' with the farm manager and he states that he is not surprised with the outcome, as to date, no one has ever made a recovery and he offers me an ice cold beer. However, as I have a large amount of water sloshing around inside my stomach, with great reluctance I decline. About an hour later our Land Rover arrives and we head for home. I sit beside the driver, answering his many questions and interspersing these are my thoughts of a shave, a nice hot bath and dinner. Suddenly I feel very tired and silently pray to God that we do not have any Mau-Mau alarm call-outs during the night from the local farmers.

Arriving at the Police Post we de-bus and as I walk towards the farmhouse Tumbo sees me and comes galloping across the dry dusty earth and I receive a very enthusiastic greeting! He barks with his tail wagging furiously and constantly licks my free hand. Still excited he scampers and jumps around me as I make my way to my room. I remove my boots and stretch out on the bed and in relaxing my right arm dangles over the side. Tumbo, taking this as a gesture of affection, licks my hand again. I turn onto my side and look down at him.

"Tumbo, those Masai have beaten us this time, we'll have to try harder won't we?" I scratch behind his ears. Tumbo looks at me expectantly and furiously wags his tail. Placing my head back onto the pillow I start to doze off but I arouse myself and head for the bathroom. In less than an hour it will be time for dinner.

I discard my dusty, smelly clothes and sink into the bath until the deep hot water covers my chest. With my head resting back onto the bath I watch the steam rising and savour the feeling of the hot water on my body and can feel the relaxing effect that it has. I splash some water onto my face and for a moment I stare at my toes protruding from the water; then I close my eyes – this is utter bliss! I muse how odd people back home would think it was to have a loaded machine carbine beside their bath. As we are within a Mau-Mau area, where I go it goes, it never leaves my side.

Having lathered myself all over and sunk back into the bath, now comes the difficult part – shaving off three days growth of beard. Having removed this, and with fresh clean clothes I feel civilised and revitalised! As I pass the kitchen there is a delicious smell of roasting meat with overtones of apple pie, or is it apple sauce? This immediately reinforces the thought that I am ready for a hearty dinner and a good night's sleep.

My prayers must have been answered as it's been a quiet night. Due to the distance to the Police Post I have organised a communication system: one blast on my police whistle for the driver, two for the Corporal and three for the Sergeant Major. The system works very well. I give three blasts and the Sergeant Major comes trotting across to the farmhouse. I receive his usual 'big' salute.

"*Jambo Effendi, habari gani?*" (Morning Sir, how are you?) We discuss our failed 'chase'. He tutts and agrees that these Masai are *mbaya sana* (very bad). He informs me that there aren't any problems, except Kipchunga's wife is sick and Kipchunga wants to go home to see her, the driver has told him the Land Rover needs servicing and one man is sick and needs to go to hospital.

"Is Kipchunga's wife really sick, or is he looking for a few days off?"

"He's a good man Effendi, I'm sure it's the truth." I open up the radio to Divisional Police Headquarters and make arrangements. Later I organise a night ambush of a footpath that may be used by Mau-Mau terrorists.

At dusk, and driving without lights, the driver drops off our ambush party about two miles from the footpath, and we make our way to it heading towards the escarpment. There is very faint moonlight and we can see quite clearly as we make our way through the bush. It is going to be a long night and we will not be withdrawing until about 5am. We 'go down' into our prone positions and all we can do is wait. The moon sinks lower into the night sky and I have to pull the brim of my jungle hat down to prevent its light affecting my vision. The hours tick by. It's very difficult to keep fully alert and from time to time your vision plays tricks on you. That shape and shadow, I'm sure it moved. Suddenly there is a shape and it is moving! What is it? It's not a terrorist but a hyena! It stops about thirty yards away and obviously senses our presence, and now I can see there are five others with it. Their strange shape with their shoulders being higher than their hindquarters is clearly discernible. The lead hyena makes that weird high-pitched 'whooping' noise constantly looking in our direction. Now hyenas have jaws that can crush bones like matchsticks and if they come any closer we may have to open fire to scare them off and give away our position. To my relief they turn around and slink away and some minutes later I can hear their strange cry in the distance.

The night passes without incident and we make our way to the 'pick up' point. On the return journey the driver informs me that it has been a quiet night. Back at the farmhouse I have a quick wash and just as dawn is breaking I 'fall' into bed and I'm asleep within seconds.

Tumbo's growling wakes me up (as it always does).

"What is it Tumbo?" The Corporal appears at the French window and Tumbo erupts into his usual frenzy of barking. I look at my wristwatch; it's just after 11.00am. I feel 'half daft', everything seems to be coming from a distance and the bright sunlight hurts my eyes.

"Effendi, we have been talking to one of the farm labourers who works on the next farm. He tells us that a small Mau-Mau gang visited there last night to obtain food."

"What time did he tell you this?"

"About ten minutes ago Effendi."

"OK, alert the driver and I'll need Kipkoske and three others. They'll need one day's rations and a full water bottle each."

Here we go again! I haven't had any breakfast yet, so as time is short, as usual, I grab some bananas and drink some milk.

The farm is only about three miles away, with the labourers' housing just across the river from the main farmhouse. We do not want to make it too obvious that we are acting on information received so I decide we will make it appear like a normal foot patrol.

As it's the 'dry season' the Land Rover easily fords the river, the water not even coming up to the lower edge of my door. We surge up the opposite bank passing the farm labourers camp with its typical thatched round mud walled huts and with the usual chickens running around plus two or three emaciated dogs. As we pass by the women simply stare and one of the children, who cannot be more than four years of age, gives us an enthusiastic wave, which I return.

The gang would have come from the direction of the escarpment, not from the Masai side, therefore, if we patrol along the base of the escarpment, which is due North of the labourers' housing, we may stumble upon their tracks and be able to follow up. The majority of the labour at this farm are Kikuyu (the same tribe as Mau-Mau) and will be Mau-Mau supporters, no doubt supplying food and money. To have stopped to ask questions would arouse their suspicions that someone had talked.

About two miles further on we de-bus and I tell the driver to return to base and I will telephone from the farm when we need collecting. The base of the escarpment is no more that a quarter of a mile away and once there I plan to head back along its length and hope we can find something.

We have been in position and walking for about twenty minutes; Kipkoske leads the way constantly scanning the ground. Suddenly he raises his hand and stops.

"Effendi, look here." He points to some very faint marks on the ochre coloured earth that appear to me almost like scuff marks.

"Are they footprints?"

"Ndiyo Effendi and heading over there." He points roughly in the direction of the farm which is about two miles away.

"How many men?"

Kipkoske studies the ground again and walks up and down beside the tracks. The ground here is very hard, yet despite this he comes up with an answer

"Definitely two, and there could be a third. Look here." He points to several very faint marks and how he defines that two or three people have walked here almost defies belief.

"Are the tracks also leading back on this same route?"

"No Effendi, only just this way." He makes a sweeping gesture towards the farm. We continue ahead with Kipkoske again studying the ground very intently. After about two hundred yards he stops again, bending down to take a closer look at his find.

"Effendi these tracks are going this way." He points towards the escarpment.

"Right... let's follow them."

The ground starts to rise very steeply and there are plenty of rocks, which makes tracking difficult, and we have to pause from time to time as Kipkoske studies the ground, thus giving us time to recover our breath before he leads on again. If there are any terrorists manning an O.P. (observation post) they will see us coming so we need to be cautious. Kipkoske continues to look down; we look ahead and are well spread out. After some hours we arrive at the edge of our patrol territory. This small gang have crossed the Nairobi-Naivasha road, but to continue to follow up could be dangerous as we might stumble upon another security force patrol, or one of their ambushes. We make our way back to the farm and I telephone for the driver to pick us up.

Back at the Police Post I radio HQ and report that we have been following tracks of two or three suspected terrorists and give a map reference where the tracks crossed the road. At some future date I will organise an ambush near the farm labourers housing.

I am starting to realise that I am short of manpower. I have a dual role: to prevent stock thefts and to be responsible for the safety and security of local farms. Based on my brief experience, I am aware that following up on a stock theft can take at least three days, and if I am away chasing stock thieves, the Sergeant Major and the Corporal will have to take responsibility for all other tasks. I cannot afford to have too many men on any one exercise. The Post still has to be manned and guarded and also be able to respond to an emergency. I am to face this manpower problem throughout this posting.

One evening I visited a Police Mounted Section (we called them 'Kenya cowboys') who were camped under canvas in the bush. I had been invited to dinner and it was excellent. We had ice cold beer (which had been kept under rocks in the nearby river) followed by roast buck with all the trimmings and a sweet followed by coffee. All this was produced by their African cook using a field oven made from an ex-army 14lb biscuit tin covered by a mound of earth to keep the heat in, with a small trench under the tin for the heat source, and surmounted at its rear end by a small chimney made from discarded tins. The stars twinkled in the clear night sky, hyenas could be heard in the distance making their weird call, the horses were snuffling and the camp fire threw flickering red and gold images onto the tents and our faces. The conversation dwelled on past exploits and days to come. I sat there thinking that people would pay thousands of pounds to experience this, and here I was enjoying it for free. I could well understand why the Police Mounted Section was so popular.

We have another stock theft. This time, to overcome the water shortage, before setting off in pursuit, we all drink as much water as possible, and I tell Kipkoske not to let any Masai that we meet realise that he understands their language. We will only speak to them in Kiswahili and hope when they converse amongst themselves, they might 'give the game away'.

Both of these new approaches work reasonably well, but we still return empty handed. There are two reasons: the speed of the thieves compared to our estimated three miles an hour when tracking and the 'conspiracy of silence' that we face from the Masai population. Out in the Masai Reserve there are some thieving b******* making fools of us! I consider changing our 'modus operandi'. The local District Officer may not like it, but this blatant thieving has got to stop! We only have two weeks to wait to apply plan number two.

This time twenty head of cattle are stolen and the thieves make their first mistake. They head in a different direction where the ground is dry and soft and the going flat. Kipkoske is sitting on the bonnet of the Land Rover and hanging on to the wing mirror for support. The driver follows his constant pointing and we are travelling at about ten miles an hour. I knew from previous 'recces' in the area that the tracks are leading towards the Government installed water tanks, and 'I will put a pound to a pinch of snuff' what our thieving 'friends' will do. Just as I expected, the tracks lead directly into hundreds and hundreds of other cattle tracks where they are brought daily to drink. I tell the driver to slowly circle the water tanks at a distance of about one mile, and I tell Kipkoske to watch out for the tracks of the stolen cattle. We circle at a 'snails pace' constantly stopping to examine tracks leading away from the water tanks. When we are about 200 degrees from our entry point, Kipkoske again holds up his hand to stop. He alights and examines some tracks walking backwards and forwards.

"It's them Effendi, three men and our cattle." He gives me a grin and off we go in pursuit with Kipkoske again sitting on the bonnet of the Land Rover pointing the way.

We are driving across virgin bush country and it's very slow going. At about 4.00pm the terrain becomes too rough even for the Land Rover. We alight and continue on foot, and I tell the driver to return to base. An hour and a half later the tracks pass within a hundred yards of a *manyatta* and I speak to the headman in Kiswahili. In response he shakes his head and replies in Masai. I shake my head and make gestures that I do not understand. Being an elder he is wearing a blanket across his body affixed at one shoulder and he is wearing the usual truncated copper earrings. His spear, unlike the young men (*moran*), has a short blade; protruding beneath the blanket is his wooden club (*rungu*). On his feet he is wearing typical Masai sandals consisting of square ended very thin leather soles with plaited leather thongs passing between the big and second toes, then tied around at the ankle. Soon he is joined by another man and they rapidly converse. If you have ever seen an old silent movie film of someone listening to a conversation, Kipkoske's facial expression and body posture would make him an excellent 'stand in'.

"Effendi, they are saying that these police people are fools and will never find the cattle, but we'll give them milk and tomorrow they will go away."

If this is what they believe, then they are in for a shock!

In order to avoid the usual swarm of flies, we organise ourselves to sleep at least three hundred yards from the *manyatta*, and at this stage, we do not 'go down' into our usual triangular formation but I post one man on guard duty.

Within thirty minutes the headman arrives with three women carrying large gourds heavily decorated with beads and stoppered with maize husks. The first gourd is offered to me and, by sign language, he gestures that I should drink. The women are bare footed and have shaven heads, showing that they are married; their clothing reaches almost to the ground and is made from skins that look like soft, almost shiny suede. Around their necks are many hoops of brass. Their ear lobes have been slit when children and, as a result, the bottom of the lobe almost touches their shoulders. Inserted into these huge holes are leather earrings, again heavily beaded, causing the slit lobes to appear taut due to the weight. Their bare upper arms also have copper and 'silver' wire wound around them. Their posture is very upright and they walk with short steps in a very graceful manner; like the males they have high cheek bones and almost oriental eyes; their faces are expressionless. Having placed the three gourds onto the ground in front of me the women depart without having spoken one word, and again I cannot help but notice their graceful posture and their short unhurried steps.

Being asked to drink some of this milk I am now faced with a very real problem. The cattle within the Masai Reserve are riddled with every bug and microbe known to man. Just to add to this junket, due to the lack of water, the milk gourds are washed with cow's urine. As the cow urinates, the women hold the gourd under the stream of urine, shake the gourd vigorously, then empty the now 'washed' gourd and hang it inverted over a smoking fire. I smile, accept the gourd and remove the water sterilising tablets from my pack, put five into the gourd and shake it. The headman looks on in wonderment.

"Kipkoske, tell him I am doing this because it is good for making babies."

Kipkoske translates and the headman smiles. Suddenly his expression changes as he realises we would have understood his previous conversation.

"Kipkoske, tell the headman that we know the stolen cattle passed by here, and tell him the police are not fools. We want the stolen cattle and the thieves delivered here and we will wait for a maximum of one day only."

Kipkoske translates and the headman responds rapidly in Masai.

"He says, Effendi, that he saw the cattle, but doesn't know the thieves."

I turn to the headman, glare at him and say in Kiswahili "*Upusi!*" (rubbish). "Tell this headman if we do not have the thieves and all the stolen cattle within one day from now, I will confiscate all the cattle in his *manyatta* and take them to the Government cattle *boma*."

The headman looks shocked and speaks rapidly to Kipkoske.

"He says if you do this the children will starve and no one will have anything to eat."

"Tell him he has one day, and one day only. Then tell him to find the thieves starting now!" I raise my voice for this final word and look as stern as possible.

Kipkoske translates and the headman runs off at speed. I hope that he doesn't call my bluff. I don't have any legal right to confiscate his manyatta's cattle, and I hope and pray he will not lodge a complaint with the local European District Officer who is based in Narok. If he does I will be in for a 'very hot time'.

I put sterilising tablets into the other two gourds and wait for the chemicals to take effect, then, using our empty ration tins, the men make a small fire and we boil the milk in the tins for at least ten minutes. When it has cooled I pick up my corned beef 'saucepan'. The milk tastes very smoky and contains the odd fragment of corned beef, but it makes a welcome addition to our safari rations. Strangely enough I find it very filling. Due to the amount of milk we will have sufficient for the morning. I organise the guard roster and opt to take the first 'stag'. I brief the men to be very vigilant; we are a long way from base, and due to my threat we may be attacked during the night.

We settle down in our usual formation with our camouflage smocks providing cover. As usual I slip on my police issue sweater, tighten the draw cords on my smock, cock my Patchett machine carbine and sit down, adjusting my eyes to the starlight darkness. I listen for the slightest sounds, but all I can hear is the usual lowing of the cattle interspersed with the soft clanging of their cowbells. I feel hypersensitive tonight; I've gone 'out on a limb' and anything could happen. Eventually I hand over my guard duty and, removing my smock, place my bent knees inside the hood and cover myself with the remainder. It takes me ages to go to sleep. Will the headman believe me, or will he call my bluff? My other thought is, "we haven't been into this area before and I wonder if there are lions around?"

I sleep very lightly and awake just after midnight. All is quiet and I signal to the man on guard who is about five yards away. He gestures in response. I settle down again but sleep eludes me and I wonder what will happen tomorrow? I must have dozed off as when I next open my eyes it's almost dawn. I put on my smock and walk over to the man on guard. It's Kipkoske. In a whisper I ask if everything is OK?

"*Hakuna matata Effendi,*" he whispers (there isn't any trouble Sir) and grins. We are going to be here all day, so there is no point in waking the others. I rub my hand over my chin and face. It's amazing how quickly my whiskers grow in this hot climate and I think, "if only I could wash and shave."

We remain near the *manyatta* and as the sun rises we use what shelter we can find beside some thorn bushes. We still remain alert and I organise the day's guard roster.

At about 5.00pm the headman arrives, and through Kipkoske he informs me that the thieves have been arrested and the cattle recovered and they will be with us by early next morning. I tell him if they fail to appear we will confiscate his cattle. He assures me that they will be here and hurries off. The evening light starts to fade and we settle down for another night out in Masai. Thank goodness it's not the rainy season!

As we settle down for another night in the open again I take the first 'stag'. My thoughts turn to lions and I recall the story told to me by a Game Warden about how the lions catch and kill Masai cattle. At night the Masai protect their cattle with a circa five foot high corral made from thorn bushes with very sharp thorns. The lions who normally hunt in packs, go up wind of this and urinate, the cattle smell this and in their panic smash their way out of the enclosure. The lions now take their pick! To date we have never encountered lions when out here in Masai; is it possible that we could detect them if they were stalking us? I hope that by choosing 'camp' sites devoid of bushes and long grass it gives us a slight edge. These thoughts heighten my awareness and I strain to catch the slightest sound.

My two hours are up and I hand over to the next man on duty. As I snuggle under my camouflage smock my mind turns to lions again. My thoughts couldn't have lasted very long as when I awake the sky in the east is just being tinged with a pale purple and in stirring I am conscious of the heavy dew on my smock and the surrounding grass and I shiver with the cold. Who would believe that it can be so cold in Africa!

Soon after first light a group armed with their usual spears, appear with three men with their hands tied behind their backs and, being driven along behind them, twenty cattle. The headman speaks to Kipkoske, who then translates.

"He says these are the bad men that you want and they have confessed to stealing the cattle. Every cow has been accounted for, and he has kept his promise."

"Tell the headman that the *serkali* (government) will be very pleased with him, and give him my thanks for helping us."

It is only the second time that I have seen the headman smile. We now replace the cords on the prisoners' wrists with handcuffs and two pairs suffice for the three men and, using their 'services' to drive the cattle (after all they have met before), we set off for 'home'.

My men are in high spirits! They sing and whistle at the cattle, and we halt from time to time to rest and consume some water, some of which is offered to our prisoners, but it is refused.

By evening we arrive at the farm and expect a hero's welcome. The farmer, alerted to our arrival, comes out to greet us. He is not smiling.

"Well, we have recovered your cattle and have arrested the thieves!" I feel jubilant, but something is wrong!

"What the bloody hell do you think you're doing bringing these cattle onto my land!"

"But they're yours, not Masai replacements, and we've checked the brands.

"I know that they're my cattle, but I don't want them here!"

I was dumbfounded!

"Why not?"

"Because they have been into an infected area and may have picked up rhindapest, black leg fever and God knows what!"

"So where do we take them?"

"The one and only place, the Government cattle Pound which is just inside the Reserve, and they stay until the Government vet has inoculated them and cleared them for release."

What a greeting! And we were expecting 'medals'.

I contacted the Police Post and explained that we needed at least four men, plus the Corporal to guard the recovered cattle at the Government *boma* until they are relieved by the Veterinary Scouts and that they would need rations and water. When they arrived we thankfully clambered aboard the Land Rover and headed for home.

The men sang all the way back to the post and, when I had grasped the rhythm and the words, I joined in the chorus with gusto! We'd done it! The first ever arrest and recovery in this area of stolen cattle!

The three stock thieves subsequently appeared in Court, pleaded guilty and received prison sentences. I hoped that this information would go into circulation within our area of the Reserve.

I decided to carry out some tests with the Land Rover. As the terrain along the edge of the Masai Reserve was fairly flat, I discovered that if the gearbox was put into low ratio, the accelerator pedal hardly touched and all loose items secured, it was possible to drive the vehicle to within less than one hundred yards of our Police Post before anyone could hear it. As a result, just inside the Masai boundary we carried out a series of mobile night patrols without lights. There were two reasons for this. One, we may stumble onto some stock thieves, and two, which was the main reason, in the morning the Masai would see the Land Rover tyre tracks which were not there the night before. Just like Kipkoske, the Masai are keen-eyed and would not miss this evidence that either we, or some other Government vehicle, had been roaming around at night and they had not been aware of its presence. I felt sure that this news would also be spread around our area of the Reserve.

My next step was to introduce foot patrols lasting two to three days into the area and, as part of this 'showing the flag', or 'awareness campaign', we would also check any cattle for obliterated, or partly eradicated, European brands. By these new tactics we would be adopting a pro-active role to deter stock thefts, rather than the previous re-active method. This was partly underpinned by Akira Ranch who now armed their stock guards with single barrel, twelve bore shotguns.

With this new approach in place stock thefts ceased, but I realised that the 'carrot' of hundreds of head of fat European cattle spread along the Masai boundary just within 'striking distance' would be hard to resist, and at some stage some of the young Masai *moran* would risk another raid. If this occurred, I had every intention of repeating my previous ploy of threatening to seize the cattle of any *manyatta* where the tracks of stolen cattle had passed close by.

Some weeks later we received a call from Akira Ranch. During the night some guarded cattle had been attacked, not by Masai, but by hyena. We were not game wardens but I went there to see what, if anything, we could do to help. For the first time ever I was to witness the sheer strength of a hyena's jaws. One cow had a large hole bitten into its side, the single bite crushing straight through the rib bones as if they didn't exist. The armed stock guard hearing the noise had approached and, perhaps because he disturbed what was about to be the hyenas' meal, one had sprung at him and he had instinctively held the shotgun across his body as protection. The hyena's bite had severed the weapon in two just behind the trigger-guard, crushing the wooden butt and leaving gouge marks in the metal where it joined the wooden butt to the actual shotgun. I had never heard of hyena attacking either cattle or man. The farm manager said it was because there was little carrion about at this time of the year, but it was also a first in his experience.

The farmer's wife at Akira had been trained as a nurse. As a result most mornings it was not uncommon to see several Masai of all ages and sexes arriving there for medical treatment, which was provided free of charge. I always found it difficult to understand the Masai mentality. Here at Akira they could receive free medical treatment, yet despite this, they were not averse to helping themselves to Akira's cattle. To add another twist, from time to time they would bring in young wild animals when the mothers had been killed by lion, hyena, or wild dogs. During one of my visits there was a very young zebra with a dark brown and white coat (the brown turns to black later), and a very young giraffe that the farm had named 'Belinda'. Even at this early age 'Belinda' was seven feet tall and very tame. I made the mistake of stroking her nose. In milliseconds my hand was in her mouth and she had a suck like a corporation drain, plus a very rough tongue! She was fed milk daily and, due to careful nurturing, survived and became a film star.

Vultures are incredible birds and I have carried out the following experiment many times 'when shooting for the pot'. Look up into the sky in every direction, there is not a vulture to be seen. Now take careful aim and shoot a buck. Wait just thirty to forty seconds and look up into the sky again. There, circling at a very high altitude will be two or three vultures! Within minutes there will be twenty or more. Where have they appeared from? If you are thinking, "Well it's obvious, they've been sitting in the nearby trees." But what if there aren't any nearby trees? On one foot patrol we came across a dead giraffe and it was smothered in at least a hundred vultures, all using their powerful hooked beaks to tear at the flesh. Some were so gorged that on our approach they had great difficulty in taking off to fly and reminded me of the albatross who needs a very long run to get into the air. The vulture is such an ugly bird with its long neck looking as if someone has plucked it bare and their large black-feathered bodies, with a white ruff of feathers at the base of their bare necks. Once aloft their large wings are designed for soaring and, using the thermals rising from the hot earth, it appears to be effortless flight. Despite their ugly appearance, they are Africa's number one 'dustmen' and anything that they leave, (normally just bare bones), is eaten by the hyena and silver backed jackals.

Within my police area, from time to time, I would 'do a round robin' of all the farms in order to stay in touch with their owners or managers and to 'keep my finger on the pulse'. On one such trip I arrived at a farm very early in the morning and was invited to stay for breakfast. It was sumptuous! Paw-paw with fresh limejuice squeezed over it, toast, butter and marmalade, all home made. Then a large salver arrived and was placed onto the middle of the table. It contained eggs, bacon, sheep's' kidneys, steaks and chops of Thompson's gazelle meat, and lightly grilled tomatoes. All of this was accompanied by excellent Kenya grown coffee and sparkling conversation.

It was at this same farm that some months later I was invited for lunch. The owner's wife was away in Nairobi and as a result, and unbeknown to me, he had asked the cook to produce his favourite dish. Boiled sheep's head! Had I known this, I would have found some excuse to stay away.

I arrived full of expectation for a lunch, which was based on my breakfast experience. Following an excellent soup, my plate duly arrived. It held half a sheep's head cleaved in half between the eyes, with a long row of grinning teeth and one watery eye looking balefully in my direction. The head was displayed surrounded by boiled potatoes and cabbage in a sea of gravy. How did one eat half a sheep's head? It was far too large to pick up like a leg of chicken and I waited for "mine host" to lead the way. Using only his fork, he commenced with gusto to pick the meat off the half skull. I stared back at the watery eye and the teeth. It was no good I had to make a start. Being watched all the time was quite off-putting; I commenced to gingerly follow the example of my host. He was ahead of me, and now turned the bare skull over and commenced to eat the brains. I was determined that my skull would remain in the position as served! By now his plate, apart from the now totally bare skull, was empty. Thank goodness he hadn't tackled the eye! He looked at me and poured some more cold beer into my glass.

"I can see that you really enjoyed that," he said and called to the houseboy, "*Lete kichwa ngini*" (bring another head). There was to be a slight difference. This time I had a watery left eye looking at me.

A very similar situation occurred some years later. I was invited to lunch by a retired magistrate. This time it was tripe and onions served in a white cream sauce. Again it was a struggle to eat it, and he insisted that I had a second helping. The only blessing was the glass of chilled white wine that accompanied the meal.

You will recall that there is not a great deal of water in parts of the Masai Reserve. One day we received a radio message that a private single-engined light aircraft was well overdue on a flight from Nakuru to Nairobi and that its filed flight path would have passed over the part of Suswa covered by our area. Having been alerted we quickly 'scrambled' with the Land Rover, with four men and two days rations, plus extra water. The Police Airwing were also involved in the search, as were other Police Posts along the flight path. Looking at our map, if the pilot had landed in our area and stayed with his aircraft then I felt confident we would find him. Before the end of the first day we heard on our radio that the Police Airwing had found the aircraft, but there was no sign of the pilot. According to the map reference he had landed on the extreme edge of our area, and the shortest route to safety was towards us. We continued our search but found nothing. Near the end of day two the pilot was found dead by another patrol; he had been walking in the direction of Nairobi, deeper and deeper into the bush and away from the obvious route that would have ensured his survival.

He had died from dehydration. What a pity he had not stayed with his aircraft.

It was a quiet Sunday morning. After several weeks of anti-stock theft activity, plus night ambushes without any break whatsoever, I decided that we needed to 're-charge our batteries'. The farm owner had gone off to see his girlfriend in Nairobi for the weekend and had stressed that I needed to be aware of any reports of sick cattle as this is the standard approach by the farm labour to obtain meat in abundance...

I am on the veranda sprawled in a comfortable armchair and reading a very good book which transports me to another era. Tumbo is curled up at my feet fast asleep and I note that he twitches from time to time, no doubt dreaming about some canine escapade. The 'house boy' has just produced mid-morning coffee and I am now partly through my second cup. With cream and just a touch of brown sugar, this coffee is delicious.

Suddenly Tumbo stirs from his slumbers and starts growling; his ears are erect! Chui, the head herdsman appears looking very agitated and carrying a spear.

"Effendi, a lion has killed a bull in the donga about five hundred paces from here."

I cannot believe what I am hearing! I was warned about this!

"Right Chui, show me the bull." I tell Tumbo to "stay" and he sits beside my chair looking very expectant. I never ever go anywhere without my Patchett 9mm machine carbine and I casually place this onto my shoulder as if going for a Sunday afternoon stroll.

Chui lopes ahead of me. He's a Turkana from northern Kenya, yet despite the heat, he's wearing an old army khaki overcoat and an old wide-brimmed felt hat of matching colour, now very badly stained, covered in dust and showing its age. His lower lip is pierced and into the hole he has placed a small wooden plug where normally he would be wearing some ornament. The wooden plug obviously doesn't fit very well as spittle is leaking and running down onto his chin. On his feet he is wearing 'chupplies' (sandals). The soles are made from the tread of a car tyre and the cross straps, which are nailed into the sides of the tread, are made from the tyre side walls stripped down to just one layer. As I walk behind Chui I am conscious of his body odour; where he comes from water is very scarce, as a result Chui very seldom washes, preferring to rub his body with oil.

By now we are within a hundred yards or so of the *donga* (dried up river bed) and Chui now falls back behind me and looks very agitated. My thoughts are, 'Now we are nearly there he's going to have to show me how the bull "died" and he knows that I will not believe him.'

We are within thirty five yards of the donga when suddenly and without warning there's a sound of crashing in the bushes.

I freeze in my tracks. Facing me is a male lion with his head poking through the foliage!

For a second we look at each other. If he charges, the chance of taking my Patchett from my shoulder, cocking it and opening fire, is just about zero. With another crash he withdraws his head and is gone. I can feel my heart thumping in my chest and turning around I go to speak to Chui.

He is nowhere to be seen. He must have run at the speed of a cheetah! I hurriedly cock my Patchett and slowly walk forward. There is no sound from the donga – all I can hear is my own heart thudding in my chest. I feel as if I am 'walking on eggs'. Every step that I take forward heightens the tension and I am hypersensitive to the slightest sound. Finally, I reach the edge. There below is the dead bull, but how did it get away from the main herd? It must have been grazing alone and was chased here by the lion. Anyway, speculation will not alter the current situation. Now what do I do?

A few moments later Chui arrives and very cautiously peers down into the donga, shaking his head from side to side and making 'tch-tch' sounds.

"Chui, go and find the tractor driver and some *watu* (people) and drag this bull near to the farmhouse. You will be in charge of cutting it up and giving everyone a fair share." I know that the Turkana will eat anything, including snake, but I am not sure about the other labour. Chui's eyes are like diamonds; masses of meat! He runs off in the direction of the labourers' camp and I stroll back to the farmhouse somewhat shaken, thinking how utterly stupid I had been in not believing Chui's report. I should have cocked my Patchett in order to be ready for any eventuality.

The share out of the meat is frenetic with Chui cutting up the carcass and Turkana women shouting at each other in a tongue I cannot understand. There are a number of disputes. Men are carrying off hunks of raw meat and others lashing out with sticks at the six or seven dogs that have appeared from the labourers' camp. On the fringe are small children, some just peering at the dwindling remains of the bull, with one small child crying for no apparent reason and he appears to be on his own.

Within twenty minutes nothing remains, not even the guts. The only sign is the bloodstained earth and this is attracting flies. I call the 'shamba boy' (gardener) and tell him to place fresh soil onto the area. Chui has claimed the skin as his special prize and prior to this his wife has walked away with a large piece of meat covered in flies, but where she comes from flies are flies; they are always around.

The Turkana women are very small in stature compared to the men and like their menfolk very dark skinned, almost black in colour. They are dressed in skin skirts that have never been cleaned since the day they were first put on. They are all bare footed. The majority do not clothe the upper part of their bodies, revealing the very withered breasts of the older, grey-haired women. They have loose brass rings around their necks, the sides of their heads are shaved, and the married ones carry leather whips.[3]

With the tumult died down I have a light lunch of cold (farm bred) lamb with some trimmings and return to my book. Tumbo is beside me and I am thankful I told him to "stay", as, without any doubt, he would have rushed at the lion and then anything could have happened. I was looking at the book, but not seeing the words; in my mind's eye I was picturing what might have been. Evidently, what saved me from the attack was the fact that I didn't run away.

It will soon be Christmas and with it comes a historical Christmas tradition. The Officer in Charge of a Police Station, or Post, purchases a bull for the 'troops'. This involves much discussion by the NCOs and many visits to several unsuspecting bulls. Finally one is chosen and is shown to 'the man with the money' for final approval. The poor bull, still blissfully unaware of his fate, continues to eat well, much to the approval of his admiring onlookers. On the day, and having received

---

[3] The farm labour were paid monthly and it was not uncommon to see a wife pursuing her much taller husband with a whip and shouting at him in the process! This was 'women's lib' before it was even thought about in the West.

the *coup de grace*, the bull's remains are distributed by the Sergeant Major, and by tradition the officer in charge receives a small choice cut.

There are 'two flies in the ointment'. Neither the Mau-Mau or the Masai 'down tools' at Christmas, therefore, we must be able to respond to any threat or theft. This means that any drink will be very restricted, and I remind myself to discuss this with the Sergeant Major well in advance of the celebrations.

Later that night I walk over to the Post and I'm challenged by the sentry and enter into the enclosure.

"Jambo Effendi." He's heard all about the lion and asks me how big it was and what happened? Hearing my voice the Sergeant Major joins us and I have to repeat my story.

"Sergeant Major, unless we have an emergency, tomorrow morning I want to take a patrol into the Masai again. Alert the driver, and as usual I need six men armed, with three days water and food. We'll leave at 7.00am."

"Ndiyo Effendi."

I say goodnight, walk back to the farmhouse, wash, change into my pyjamas and climb into bed. Tumbo as usual is on the bedside rug between me and the French window. With him there I know that I can sleep soundly.

I am up early and have a substantial breakfast. This time I plan to 'show the flag' on the Eastern side, so as soon as we arrive at the boundary we will turn left, head towards the Government water tanks and keep going. When the Land Rover finds the going too tough we'll 'de-bus' and continue on foot, telling the driver to pick us up at the same point in two days time.

There is still dew on the ground and as usual we leave a faint dust trail in our wake. Part of this area will be new to me and I'm looking forward to being away from base and 'out in the wilds'.

We keep passing small herds of cattle being driven towards the water tanks, and we greet the Masai herdsmen in their native tongue with "Soba" which they repeat in reply. As we pass by the tanks the area is milling with cattle which raises the dust which we have first seen from a distance. Their lowing is inter-mixed with the whistles and shouts of their owners. There is the usual, almost sweet smell of cow dung and urine. Now we are leaving a heavy dust trail and the 'troops' in the back of the Land Rover have put the hoods of their camouflage smocks over their heads.

An hour later the terrain brings us to a halt. We de-bus, the driver and his escort return to base and we continue on foot. Now that we are walking, and without the cooling breeze generated by the Land Rover, despite the early hour the sun already feels hot and later as we commence to ascend the lower slopes of Mount Suswa I can feel the heat radiating off the rocks that sometimes bar our passage. Soon we come across a large rock and on one face in white paint are the words FAINT NOT NOR FEAR with an arrow pointing to the East. I know that 'The Desert Locust Control' operate in this area and I can only assume that this is where even their Land Rover couldn't go.

Throughout the day we constantly encounter Masai herding cattle, some with as few as twenty head and others with well over fifty. We greet them, "Soba" and examine the stock for brand marks. This news of our checking cattle will also spread and hopefully make any would-be thieves aware that the police are around the area.

Their dress is sometimes a blanket slung across the body, and affixed at the shoulder. The younger men wear an ochre-stained cloth worn in the same manner, and their hair is plaited into thin ropes and tied back at the nape of the neck, with a small fringe also tied in the same manner on their foreheads. The hair is covered in a mixture of red ochre and sheep fat. Their ears have been slit at childhood and they all wear the same design of earrings; two copper truncated cones about half an inch long and joined by a loop of copper wire affixed onto the apex of each cone. Some wear necklaces of fine beadwork threaded onto a thin leather thong. Their weaponry is also standard. Attached to their bare waist by a thong is a *simi* (a short sword about eighteen inches long, double edged, with the blade being widest just back from the point, quickly narrowing at the handle and contained in a red leather scabbard). A spear with a long narrow blade about three feet long and again double edged. This is forced onto a short wooden haft no more than ten inches long, with the metal tail of the spear commencing at just over an inch round (cross section) where it is forced onto the wooden shaft, rapidly converting to a half inch round cross section, and the same length as the blade. The final weapon is the *rungu* (wooden club) with an almost sphere-shaped head about four inches in diameter with a thin, stick like grip of about eighteen inches. This is made from one piece of wood. When standing a Masai will rest the tail of the spear onto the ground and raise one leg so that the sole of one foot is resting against the inside of the other leg, just above the knee. As I have noted before they have very striking features, with high cheekbones and eyes that look slightly oriental. Their bodies and limbs are very slim and they have a proud bearing that reflects their ancestors' prowess as warriors. They look so very different to the average African.

We continue heading roughly in an easterly direction encountering more Masai with their cattle which we subject to checks for obliterated brands.

At about 6.00pm I call a halt, it will be dark in an hour and we must find a suitable site to spend the night. We 'go down' into our usual triangular formation and as usual I opt to take the first 'stag'. There is nothing to cook, so we open our tins and commence to eat. The 'troops' have special African type food. Each tin, about the size of a standard soup tin, contains hunks of meat mixed with maize corn and suspended in gravy. Their biscuits are the same as mine. Back at the Post the 'troops' standard fare is maize flour (*posho*) mixed with water, then heated until it is very thick and almost like a slightly moist dough, cabbage, which is boiled for ages and ages, meat, and, as we are on the farm, plenty of milk. The thick *posho* is picked up by hand, made into a ball and dipped into the meat and cabbage mixture, and also used to mop up any remnants of gravy. Despite this almost mono-diet, they are fit and healthy. When we have finished eating the tins are crushed and buried, we never, ever leave any litter.

I have had my usual corned beef and tested my teeth on the 'bullet proof' biscuits. I take sips from my water bottle and place it into the thick grass; by morning it will be ice cold and delicious to drink. The other bottle stays attached to my waist belt. I am a great believer in 'always being prepared'. If we have to move quickly during the night, to be out here without water could mean disaster.

On this trip, as usual, I am wearing a lightweight khaki woollen shirt with the sleeves rolled up. On balance I prefer this to cotton. The back has still become soaked in perspiration, but I have the impression that it's cooler, plus the fact it has added advantages at night.

It is almost dark. Having rolled down my shirtsleeves, I put on my sweater and smock, tightening the neck and lower body to keep the heat in. I cock my Patchett and, in a sitting position commence my two hour stint. I look to the East, in the far distance on the horizon I can just see the glare of Nairobi in the night sky. How far away must it be from where we are tonight? I look up and just catch sight of a shooting star and as usual the stars seen through this clear air and from this altitude are like brilliant multi coloured diamonds. Now the night has arrived and I must concentrate on the job in hand. Are there any lions around? I hope not.

My eyes adjust to the starlight. It is so quiet that I can almost hear it. It seems a strange thing to say but perhaps it's the blood flow in my ears. In the far, far distance I can now hear the sporadic lowing of cattle, then all is silent again. Thinking about lions my thoughts turn to the lion in the donga. "Hell I was lucky, had it charged I wouldn't be here tonight." My thoughts wander again. Here in this part of Kenya it is so different from the 'White Highlands'. During the dry season everything dries up, and when it does rain, dry rivers become raging torrents. It's really hot during the day, and despite being very brown, far darker than the usual UK tan, some days when walking with bare forearms, at the end of the day if I rub them they can feel mildly sore. I muse that I have 'the best of both worlds', a comfortable well furnished room to sleep in; good food, and at the 'other end of the scale', this wild untamed place and tins of corned beef.

Suddenly a sound disturbs my thoughts, but it's only one of the men turning over in his sleep. I look at my luminous watch, just thirty more minutes and I can curl up underneath my smock.

The second day we head back to our pick-up point, but in order to cover more of the area, return by a different route and in so doing stumble across a deserted *manyatta*. It must be quite old as some of the cow-dung huts have holes in the roofs and despite the passage of time, there are still flies around. Our arrival activates them and they try to settle onto our faces to lick up our sweat salt. We constantly swat them away with our jungle hats and, as there is no point in hanging around, we set off at a fast pace, still being pursued by flies.

We are walking along the lower slopes of Mount Suswa and from this elevated position we can see for miles and miles but our views are distorted as the ground shimmers in the heat. Finding some limited shade we take a brief rest and I take a long drink from the water bottle. The water is warm but still delicious and refreshing. I sit in the shade of a leleshwa bush and recall some of the words from a poem by Rudyard Kipling about the British troops under fire in the heat of India's Khyber Pass.

"And when it comes to slaughter,

yer dus yer werk on water,
and you'll lick the boots of any man as got it."

I can well understand the sentiment behind those words. The picture in the mind's eye of a long, cool beer, doesn't help. Out here, as in India, you survive on water.

We continue on our return journey and from time to time come across Masai and their cattle which we check and exchange the standard greeting.

"*Soba.*"

"*Soba.*"

There is no animosity showing in their faces, but neither do they go out of their way to make contact; they simply observe what we are doing. With one group I use the Kiswahili greeting "*Jambo.*"

The man looks at me and replies "*Munning Swahili.*" (I don't speak Kiswahili). He is with a small boy and the herd is grazing and he is using the usual resting posture of spear tail on the ground and one foot resting on his other inner calf. The boy, who must be about seven to eight years old, carries a *fimbu* (a thin stick about three feet long) and he tries to emulate the posture of his senior. He stares at me all the time we are checking the cattle – perhaps I am the first European he has ever seen.

Now we are moving lower down Suswa's slopes and almost onto the plain and in the far, far distance I can see a faint plume of dust heading in our direction; it must be our Land Rover. The driver greets us and he informs me that all is quiet and there are no problems or trouble.

"*Hakuna matata Effendi.*"

Just before leaving the Reserve, ahead of us, about quarter of a mile away is a huge herd of about four hundred zebra. I tell the driver to partly circle them as I wish to ensure that there aren't any Masai cattle grazing within the area. I take one of the askari's rifles, adjust the rear sight and fire a shot across the herd. Being startled they stampede, raising a huge cloud of dust and gallop in a large sweeping circle. After about three hundred yards they stop and commence grazing again. What a magnificent spectacle to see all those zebra at full gallop!

Our next and almost immediate encounter is with a cheetah. My shot must have disturbed it and by its manner my 'troops' say there must be cubs nearby. And there they are! Four tiny spotted cubs. I ask the driver to stop and I walk over towards them. They are making an almost mewing sound and I wished that I had not left my 35mm camera in the Land Rover. The mother is standing off at some distance and, in order not to cause any further disturbance, I return to the vehicle and we continue our journey home.

As we have been engaged in another long period of intensive activity I decide that this coming Sunday we will all have a day of rest.

It is early afternoon, and from the edge of the veranda I watch as just beyond the garden boundary the 'dust devils' whip across the dry land. Overhead I can see the hawks wheeling in the clear blue sky waiting to snatch up any unsuspecting chicken, and in the far distance the farm's cattle are too hot to graze and huddle under the small amount of shade given by the acacia trees. Here under the veranda the air is cool, but beyond its reach the sun beats down, making it feel hot and airless. We have just had an excellent curry lunch, and here in this comfortable chair I am finding it difficult to keep my eyes open. From time to time I nod off, quickly awakening as my head lolls off to one side. I feel at peace with the world.

The farm owner has gone to Nairobi for the weekend leaving me with various instructions regarding the farm's electrical generator, to keep an eye on the thieving farm labour, and what to do if a cow goes lame or becomes sick. In my slumber all is perfect. The scenes in my mind's eye are of home, the last patrol, the Australian nurse I met in Nakuru...

Nyoka!

The word is repeated and penetrates my dulled senses.

SNAKES!

I sit up to see the 'shamba boy' (gardener) brandishing a stick and pointing excitedly at a bush. I stagger into the garden trying desperately to wake up. However, the curry and the pre-lunch pink gin have other ideas. By this time other farm labour and some of their wives have arrived in force. Some braver than others poke at the bush, then leap back like startled stags. The women hang onto infants, some suckle their young. Everyone is trying to look fearless, including me.

"It's about five feet long Bwana and very upset!"

The 'shamba boy's' information causes much sucking in of breath over twenty odd sets of front teeth, except for one old woman, who manages to produce the same sounds over a set of worn stumps.

All eyes turn to me. The Bwana will know what to do.

I order a hose to be rigged up and arm the bravest with sticks from the woodpile. I explain the plan. I will hose the bush, the snake will not like the water and will slither out. The gang of stick wielders will then 'clobber' it. The crowd nod like old sages except for the woman suckling her child who now decides it is an ideal moment to swap supply lines. The old lady with the now defunct 'Colgate' smile scratches her armpits, and I make a quick mental note that if we are successful, I won't shake her by the hand. The hose is turned on and the snake's head appears! My 'war party' are all of a quiver, sticks raised ready to attack. I note that the 'shamba boy' has worked himself into the rear of the 'war party' and is shouting the loudest just to prove to everyone that he is still brave, but has no intention of being bitten by a five foot cobra.

The snake refuses to leave its lair, and is obviously enjoying this cooling shower provided by these mad humans. It merely moves its head slowly from side to side, its forked tongue flickering in and out, whilst I continue to provide its ablutions. The crowd is not impressed. I can sense their thoughts.

"Bwana Stephens would have killed it by now."

I discard the hose, draw my .38 'Smith & Wesson' and kill the snake with one shot. The 'war party' now rushes in for the 'kill'! With much yelling and thumping they attack the snake, even the 'shamba boy' is in the thick of the fray.

The crowd love it! The now battered remains of a pulverised cobra are removed by a Turkana herdsman for his supper.

The crowd disperses, each one of the 'war party' telling in great detail their feats of 'derring do', that over time will be added to, no doubt to impress the comely maidens they have been fancying for months. I return to the veranda. The houseboy arrives with a glass jug full of ice-cold real lemonade and informs me that dinner will be at 8.30pm. Peace and tranquillity returns once again.

Mrs Stephens and I dine alone. The three-course meal followed by coffee and a brandy was excellent. We retire to the lounge, exchange polite conversation and read. At 10.00pm Mrs Stephens, closes her book, wishes me "Good night" and reminds me to switch off the diesel generator.

I recall Arthur's instructions.

"Go around the house switching off the lights and ensuring that all doors and windows are secure. The last light to be switched off also automatically switches off the generator."

All very simple.

I flick off the final switch and walk around the veranda to my room. I can still hear the soft thud-thud of the generator and assume it will soon stop. I enter my room have a quick wash, put on my best pair of pyjamas and slip between the cool crisp sheets. Tumbo beds down on the rug beside my bed. Through the room's French window I can see faint moonlight outlining the veranda rail and casting soft shadows onto the lawn. It has been a very relaxing and enjoyable Sunday. I close my eyes ready for sleep. I feel at peace with the world and start to doze.

Suddenly I sit up in bed! I can still hear the thud-thud of the generator; something must be amiss! Finding my torch I walk across to the engine shed. The light of my torch reveals an ancient diesel engine that must have come from the British Museum, with a large pipe feeding into a forty-four gallon fuel drum. From the engine are some thick cables attached to banks of over-size car type batteries. What can have gone wrong? Then I note the solution! Just before the pipe disappears into the inner workings of the engine, there is a stopcock.

"Obvious really. Turn off the fuel and that's it fixed!"

Three quick turns and I leave the shed for my room. It will take some minutes for the fuel to be exhausted, so the initial thud thuds are to be expected. I clamber into bed once again, thinking about the snake, this Colonial life style, and close my eyes ready for sleep.

What's that noise? Suddenly I become aware that the thud-thuds haven't stopped! Again I grab the torch and enter the engine shed. The old diesel engine is still 'going strong' and I realise that there is an urgent need to sort out what is going on.

Obvious. The stopcock being old doesn't work anymore! Solution? Remove the pipe from the fuel drum. I do so, dripping diesel onto my pyjama trousers, and reminding myself to somehow let Mrs Stephens know when I hand in my laundry that I am not suffering from 'Montezuma's Revenge'. I leave the shed and, having changed, finally retire for the night. I close my eyes congratulating myself at the obvious method used to solve the problem. I feel tired and look forward to a good night's sleep as Tumbo once again settles down on the rug and I start to doze off again.

What's that noise? It's that damned diesel, its still going! Impossible, it hasn't any fuel! Again I grab the torch and set off to see what can have happened. As I get closer to the engine shed I am aware that the soft thud-thud has now changed to a sound as if someone is banging metal with a 14lb hammer! As I enter the shed the noise is deafening and the diesel engine is shaking all over! I cannot believe it, purely by accident I've discovered perpetual motion! Or have I? Then I recall my physics class at school regarding generators and electric motors. Could it be possible that the batteries are feeding back through the electric motor and driving the diesel engine? Something has to be done.

I look at the bank of over-size batteries and calculate that at X amps per battery I could be welded to the ground! The Mau-Mau couldn't get me, and here I am about to be 'snuffed out' with about 60 amps provided by a diesel engine designed by the British! Finding an old pair of 'wellies' I slip these on and, searching around find an adjustable spanner. Now holding it in some dry sacking, and using only my right hand, I unbolt the cable. The final disconnection is greeted with a shower of blue sparks, and the engine stops!

Thank God! The farm is now without power, no lighting, no refrigeration. No doubt Arthur will know what to do. At least I hope so!

I return to my room to find Tumbo sitting on the bedside rug and upon seeing me he wags his tail and, as I climb into bed he finally settles down for the night. Before going to sleep I wonder what I can say to Mrs Stephens in the morning? I drift off into a deep, deep sleep.

I am awoken by Tumbo's growling as the 'houseboy' arrives with tea. It's 6.30am and a typical Kenya morning. At this hour the air coming through the open French window is cool, the sun is already rising in the sky and the 'nightmare' of the diesel engine is pushed into the background as my senses absorb the sights, the sounds, and smell of the earth. What will the day bring forth?

What was the outcome? The old diesel sometimes 'went off the rails', and my final solution was the standard procedure to bring it to a halt. Evidently a badly corroded valve had been sucked into the cylinder head and pounded into a very odd shape. It was soon up and running again as it had been for the last thirty years.

They don't make them like that any more!

There was a radio message for me. A British army unit was moving in next to our area and a Major would be arriving to meet me. The following day an army Land Rover with an armed escort arrived and I met Major Coxsedge. I showed him my wall map of the area and discussed with him areas of possible terrorist activity. We agreed that the following day I would show him around the area. The European farmers were well known for their hospitality and therefore it came as no surprise when Mrs Stephens invited him to stay for dinner.

The following day we toured along the base of the escarpment and quickly visited the farms in the area. Following this, we headed into the ranching area and then into the Masai Reserve. As usual it was teeming with game, which obviously delighted my guest, and we kept stopping in order for him to obtain a better view. We then turned westward onto the Narok road and headed towards Akira.

We passed some ostriches which must have had chicks as, in order to lure us away, the birds ran away from the nesting site and used their usual 'trick' of constantly flopping over to one side then dragging their short wings onto the ground, giving the appearance of being severely wounded. We also passed a lonely warthog with a magnificent pair of tusks. It hurried away with its tail in the air and promptly went down a hole in the ground in reverse gear. This way their tusks can be used for defence. As usual in this part of the area there were hundreds of wildebeest who were quite unperturbed by our passing.

On the return journey, as I held a game licence, I shot a Thompson's gazelle for Major Coxsedge to take back to his Mess.

Our job here in the Kedong is to constantly strike a balance between Masai patrols and Mau-Mau patrols. As a result, today we are on an anti-terrorist patrol along the edge of the escarpment. From time to time when the foliage thins, we can see the crops of tobacco and maize in the fields below. We are following an old footpath, almost over-grown, that in the past must have led from the valley floor up the escarpment and onto the plateau. As usual we are well spaced out and have been in this area since 6.30am. Now it's close to mid-day and we haven't seen any tracks. Suddenly the tracker stopped dead. There wriggling ahead of us was an enormous python! It must be in excess of fifteen feet long with a girth of about twelve inches. We prudently wait until it has disappeared into the undergrowth and then continue with the patrol.

Just two days before we had been returning to base by Land Rover when an African boy aged about ten had run onto the dirt road, waving his arms for us to stop. He said that a very big snake had just killed his dog.

"*Kuja Bwana, kuja.*" (Come Bwana, come). He was very excited. I grabbed one of the askari's shotguns and followed him. He suddenly stopped.

"*Uku, uku!*" (There, there.) I couldn't see anything.

"*Uku, uku!*" He was very agitated and pointed towards the grass about ten feet ahead. I still couldn't see anything. Suddenly a python reared up! I instinctively reacted and fired from the hip, taking its head clean off. As we moved forward its body was still writhing on the ground and almost beside it was the boy's dog – it was dead, having been crushed to death by the python. Had I not killed it, the python would then have proceeded to swallow the dog whole. It would then have rested for two or three days while its very strong digestive juices consumed every part of its victim.

By this time I had been joined by my patrol.

"*Una taka ngosi Effendi?*" (Do you want the skin Sir?) The boy brought an old sack and placed the still writhing body of the python into it. Back at the farm one of the labourer's skinned the snake and the meat was taken by one of the Turkana herdsmen. Some weeks later I sent the skin to 'Zimmerman's' in Nairobi for curing. I took it home on my first leave with the intention of having a handbag made for my mother. It never transpired and I have no idea what happened to the skin.

It was not surprising that in the Kedong we were continually encountering wild animals at close quarters. During one foot patrol we were just about to cross a farm track. Round the bend at full gallop, and with their eyes rolling with fear, came a herd of sheep. Following them, and also at full gallop was a leopard! Seeing us it stopped at a distance of no more than twenty-five yards, its tail lashing backwards and forwards. As we were on patrol and armed and my 'Patchett' machine carbine was cocked all I had to do was flick the safety catch forward with my right thumb and pull the trigger at the same time but it would have been a crime to have shot such a beautiful animal. For several seconds it stood looking at us, then suddenly turned and went off into the bushes.

Within less than a week after my first meeting with Major Coxsedge I received a radio message to report to his camp site for an urgent 'O' Group (group discussion on forthcoming anti-terrorist activity). Arriving there he told me that the K.A.R. (Kings African Rifles) had found a small boy during a patrol above the escarpment, who had told them that his father, who was a terrorist, was with a small gang of about ten in number and that they were camped in a cave on Mt Longenot. Major Coxsedge said that he proposed to attack the camp that night and outlined his plans, which involved a force of about fifty plus. I could foresee several problems. We would be operating in very faint moonlight and large numbers would be difficult to control, plus they would make a lot of noise. My counter-proposal was that he and I should lead the patrol, plus my tracker and only five of his men. The remainder should follow at a distance and be guided by 'scouts' left along the route. I also suggested that the follow-up party should not have their weapons loaded and cocked. To this he reluctantly agreed.

We set off in a number of vehicles without lights and de-bussed on the Narok road. Led by the boy and an African K.A.R. Sergeant we made our way towards Longenot's lower slopes being trailed by the large well-armed follow-up party.

The boy led without any hesitation, which confirmed that he had been here before. After about an hour we encountered a herd of buffalo which stampeded at our approach. We now commenced ascending the lower slopes. After two or three miles the boy stopped and whispered something to the K.A.R. Sergeant.

"Effendi, he says that they used to post a sentry here." This whole situation struck me as being very bizarre. Here we were on our way to an encounter with his father and the gang, and it was highly likely that his father would be killed. Were we being 'led up the garden path' in order to give the Mau-Mau an unopposed opportunity elsewhere? I had already briefed my 'troops' to be extra alert and for the Corporal to be ready with six men to 'go' if any farm came under attack.

By now we were well up into the lower slopes and the boy continued to unwaveringly forge ahead. He suddenly stopped and whispered to the Sergeant again.

"He says that about a hundred yards ahead is a large rock where they now post a sentry." In whispers I conferred with Major Coxsedge and suggested that the boy should now go to the rear of our patrol with the Sergeant. Then he and I, plus my tracker, should slowly move forward and see if it was possible to surprise the sentry. His men should stay back. By now it was about 2.00am and the sentry might be asleep. He nodded in agreement.

We moved forward very slowly like ghosts and well spaced out. It was important not to make the slightest sound. We arrived at the rock – nothing! We signalled to the others 'down the line' to come forward. Again the boy whispered to the Sergeant. Crouching down by the rock the Sergeant pointed. In the faint moonlight I could see a dark shadow at the base of a rock face.

"Effendi, that's the cave where the gang are." I eased myself close to Major Coxsedge.

"I'll crawl forward with my tracker to the cave entrance, if we can hear any sounds of breathing I'll lob in a grenade. When it explodes you come running." He gripped my forearm and whispered,

"No way, we'll share this moment together!" In whispers the Major briefed his men what we were going to do.

The three of us, well spaced out, crawled very slowly towards the cave entrance. It seemed to take an age to arrive on either side. We lay there, ears straining for the slightest sound from inside. There was utter silence. I signalled to the Major that I would switch on my torch and that he should be ready to open fire. He gave me a thumbs up in acknowledgement. I eased myself closer to the opening until I would be able to switch on the torch and still have some form of protection from the edge of the entrance. I signalled, ready? He acknowledged. I switched on the torch – the cave was empty! It was about six feet high tapering to about two feet and about eight feet wide. There were signs of occupation but, according to the tracker nothing was very recent. I had reason to believe that the boy was aware of what we would find and had given this information in order to be 'in the good books' of the K.A.R.

We retraced our steps. Encountering the follow-up party we made our way back to the transport. Back at the army camp the cooks had not been idle and we were given a steaming hot mug of oxtail soup. 'It really hit the spot'! Back at base I 'fell into bed' and was asleep within seconds.

The following morning, many miles away in the direction of Suswa and Akira, I could see smoke rising into the sky. It was a grass fire in the

Reserve and with the ground so dry it would soon be totally out of control! Giving three blasts on my whistle I ran over to the Post to alert the Sergeant Major to raise six men plus the driver as soon as possible. He saluted.

"*Hakuna matata Effendi, Masai wanachoma mchani mbila mvua.*" (There is no trouble Sir, the Masai are burning the grass ahead of the rains). It looked highly dangerous to me, but evidently they had been doing this ever since anyone could remember, and it was their method of fertilising the land. I returned to the farmhouse to finalise some reports that were almost overdue.

Some two day later I was again engaged in bringing some more paperwork up to date, when suddenly I was aware of a roaring sound. What could it be? I came out onto the veranda. There in the distance was a 'black wall' moving towards us. Ahead of it dust was rising into the air. The rains had arrived! The wind was the first thing to strike the farmhouse causing unclosed doors and windows to crash backwards and forwards, then the rain hit us. I had never, ever seen rain like it! It thundered onto the corrugated roof making conversation impossible! The noise was almost deafening. Due to the sheer volume of water visibility was down to less than ten yards. It was like being under some giant waterfall!

Beyond the veranda everywhere was under water; despite the dryness of the ground it could not soak up this continuous torrent. It lasted for about twenty minutes and then the rain eased. I sloshed my way across to the Post to ensure that the men and their quarters were OK. Two of the rooms were flooded and the men were bailing them out. Only the floors were wet and their bedding and clothing remained dry.

All the farm's earth roads were like rivers and I could hear the roar of water in what, half an hour ago, had been a dried out riverbed. The following day I had cause to use the Narok road. It was only of graded earth construction. Due to the floodwater, huge gouges had been made in the road's surface, some up to three feet deep. This would not impede the small number of vehicles using this road; all they had to do was to drive around the deep holes and continue on their way.

Nature is incredible. Within just twenty-four hours of the deluge small green shoots of grass started to appear and within forty-eight hours small wild flowers in bud. Within a week the farm's cattle had visibly fattened and there was an excess of milk, which both my 'troops' and the labour enjoyed. Soon the whole area would green up and be almost unrecognisable from its former parched self.

Following the usual Masai anti-stock theft patrols, daylight patrols and night ambushes, I thought that it would be opportune to scour the area around the deserted cave. We took our usual three days rations and water and, with Kipkoske, plus five of the 'troops', the seven of us were dropped off on the edge of the Narok road where the army lorries had awaited our return. Once onto the lower slopes of Mount Longenot some heads popped up above some large rocks. Baboons. It was almost as if they were playing hide and seek. Up would come their heads and down they would go again. As we drew closer they became braver and sat on the top of the rocks, but I could see that they were ready to run at the slightest sign of danger. As we passed below, the males made grunting noises and walked on all fours along the rocks looking down at us and tracking our passage.

We continued and with extreme caution approached the cave. It was empty and there were no signs of recent habitation. We commenced to scour the general area and just before 5.00pm we discovered another old hideout. It contained a withered cow's tail (obviously they had dined well) and the partly finished butt of a 'home made' gun. It was cleverly concealed as the entrance was almost covered by a large bush. We continued our search for further traces of Mau-Mau activity, but found nothing. Just before dusk we 'went down' into our usual triangular formation, then later when it was dark, moved to a new location and I took first 'stag'.

We continued our search on the second day, but we drew a blank and despite Kipkoske's 'eagle eyes' he did not spot any signs of human activity.

It was late after-noon and we were making our way down the lower slopes towards the Narok road. This part of the area was covered in long grass and numerous bushes. Suddenly there were numerous crashings in the undergrowth! We had disturbed a large herd of buffalo, who are not known for their friendly nature. A large bull appeared and started walking towards us. I always carried two clips of soft nosed .303 bullets, which I had exchanged with one of the farmers for our standard issue hard nosed. I quickly asked one of the men for his rifle and handed him my 'Patchett' machine carbine. Then I rapidly loaded five rounds of soft nose .303 on top of the five hard nose bullets in his rifle's magazine and 'shoved one up the spout'. I had always carried them for just such an emergency.

At a range of about thirty five yards the bull stopped. By this time I was at the rear of the patrol and facing him. What would he do? He stood stock still sniffing the air with his head raised clearly exposing his huge set of curving horns with the solid bulge of the boss in the centre. I assumed from this that our scent was not blowing towards him. I told the patrol to stay still. We stood like this for several minutes then I motioned for them to move on. As we did so, the bull followed, matching our walking pace. We stopped and again I faced him with the rifle ready to fire. The bull also stopped at roughly the same distance and raised his head sniffing the air again and emitting the odd snort. Would he charge? Obviously he had been with a large number of females so was he merely 'escorting us off the premises', or just curious, which could be the cause of his sniffing the air.? This 'cat and mouse game' continued for about 400 yards and, at long last, he lost interest and we continued on our way.

Talking to a Game Warden some weeks later he told me that had the bull charged, at a range of thirty yards, at best, I would have only been able to fire twice, and it was highly likely that the .303 would not have been sufficient to have stopped it in its tracks. He suggested the minimum rifle would be a .375 magnum. I was sure that Major Thompson (K.P.R) in charge of Divisional Police Stores would 'have a fit' if I ever placed an indent for one of these. He normally complained when I indented for standard items.

I was asked (or should I say told?) to work with the army again. It was to be with a Captain of a recently arrived British regiment, who was keen to lead a small patrol along the lower slopes of Longenot which faces onto the main Nairobi Nakuru road. I was to supply myself and a tracker. This brief exercise was for one day only.

The army patrol consisted of five men, a Corporal and the Captain. He briefed his men on where we were going and informed them that it was a very arid area without any known water supply. As a result there was very strict water rationing. We would stop every hour and they would only drink one capful of water from their alloy water bottles, per stop.

We set off, with Kipkoske leading the patrol with his eyes 'glued' to the ground, I followed watching ahead with the Captain behind me, then the rest of the patrol. Just before 1.00pm the Captain looked back and spotted one man taking an 'illegal' drink. We halted. He ordered the man to hand him his water bottle and then poured the entire contents onto the ground! I could not believe that anyone could be so stupid! It was hot, the men were not accustomed to walking in these temperatures, and the outcome was a foregone conclusion. I took the Captain to one side.

"Do you appreciate what you have done? This man will now have to share our water, and we are only carrying a litre each. Surely you could have placed him on a charge and dealt with him back at camp!"

"When I give an order I expect it to be obeyed, and he will not share anyone's water."

At 4.00pm the man collapsed; he was white and felt clammy to the touch. It was heat exhaustion. We carried him into the shade of a bush; he was looking ghastly. I always carried some salt. Shaking about half a teaspoon into the cap of my water bottle I filled the cap, stirred in the salt and gently poured the mixture into his mouth. I repeated this and then gave him a long drink of water. Within ten minutes the salt had reactivated his natural cooling system, and within twenty minutes we were able to move forward but at a much slower pace. I agree that discipline is necessary but this was a thoughtless act.

I realised my home leave date was very close and therefore I was not surprised when Headquarters gave me a date when my relief would arrive. Following this I would be heading for home with nearly six months fully paid leave!

It is amazing how news spreads. Within days I had a job offer from the 'no nonsense' widow to become her farm manager as her current manager had obtained a Government job in the Seychelles. Most surprising of all, the Sergeant Major said that two of the men wanted to see me in private. I saw them the following day.

"Effendi, we have spoken with our Chief in the Reserve and he says that he will accept our word. We want you to come and work for us."

This was totally unexpected.

"Why me, and what do you want me to do?"

"In our Reserve Effendi we have a small gold mine. Every African we have employed to run it and look after the money has stolen from us. We know that we can trust you. We know that very soon you will be leaving here to go back home, but before you do so, will you please consider our offer. We can pay you well."

I didn't quite know how to respond. I did not wish to offend them, it was a sincere offer and I was almost lost for words.

"First, thank you for your offer and I feel very honoured that you want me to work for you. I don't know what to say. But let me consider it and I will come to some decision before I leave here." They saluted and returned to the Post.

The following week I asked to see them again.

"I have given a lot of thought to your offer, but many, many years ago when I was a very young man (*kijana*) I wanted to be a policeman in Kenya. I have done this job for three years and I know it is the work that I want to do. Please thank your Chief for his offer, and thank you for giving him my name." They looked very crestfallen, and I felt as if I had almost betrayed the trust they had placed in me. I often wonder what happened to their mine. I hope that it prospered.

It was with a sad heart that I bade farewell to the Stephens, my 'troops' and Tumbo. As the Land Rover bumped its way towards the main Nairobi Nakuru road, I wondered if I would ever experience something like this again? It had been a unique experience and I had grown to love this place, its diversity of wildlife, its remoteness, the heat and my very fortunate position of living in the farmhouse with all its home comforts.

6   Home leave

Having ensured that Tumbo would be cared for during my absence, and having deposited my kit at the Government Store in Nairobi, I spent the final day in the city shopping. During the early fifties, ivory was plentiful and very reasonably priced. As a result I purchased an assortment of ivory items for the family, plus a very exotic Indian rug for my Mother. Also in my baggage was the cured python skin. This I intended to have made into a handbag for my Mother, plus a pair of shoes if there was any surplus.

The following day, there on the tarmac at Nairobi airport was the now familiar 'Canadair Argonaut' aircraft. I had arranged to have a window seat and also, in order to 'shake the dust of Africa from my shoes', I had arranged to break my journey in Rome. Having boarded the aircraft and taken my seat, sitting on the opposite side of the cabin was an Italian, about my age, who introduced himself as Benito. He was on his way for an eye operation in Milan. His English was very limited, so we tried to converse in French. Finally, we discovered that the best solution was to use Kiswahili, and this we proceeded to do until we finally parted company some six days later.

On this return journey to the UK we landed at Khartoum, not at dawn but at 2.00am. Outside the airport building there was a hot breeze blowing and I was glad that we were not staying there over-night. What an environment; 'roasting' during the day and a hot breeze at night! I was looking forward to Rome and a week of sightseeing. Benito informed me that he was booked into an hotel on the Via Natzionale and that during my stay he and his friend would show me the city sights.

Having landed at Rome Airport and de-bussed outside the BOAC office near the city centre, I asked a member of staff there to find me a small family-run hotel. Their choice was within walking distance and I set off with my pile of baggage. I arrived at the hotel covered in sweat, booked in, had a shower and a meal, then 'slept like a log'.

Following breakfast, next morning I set off to find Benito. His greeting was totally unexpected.

"Have you had a woman yet?"

Considering that we had landed at about 9.00pm, and by the time I, and no doubt he, had had dinner, it must have been around 10.15pm, how was this possible?

"Where did you find a woman so quickly?"

Benito smiled knowingly.

"Did you pass a cleaning girl in the corridor? It was her, about fifteen minutes ago. I gave her the equivalent of ten shillings."

Until now I had always assumed that Italian women were very chaste, perhaps the word should have been chased! Benito seemed very surprised that to date my visit to Rome had been so uneventful!

That day we carried out a rapid tour of Rome. I wish to stress the word rapid! Our various taxi drivers must have been ex-racing drivers as the speed of our tour was conducted in direct competition with every other vehicle, accompanied by many blasts on the horn and many hand gestures, some of which were obviously very rude as other drivers gave us a similar gesture in return. In addition, there were many exclamations! Even though I didn't speak Italian, I suggest they were unprintable and these two reactions were directed at any impediment to our high speed progress.

To my 'Kenyan eyes' Rome was an extraordinary and beautiful city. The main railway station was stunning, with a huge glass window at one end, displaying through the glass some of Rome's ancient ruins. The whole complex was vast, with underground shops offering a huge variety of choice. It must have been possible to have arrived unkempt and in rags and to have left well fed, well groomed and smartly attired in the latest Italian menswear.

There were smartly dressed girls everywhere and I have to admit that the girls were very beautiful. With Benito as my procurer, had I not been English, I could have departed from Rome physically exhausted! You will recall that Benito and I were conversing in Kiswahili, so upon meeting a lovely shop assistant Benito would ask me "Do you fancy her? If so I'll ask her." He must have thought that all Englishmen were 'queer', as I always refused to pursue this embarrassing and very direct line of enquiry.

During our first day in Rome Benito took me to an Italian barbers. What an experience! Hot towels, a vigorous shampoo, followed by a haircut and a head massage of eau de cologne, then more hot towels. The barber eyed my bristling English moustache and, through Benito, said he could trim it down into an Italian model. There was much merriment when I flatly refused. We left, and as we walked in the hot morning sunshine leaving a cloud of eau de cologne in our wake, we were feeling, if not looking, like two film stars.

Our next port of call was a gentlemen's outfitters. Benito 'splashed out' on two suits, shirts and silk ties and shoes. From his image on the plane to what was before me now, was a complete transformation. With the haircut, plus new attire, he looked the immaculate, suave, sophisticated, Italian predatory male. After lunch we parted company, arranging to meet later that evening when his friend would join us for dinner.

His friend worked in a drawing office and spoke only Italian, but through Benito I was able to establish a rapport based on my cartographic experience. His friend suggested that I should leave the Kenya Police and obtain work in a drawing office in Rome. After all, he had connections and in Rome there were lots of very pretty girls!

Our first 'port of call' that evening was a typical Italian restaurant run by a husband and wife. There were very few tables and each one was covered with a red checked tablecloth. Benito ordered the not unexpected spaghetti with a thin veal steak and a delicious tomato sauce; this to be 'washed down' with a large bottle of Chianti. The 'Mama' saw me struggling to master the Italian art of spaghetti eating. She came over to our table, then placing my napkin underneath my chin and taking my spoon and a fork, she stood behind me twirling the spaghetti into the bowl of the spoon and then feeding me, much to the amusement of my new found friends and the regulars. Having fed me five mouthfuls, she then motioned for me to try. I wasn't very good but she patted me on the shoulder saying "Bueno, bueno."

It was a very enjoyable meal and I had even been shown how to eat spaghetti, although I must confess that despite this lesson, to this day I still chop it up, as this saves the long dangling pieces dripping tomato sauce onto my tie and shirt front.

I had considered Benito's approach to the opposite sex somewhat forward, but that evening his friend proved that Benito was a mere starter. Being English, my attitude to girls was somewhat more restrained, and I am sure that they both wondered if I needed to see a doctor. My idea of beautiful, chaste, Italian girls was 'turned on its head'. Here in Rome it was *La Dolce Vita*! Our nightly routine was a good meal in a family restaurant, visits to the floodlit La Fontana de

Trevi and other places of interest, then taking a horse drawn buggy around Rome. And for them, 'chatting up' everything with a skirt and two legs and using me as the lure. There was lots of fast talking and lots of laughter. My part was merely to smile. I had no idea what was being said, but my two P.R. men were obviously giving me a big build up.

During the day we visited St. Peter's with its colourful Swiss Guards dressed in medieval uniforms and where the size of the cupola (inside St. Peter's) has to be seen to be believed. The Coliseum is where every Italian driver, irrespective of the vehicle's size, is convinced he's driving a racing car. As a result, if you ever visit Rome, you will see that the road around the Coliseum is covered with residual rubber from thousands of screaming tyres, accompanied by other residual rubber from the soles of tourists shoes, as they have tried to avoid annihilation when attempting to cross the road!

To reach the Coliseum we boarded a tram. One of the passengers was a very beautiful Italian girl. Benito noticed my glances and asked the usual question. To our surprise, the Conductor said in Kiswahili "Eyes off our women!" We were stunned. Evidently he had been a prisoner of war in Kenya and could still speak the language!

So my brief stay in Rome was educational and enjoyable. Now Benito was off to Milan for his operation and I needed to be heading to England and home.

I told the lady owner of the small hotel where I was staying that I was leaving in the morning and asked if I could pay my bill as I had to be at the Airline office by 6.00am. Repeated requests failed to produce my bill. Finally I tracked her down in the kitchen. The bill was ready, but it was for twice the price stated by both the Airline office and herself when I first arrived. I said that I would pay the correct price. She said she would call the police. I then produced my Kenya Police warrant card and said I was calling the police. She looked shocked and took the correct money with obvious ill grace.

The hotel was situated on the third floor of the building and was serviced by a lift. The next morning the lift was locked and she refused to open it. As a result I staggered down to the ground floor with two very heavy bags, then on to the Airline office, where I had to change my sweat-soaked shirt. It was an unpleasant finish to my brief stay in Rome.

This time the aircraft was the new 'Viscount' which had four turbo-prop engines and a very unusual feature, elliptical windows. On take off the power could be felt as the pressure pushed me into the back of my seat, which increased as we sped down the runway. These new turbo-prop engines were quiet compared to the 'Argonaut' and there was none of the usual roar and vibration. We continued to climb, leaving the city far below, and then the aircraft turned West towards the Italian coast. Having crossed the coast there was another change in direction as we headed North, with the coastline almost below our starboard wing and the early morning sunshine pouring through the starboard cabin windows. It was the same kind of cloudless day that I had experienced almost three years before, the sunlight reflecting off the tips of the four-bladed propellers causing a large halo effect around each engine, and there below our aircraft, the brilliant blue sea glistening in the early morning sunlight, with the paler blues clearly defining the shallows. Now it was time for breakfast. It was typically English – and I enjoyed every mouthful.

Some hours later, the snow-capped Alps were just coming into view. It was at this juncture that the Captain's voice announced over the intercom.

"Ladies and gentlemen, in approximately twenty minutes we will be passing very close to Mont Blanc, which will be clearly visible from the port side of the aircraft. I will alert you in good time should you wish to take photographs. Thank you."

The aircraft was not full so, following the Captain's next announcement, I occupied a vacant port side window seat and secured some excellent shots of the cap of Mont Blanc, which I still have to this day.

On arrival over the English coast it was overcast, and as we headed in a westerly direction towards 'Heathrow Airport' and commenced our descent, rain started spattering onto my window. I had enjoyed almost three years of sunshine, so I could hardly complain. As we continued our descent and the clouds thinned, far down below I could make out the course of the Thames, then directly below our flight-path, Windsor Castle. Soon I heard two soft thuds as the wheels were lowered, followed by a whirring noise. Looking out from my window seat I could see the landing flaps being extended, then below the wing, roads, masses of traffic, and finally the airport buildings came into view. With a soft bump and a roar from the engines as they were placed on reverse thrust, quickly softening to a deep purr, we had landed. I was home again!

'Heathrow Airport' had changed beyond all recognition. There were lots of modern buildings, so very different from the old Nissen huts. There appeared to be many more aircraft coming and going – and so many people! There was a feeling of affluence in the air.

Having retrieved my bags and cleared Customs, I went to the taxi rank and we headed for London and Victoria Station. I asked the 'cabbie' how were things in England?

"Not too bad guvnor, but we haven't had any rain for over two weeks!" I had to smile; in the Kedong Valley we hadn't had any rain for nearly eighteen months!

The journey into London surprised and saddened me. There was lots of litter on the sides of the road and the buildings looked dirty. It was not as I remembered it. The main line station was the same. It seemed dirty and unkempt. The station staff looked scruffy and they lacked an air of pride and it showed in the manner in which they wore their uniform. How very different from Nairobi. It was not just due to the lack of sunshine, it was a distinct attitude. Had it really been like this before I left for Kenya? I booked a first class ticket, checked the indicator board for my train, and headed for the platform with a porter leading the way with my baggage.

I suppose that all railways pass through some of the 'scruffiest' areas, but again I was shocked on this dull, wet day as the train passed close-packed, soot grimed housing. I was alone in my compartment and opening the sliding door I stood in the corridor; was England really like this? Soon we were passing green fields and hedgerows. This was the England I remembered. It looked so very green and I wondered what the Masai would say if they saw all this superb rich grazing and these fat cattle? The 'clickety-clack' of the train as it passed over the numerous connections in the rails, accompanied by the odd lurch, caused me to grab at the hand rail and invaded my thoughts. What would it be like being home again after all this time? Within less than an hour the train commenced slowing down; more closely packed housing, then 'my' station came into view. I had arrived!

A porter came up to me.

"I'll take your bags Sir, follow me and I'll take you to the taxi rank."

I duly followed, musing on how different our two lives were, and wondering what his reaction would be if I could transport him into the heart of the Kedong Valley? He unloaded my bags at the rank. I gave him a £1 tip, why not? I was on leave!

"Thank you Sir, I hope that you enjoy your stay here."

He walked away pushing his trolley as no doubt he had done so many, many times before.

From the rear passenger seat of the taxi I viewed my home town with 'new eyes'. It was just as I remembered it but perhaps slightly shabbier? Or was this due to the rain? The driver interrupted my thoughts.

"You're very tanned Sir, just returning from holiday?"

I explained where I had come from and as expected commenced to answer his many questions. This two-way communication lasted until we arrived at my home. He unloaded my bags from the boot and having thanked me for my tip sped away. For a few moments I stood there looking around me. It was a strange feeling, it was all so very familiar, yet somehow it wasn't home anymore. Even now I find it difficult to express in words how I felt that afternoon, which was so many years ago. I picked up my bags and headed for the front door. I didn't have to knock, it was flung open and I was hugged and kissed. There were tears, more hugs, more kisses. I was home! My sister, who had been a young teenager when I had left for Kenya was now a very attractive young woman. What a transformation! The next question did not surprise me.

"Have you had anything to eat, and would you like a cup of tea?"

Yes, I was home!

Having partly unpacked my bags, and having produced my presents which were greeted with exclamations of delight, followed by more hugs and kisses, I now produced the python skin, accompanied by how I came to shoot it and have the skin cured. To their ears I must have sounded like an African explorer.

I slept very badly that night, I seemed to toss and turn for ages. Was it the time differential, or was it being thrust so very quickly into this very different yet familiar world? Or was the cause my seeing things with 'new eyes'? I could hear the rain pattering onto my bedroom window. I looked at my luminous watch; nearly twenty past two – would I never get to sleep? I must have dozed off as the next thing I remember was the daylight coming through the material of the curtains. I looked at my watch again, it was just past six thirty. I lay there looking at the ceiling and in my mind's eye picturing the past, then conjuring up pictures of the immediate future.

That morning I collected my car, a brand new green Morris 1000 saloon. Now that I had my own personal transport I commenced to make the rounds of family and friends, answering numerous questions and handing out my African gifts. Having just arrived back in England and started to settle in once again, I almost dreaded the oft repeated question, "When are you going back?"

The other variant was, "So how long are you home for?"

Prior to departing for Kenya I had been a member of the local fencing club and had high hopes (no doubt misplaced) of representing my County. So, as soon as the first Thursday evening arrived, equipped with my old fencing gear, I made tracks for the club. I was greeted like a long lost brother by the older members and introduced to the new ones, including three very attractive girls. After some practice with our instructor using foil and sabre, I was surprised how quickly I settled in and I wasn't as 'rusty' as I had imagined. Following this I sat watching others 'going through their paces' and talking for quite some time to one of the new girls. She asked lots of intelligent questions about Kenya, my life out there, and she laughed as I related some of the funny incidents. During this very enjoyable conversation I was approached by a man with a ruddy complexion who had been introduced to me as one of the new members. He asked if I would care for a sabre match? I readily agreed.

Now with a sabre you score points with either the point or the 'cutting' edge of the weapon. If you score with the latter, the 'cut' is not followed through, but it is more like a flick. To follow through with a 'cut' is not only extremely painful (similar to being hit with a whip), but also it is 'not the done thing'. My opponent made no attempt to thrust and score with the point, every attack was with the cutting edge. Initially I managed to parry these, and at this early stage as I took each attack onto my blade, it was obvious these were 'cuts' at full force. I dropped my guard and said "Take it easy, we are not trying to kill each other."

The response was a full cut onto my sword arm and it hurt like hell! Through my mask I shouted "That hurt, take it easy!" Another strong attack and another 'cut' at full force! This was crazy, and so was he! Again he came at me lashing away with his sabre like a man possessed. I took another full 'cut' onto my body.

"This man's a lunatic!" I shouted through my fencing mask, "Let's call it a day."

The response? Another lashing attack!

At this stage the instructor came between us and seizing hold of my opponent's sword arm, said "That's enough!"

Breathing heavily, tearing off his fencing helmet and glaring in my direction, my now even redder-faced opponent stormed off to the changing room. I was stunned!

"What's the matter with that guy, he should be banned."

One of the 'old' club members said, "Normally he's OK, but the girl you were talking to for ages is his girlfriend."

So he *did* want to kill me!

Later in the changing room I had three red wheals on my right forearm and another just above my waist. A nice welcome home!

During the following weeks I invited the other two girls out for dinner, sometimes to the theatre and prolonged drives in the countryside. Both invited me home to meet their parents who not surprisingly asked the usual string of questions. Throughout my leave both girls, from time to time, proved to be delightful companions.

Being on home leave for nearly six months on full Kenya Police pay with my own car was so different from my outings with girlfriends prior to my departure, when the local buses provided the transport and the various cinemas the entertainment.

It was fortuitous that during my leave, a colleague with whom I had visited Malindi during my initial tour, was also on leave. Jim's home was in Galway, Southern Ireland, so we made plans to meet at Dublin airport, spend a day or so in Dublin and then travel to Galway. Never having been to Ireland before, I was keen to savour a new experience.

We met as planned and had lunch in the airport restaurant. What struck me immediately were the number of Catholic priests dining there and the number who had a bottle of wine on the table. It was not for me to question who was paying the bill, but as the menu was not cheap I did wonder how it was possible? These oblique thoughts were swept away as Jim and I exchanged 'notes' on our reaction to being home again, plus our immediate plans for the next few days. Plan one was a night out in Dublin. Plan two, to hire a car and drive to Galway. Plan three was to meet Jim's girlfriend and relax at his home. However, before plan No.1 could commence we needed to get to Dublin. The airport bus which was rather dated had other ideas; it broke down on the way into town and we had to wait for a replacement. Having arrived and settled in with one of Jim's family friends we went out on the town.

Having passed an establishment we heard dance music. Why not? We entered the dance hall. The men were outnumbered by Irish girls by at least ten to one. Within minutes were we approached and asked to dance. This was at odds with normal practice! We were whirled around the floor and as soon as we sat down, we were off again! By ten o'clock we were foot sore and needing a meal. Leaving was difficult as even making our way to the exit we were stopped and asked to dance. How can one refuse a beautiful Irish girl with sparkling green eyes? We managed to leave just before closing time, famished, foot sore and with enough invitations from our dancing partners to fill an exercise book! That night I slept 'like a log'.

The next day we set about hiring a car. Even on day one, what struck me as odd was not the number of cars in Dublin, but that every one appeared not to have seen water for months. A clean car was an exception. Anyway, to the car hire. We visited various hire companies and without exception, every car I tried was a wreck. Not only was starting a problem, but many had faulty footbrakes! By four o'clock we gave up and decided to travel to Galway by train.

It was late afternoon when we arrived at Dublin Central Station and we hadn't eaten anything since breakfast. As our train was yet to depart we entered the railway station restaurant.

"We're starving," I said to the waitress, "we want the biggest fried horse that you have."

With eyes like green ice and a face to match, she replied, "We don't serve fried horses here!" and with a flounce went to another table.

"Take it easy," Jim hissed. "They don't exactly love the English around here."

He ordered the meal; we dined well and then caught our train to Galway.

Jim's mother and sister gave us a warm welcome and the following morning, having had breakfast, I donned my blazer. On the breast pocket was the badge of the Kenya Police, woven in silver wire, showing a rampant lion with the words 'Salus Populi' in a scroll, surmounted with the Royal Crown. Jim's mother took one look and much to my surprise, said "You musn't wear that jacket here, it wouldn't be safe to do so. During the days of the 'Black & Tans' there was a prison here, and some people don't forget."

It would have been foolish not to have heeded her warning, so my blazer was returned to the wardrobe and stayed there for the whole of my visit.

Galway was a delightful market town, and market day was the highlight of our stay. It was a busy scene with many stallholders, donkeys bringing in produce and with much haggling taking place, which to English ears was conducted in a delightful Irish brogue. I recall crossing a small bridge in Galway and looking down into the water to be amazed that as far as the eye could see, both up and down stream, were salmon packed gill to gill, with their tails moving slowly from side to side against the current; an incredible and memorable sight.

One night, accompanied by Jim's girlfriend and his sister, we visited the local dance hall and danced the night away. We walked home in a buoyant mood, doing the 'odd' dance in the street and despite being sober, kicking the occasional dustbin. Jim's sister said with that lovely soft Irish accent, "You boys are truly mad!"

So my stay in Ireland was enjoyable and it left me with many happy memories. Now it was time to return to England. To this day Jim and I are still in touch.

Through a friend of the family I heard that another Kenya Police Officer was home on leave and living not very far away. As a result I made contact and we decided to tour the West Country.

One evening we booked into an inn for dinner, bed and breakfast. Following dinner we entered the bar to 'rub shoulders' with some of the locals. After about five minutes we were approached by an old man whom I judged to be in his late sixties. His opening statement surprised us.

"I've been talking to my old Dad. We reckon that you two fellas be policemen. Not ordinary policemen, we reckon you be foreigners."

I looked into the corner of the bar. Through the haze of cigarette smoke sat a knarled old man. 'Catching my eye' he came over, introduced himself, accepted our offer of a pint of local cider, and returned to his corner. Behind the bar, squeezed between the inverted bottles of whisky, brandy and gin, were two photographs. One was of our 'friend's' old Dad. I posed the question.

"Isn't that your father's photograph?"

"It is. A long story that. Last Summer about midnight there was a banging on my door. Trouble I says? Trouble they says, your old Dad's fallen in the river!"

Outside the inn was a small stream, and apparently anyone who was drunk and fell into the stream had his photograph placed behind the bar! We continued to talk to the old man's son.

"So where be you fellas come from?"

"Kenya," my colleague replied

"Ah, that's in India, I knows that. I've travelled in me time. I've been on two fifteen bob trips, one to Land's End and the other to East-bourne. Them postcards they sell at the seaside is disgusting, shouldn't be allowed."

I found it incredible to think that this man and his Dad had been born in the village and during his whole life (he had been excused military service), only twice had he travelled any distance.

Being home once again I 'fell into' a standard routine of fencing club on Thursday evening, and from time to time, wining and dining one of my two girlfriends. Life was very pleasant and during this period I contacted one of my schoolfriends. Neither of us had ever toured the UK, so this is what we opted to do. It would also provide me with a broader picture of my homeland and provide (hopefully) some memories to take back to Kenya. We planned a two-week tour.

Our route was to take us up the Eastern side of Britain, then into Scotland, across to the Western seaboard, down the Western side of England via the Lake District, into Wales, then into the Southwest, Cornwall and home. With hindsight our attire was not ideally suited for touring, but nevertheless decked out in blazers, 'knife edged' grey trousers and highly polished brogue shoes, we had no problems in obtaining rooms at all the hotels on route. We stayed in the best hotels, ate and dined well, and within a few days arrived in Carlisle, the gateway to Scotland! In the railway station car park was an old London taxi which must have been owned by students. It had curtains at the windows, a television aerial and painted on each side of the vehicle were the words, "Don't Laugh Sir, Your Daughter May Be Inside!"

We continued northwards. The weather was idyllic and having stayed in Edinburgh for a day, once again we headed North. By now we were well into Scotland. Having rounded a bend in the road there, trying to hitch a lift were two very attractive girls with rucksacks, wearing the shortest shorts I had ever seen. The brakes worked perfectly! They too were heading North and touring Scotland, via Youth Hostels. Yvette was French and Rosa German; both had been studying English and had decided to tour Scotland prior to returning home. We said that we would take them to their Youth Hostel. They were even more attractive close-to and spoke excellent English. What more could two bachelors want?

We had lunch together and they invited us to have dinner with them at their Youth Hostel. They said that they would provide the food and cook the meal, and it would be their way of saying "thank you" for the lift. We asked if we could stay at the Youth Hostel.

"Yes of course, you can become members when you book in."

Done! The Youth Hostel was an old, large, bleak looking house of stone construction. We parked in the drive, unpacked the boot and walked through the knarled oak entrance. You will recall that we had on our blazers and were carrying suitcases. Yvette and Rosa had on very short shorts and were carrying rucksacks. At the reception desk was an equally knarled old Scot who had summed up the situation in a trice. Yvette and Rosa produced their cards and asked, "Can these two gentlemen join the Youth Hostel Association?"

The reply was a guarded, "aye", and we paid a modest joining fee and booked in.

Looking me straight in the eye 'the keeper of decency' said "You two gentlemen, room ten *upstairrrs* and you two ladies, room two *downstairrrs.*"

"Can't you do better than that?" I asked.

He placed his face very close to mine, our noses couldn't have been more than five inches apart.

"I'll hae non of yer hanky panky here, owrrr yer oot, oot! And in the morrrning, ye'll have to get yer hands dirrrty, herrre everybody worrks. Do yer underrrstand?"

Here was a man who knew how to roll his 'R's'.

Having found our abode for the night we decided to clean up before our Franco-German dinner. Having washed, I switched on my electric razor. There was an immediate pounding of feet on the stairs and a loud knocking on the door. It was our knarled Scot.

"Can yer noo switch that thing off, it's jamming me television!"

Next morning we were washing the floors!

The meal was delightful, steak, a mixed salad, cheese with coarse bread and the girls had excelled themselves, a bottle of good red wine! This was far too good to give up! Could we give them a lift in the morning?

We spent the rest of the tour together and it was a sad day when we had to part company. I still had a reasonable amount of leave remaining so I suggested to Yvette that I would visit her in Paris.

A few days later I received her letter. Her parents would be delighted to have me stay, and as her father was an Inspector of Police in Paris, he was sure that we would have much in common. I booked a flight from Shoreham airport to Paris and, as Yvette was 'footloose and fancy free', I decided to stay for two weeks.

Do not let the words Shoreham Airport conjure up in your mind's eye some modern local high-tech facility. In 1956 it was a grass field and housed the local flying club's aircraft which were mainly 'Tiger Moth' bi-planes. Therefore it was no surprise when a small twin-engined 'DeHaviland Dove' landed and the pilot asked all the heavy people to sit in the front section, as a tail heavy aircraft might not take off! There were only ten seats in a staggered formation and no in-flight service. As there was only one pilot, I am sure that everyone preferred him to stay in his seat and not serve in-flight drinks!

Yvette met me at the airport and took me home to meet her parents. They were very pleasant people and made me welcome. Having settled in, Yvette's father took me to the local wine shop, where I was introduced and given a tour of the cellar. Yvette's mother took me shopping and remarked to Yvette that I would make "*un bon marie.*" This was greeted with a torrent of French that I found almost impossible to follow, but the gist of it was her mother was not to make any more stupid remarks!

Our normal day was a late breakfast, followed by shopping and then attending one of the many luncheons given by family and friends who had invited us in order to meet *le flic Anglias*. After five such meals I almost dreaded the next. The French certainly know how to eat! I was also introduced to a French custom. When the crystal champagne glass is empty, use two fingers to hold the stem firmly onto the table, now dip one finger from the other hand into the base of the glass to moisten the tip. Now rub the moistened finger around the rim of the glass. With six or more people all doing this at the same time, the sound produced is incredible!

In the evenings we would stroll around Paris, take a horse drawn 'buggy', perhaps dine at the Police Club close to the Notre Dame, or find some small family run restaurant for a relaxed evening meal. Some nights we would visit the normal 'tourist spots'.

Now Yvette's parents thought I looked a typical Englishman. One evening we were descending some steps in the Latin Quarter. At the bottom of the steps was a middle-aged Englishman somewhat overweight, wearing a tweed cloth cap and accompanied by (I assumed) his wife, equally overweight. As we approached he said in a loud voice with a very strong Yorkshire accent, "I'll just ask them two 'Froggies' where ter go."

I felt Yvette stiffen, as the term he used was, to any French person, insulting. He waited for our approach. In French with a strong Yorkshire accent he started "Excusez moi, je suis…"

"I'm bloody English!" I said

As we walked away we could hear him saying, "Eh mother, did you 'ear that, he was English."

Yvette couldn't stop giggling.

"What's so funny?"

"He thought that you were French!"

On our arrival back at the apartment Yvette's parents were equally amused and her mother had tears in her eyes. I gather my response translated into French was partly the cause of the merriment.

Yvette's Aunt and Uncle owned a cottage in Normandy, where Yvette and I were invited to spend a weekend. It was a lovely old converted farmhouse way out in the countryside. Grandmere was already there preparing lunch and was grilling a huge piece of steak over open coals. The aroma immediately activated my taste buds. I can still smell that wonderfully tender grilling meat. There was a huge salad, and as per our Franco/German meal, some excellent cheese and home baked bread. Now, Normandy is famous for its cider and associated products. Lunch commenced with champagne cider to give us an appetite. Then came the dry Normandy cider. After the cheese it was calvados and coffee. Following lunch, we all sprawled on the lawn enjoying the warm sunshine. I was at peace with the world. This was bliss with a capital 'B'!

I must have dozed off. I opened my eyes with difficulty and looked at my watch. It had turned four o'clock! I was alone, which was not surprising, as Yvette informed me that I had been snoring like 'un cochon'!

Yvette's Aunt, who spoke excellent English, said that the following day we would not go for a walk as it was the start of the French hunting season. It would not be safe to wander in the surrounding woods and countryside. She also said that soon after dawn we would hear shooting, as it was considered to be good luck to fire the first shot of the season.

That evening, following an excellent dinner prepared by the ladies, through Yvette I related some of my Kenya yarns and we retired to bed. I did not need any rocking. As soon as my head touched the pillow I was asleep. Calvados is a potent brew!

I was awoken by two loud bangs! I 'shot' out of bed! We were under attack! I reached down for my machine carbine, but it wasn't there! My brain was in 'top gear', but what was happening? I soon relised it wasn't Mau-Mau but some idiotic French hunter trying to be the first to welcome in the season! I looked at my watch; it was two minutes to midnight! The shots continued throughout the night and the following day, enough to herald the start of World War Three! Following breakfast, in the interests of safety, we stayed in the garden all day.

Having thanked our hosts for a very memorable and pleasant weekend, we returned to Paris for our final night out on the town. Yvette consulted *Le Spectacle* and suggested that following dinner we go and see a Spanish dancing troupe at one of the theatres. It was an amazing performance. All they had on the stage was one man playing a guitar, two female Spanish dancers and one male. The rhythm, the changes of tempo, the stamping of the feet, the swirling skirts of the women, the haughty body postures and expressions, the effort that went into every dance – we could see the sweat running down their faces – made for an electrifying performance! We were spellbound. The whole building throbbed with their pulsating and vibrant music. It was wild, untamed, stunning! When their performance ended, the whole audience rose 'as one man' and clapped and cheered until they could cheer no more. What a performance!

It was time to leave Paris. I packed my bags, thanked my hosts and said goodbye to Yvette. I was the sole passenger on the plane to Shoreham airport and within less than a week I would be on another aircraft returning to Kenya.

I sent Yvette a dozen pink roses and received her letter of thanks the day I was due to leave. The six months had been enjoyable, but with hindsight, maybe I should have done more, perhaps visited America?

I would do so during my next leave in 1959, or so I thought...

7   Back to Africa

I watched the clouds thousands of feet below the aircraft and in the brilliant sunshine it was, as always, a wonderful sight. Some clouds towered above the others almost in vertical columns and I wondered if this was caused by an updraft over a mountain range. It seemed possible that if I jumped out of the aircraft, this apparently endless sea of 'cotton wool' would gently cushion my fall.

As I looked out of the window my thoughts turned to Kenya. What would it be like now that the Mau-Mau terrorists had been beaten? Would Kenya once again be a land of peace and plenty? And how would the captured terrorists be assimilated back into their normal environment? For several minutes my mind dwelt on this topic as I recalled incidents such as the 'Lari Massacre'. Could those Kikuyu who had supported the Government ever forgive their fellow tribesmen for such pointless slaughter?

My six months home leave was finished and I was now on my way back to Kenya. I had no idea where I would be posted but I doubted very much that I would be posted back to the Kedong Valley. This thought triggered a mental picture of Tumbo – how wild with excitement he would be when we met again after all these months. Prior to departing for England I had left sufficient funds for his food, plus an extra sum in case he needed any veterinary treatment during my absence.

Some six months before, on my way home, the aircraft had flown over the Alps. It had been a cloudless day and we had passed so close to Mont Blanc that every detail could be seen. Alas, on this return journey there had been nothing but cloud cover ever since crossing the English coast. Some hours later the clouds cleared and there below and to port was the Italian coastline with its usual brilliant blue sea. The aircraft started to lose height and turned eastward towards the coast; we would be on the ground at Rome airport in less than thirty minutes.

The route had not changed since my first flight, which was now over three years ago. I knew that Cairo airport would have a strange smell, we would arrive at Khartoum about 7.00am the following morning and despite the very early hour that it would be 'roasting'. We would be having an excellent lunch at Entebbe airport, overlooking Lake Victoria, but this time the bright African sunshine, the vivid colours and the ochre coloured earth would not appear strange to my eyes – they would seem welcoming. Africa had already 'soaked into my bones' and become my new home.

The flight so far had not been uneventful. When we re-boarded the aircraft in Rome there was some delay in our departure. Evidently two passengers were missing. Finally they were found. It was a mother and her precocious little boy, who had been misbehaving ever since leaving England. The mother, looking very flustered, apologised to the various passengers as she passed down the aisle to their seats. This was not to be the last delay we would experience.

Cairo airport during late afternoon is not the coolest place to be and inside the aircraft cabin it was baking hot. There was another delay; two passengers were missing. Yes, you've guessed, it was the same flustered mother and her little boy. We continued to wait and perspire. There was a very audible 'click'. The Captain's voice came over on the cabin intercom.

"As you are aware, two passengers are missing, which is the cause of our delay. We have just received information that the little boy has climbed some structure or other and all attempts to entice him down have failed. We apologise for this delay and we will keep you informed. Thank you."

We continued to wait and sweat. A hostess came round with glasses of cool water. I took mine and downed it in seconds. We continued to wait and sweat. There was another 'click'. It was the Captain again.

"The little boy still refuses to budge, therefore we have persuaded the mother to come aboard. We will close the doors and start the engines. We feel confident that this will solve the current situation. Thank you."

The mother came on board very red in the face and looking very stressed. The doors were closed and the engines started. The result? Zero! The engines stopped and the door was opened. A steward left the aircraft with a very determined look on his face. He was back in less than ten minutes with the little boy in tears. At last we could leave! Later during the flight I asked him how he had achieved success.

"Quite simple Sir, I merely threatened to tan his backside. It's what I do with my pair back home and it never fails to get results."

Khartoum passed without incident, then later the same day we arrived at Entebbe. Following lunch we boarded the aircraft. The same two passengers were missing! They came aboard some five minutes later, again with a very red-faced, apologetic mother. We later heard that the toilet door lock in the 'ladies' room' had failed. I wondered if, when we arrived at Nairobi, the poor woman would flee the aircraft!

On arrival at Nairobi, and having cleared Customs (this time without a parcel of scanty underwear!), I took a taxi and booked into the New Stanley Hotel. It had been the usual 28-hour marathon flight and I was grateful to flop onto the bed and close my eyes.

When I awoke it was dark outside. I looked at my watch, it was nearly 7.45pm. Until I reported to Kenya Police Headquarters in the morning I was still on leave, so having showered and changed, I made my way to the dining room for a leisurely dinner.

Having been in England for nearly six months I had become accustomed to English hotel menus. Here in the 'New Stanley' I was offered an enormous number of choices, plus the usual number of courses. I was still feeling the effects from the long flight so, following dinner, I went to reception to book an early morning call. Just before arriving at the desk a very agitated woman approached me and asked in rapid French where the toilets were? I was somewhat taken aback, as only about a week before I had been staying in Paris. Perhaps the Yorkshireman had been correct, I did look French! The best I could manage was "*Je ne sais pas.*"

I went to my room and reminded myself as I climbed the stairs, to ensure that the mosquito net in my room was securely in place and to take my 'Paludrine' tablet. I need not have bothered, the bed was turned down, my pyjamas set out on the bed, the mosquito net correctly positioned. I was back to Kenyan standards of service.

I slept 'like a log' and was awoken by a gentle knock on my door.

"Jambo Effendi. Chai." (Hello Sir. Tea.)

The waiter placed the tea beside my bed and pulled back the curtains. I looked at my watch, 7.00am 'spot on' time. It was the usual brilliant Kenyan morning. Having breathed in the aroma from the hot tea and consumed two whole cups I went to the window. At this early hour there was little traffic about and the air smelt fresh and cool. I was back 'home'! It is strange how the human brain functions. Standing looking out at the early morning scene with the occasional vehicle negotiating the roundabout that housed Lord Delemere's statue, suddenly I remembered that I must put some suntan cream on my face and particularly my nose. Having been away for six months my tan had disappeared and I was well aware that the nose is the first to suffer from sunburn. Nairobi is six thousand feet above sea level, in clean air and at this altitude it does not take very long for the strong ultra-violet light to burn unprotected skin.

At this early hour the dining room was almost empty and I was looking forward to a large slice of paw-paw with lime juice, to be followed by the usual plethora of choices. I ate a hearty breakfast. Having packed my bags I deposited them with the Hall Porter, then took a taxi from outside the hotel to Police Headquarters.

The Kenya Police Headquarters building was very imposing – it was white and large, with several radio masts protruding from the flat roof. As I suspected, I was not going back to the Kedong but to a large township to be employed on normal police duties. My next port of call was to Barclays Bank to organise some funds, then on to the hotel for my bags and finally to the railway station to catch a train for the final leg of my journey.

The road from Nairobi railway station is only a short run from the city centre and during its brief history both had seen many changes from when they were first constructed. Having obtained my ticket, standing by the entrance to my carriage I met the Sikh Conductor, resplendent with his turban and uniform. He checked my ticket and I was directed to my compartment. I sat down by the window and watched the multi-coloured throng outside. As at any main railway station, everyone appeared to be in a hurry. Sitting there I recalled the display by the East African Railways & Harbours Board at the Kenya Royal Show. The centrepiece was a brand-new design for a first-class railway carriage with inter-connecting doors between compartments. The display stand was under the control of a Sikh Railway Conductor, who would explain to the visitors in great detail about the new railway carriage and its inter-connecting doors, finishing his 'lecture' with the words, "...and remember, this door can only be opened by *mutual* co-operation" – with great stress on the word 'mutual'.

I always enjoyed rail travel in Kenya. The compartments were comfortable and the food in the dining car, although limited by hotel standards, was well prepared and well presented. I sat by the window listening to the familiar 'clickety-clack' as the wheels passed over the joins in the rails and watched as a kaleidoscope of Kenya passed by the window, sometimes partly obscured by smoke from the engine. From time to time my eyes were not seeing as I was 'lost' deep in thought about what my future might hold at this new posting. Would it be possible to have Tumbo with me?

A few hours after lunch the train pulled into my destination.

Africa hadn't changed. There were the usual frenetic scenes. People hawking various foodstuffs to the indigenous passengers who, with much shouting and gesticulating, tried to attract the hawkers' attention. There were African men pushing bicycles, African women with large bundles on their heads or small *totos* (children) strapped to their backs, Indian women with brightly coloured saris, people leaving the train, people trying to push their way past those disembarking in order to board the train. There was a feeling of boundless human energy, and blanketing all of this, the noise of escaping steam from the engine plus the smell of heat and smoke that all steam trains emit.

I telephoned the Police Station and spoke to the Duty Officer. He said he would send a vehicle to pick me up and take me to the Mess. The driver arrived, with a salute and a "Jambo Effendi."

I was on my way to a totally new experience.

The Mess was on the edge of the town and about a mile from the Police Station and Divisional and Provincial Headquarters. It was large, housing the Inspectorate employed at the Police Station and both Headquarters. I was allocated my quarters and, having unpacked, went to the bar to have a pre-dinner drink and to meet some of my new colleagues. It proved to be an enjoyable environment in which I would make many new friends.

That evening after dinner I telephoned the farm in the Kedong to say that I was back and to ask how Tumbo was.

"I'm sorry to have to tell you this…" There was a pause. "He developed very bad tick fever and had to be shot."

I was stunned. It was almost like being told that a close relative had suddenly died. Somehow, Tumbo was all I had here. We had been together since he was a tiny pup. He had guarded me, been on some patrols with me and given me unstinting companionship. During my leave I had thought constantly about him and how he would be so excited to see me again. I found it very difficult to continue speaking. I simply said "Thank you for letting me know." and put the 'phone down.

Choking back the tears, I went to my room and silently wept. My reaction surprised me, but it was like losing a very close friend. Suddenly all the joy and excitement of my return had gone.

The next day, in uniform, I presented myself at Divisional Headquarters and for the first time in my life I was to meet the Senior Superintendent in charge, 'Mac'.

I entered his office and saluted. Sitting at the desk was a broad shouldered man of medium height, with thinning auburn hair and a large RAF-type moustache of the same colour. He had a ruddy complexion and my immediate impression was (to use American parlance) that here was a no-nonsense 'tough cookie'. He looked at me for some moments as if trying to sum me up, and I noticed that one of his eyes was very marginally closed, which added to his quizzical gaze. There were no pleasantries about whether I had enjoyed my leave; his words were without frills and to the point.

"Crime Branch needs some extra help, so go and report there. You can wear civilian clothes, but every Friday, you, like everyone else, will appear on parade in uniform."

"Sir!"

"One final thing... I will not tolerate slackness of any kind. Is that understood?"

"Sir!"

I saluted and left the office. I was soon to discover that Mac 'on the warpath' was a sight to behold and could 'put the fear of God' into any man.

With my arrival Crime Branch consisted of three Europeans and several African staff. Our job was to deal in the main with petty crime, such as bicycle thefts, plus anything that CID and Special Branch considered to be below their dignity. This whole field was new to me and was far removed from the Aberdares, Mau-Mau and Masai cattle thieves. We could be called at any time of the day and night, and often were. We investigated thefts, muggings, assaults, burglary and even carried out raids on illegal gambling. It was all part of my 'learning curve' which would prove to be useful in the future.

On the first raid I attended I had the backing of four of our African staff. The driver was built like an ox. He was about five feet eight inches tall, twice as broad shouldered as the average man and it was rumoured he could lift the front of a Land Rover. I didn't doubt it.

It was around 3.00pm and we had arrived unseen outside an illegal gambling den which, from information received, was being run by some African 'con' men backed by some 'heavies' to deal with any complaints. I signalled ready, steady, go and kicked the door open. The place was packed and there was pandemonium as they all made a rush for the door! The driver pushed me to one side and stood there in the doorway with arms flailing as the 'bodies' piled up before him. The final few fell on their knees pleading for mercy. He hit one on the back with the flat of his hand. The man spat out a mouthful of small white sea shells which, I was to discover, were used for gambling. This was part of the evidence we needed to secure a conviction.

"Sorry Effendi for pushing you away from the door, but I didn't want you to get hurt and I'm used to dealing with gamblers."

Apart from kicking open the door, my sole contribution to the raid, I had stood there watching in amazement as this very powerful man blocked the doorway and prevented any escapes.

My new team, after sorting out the 'fleeced' from the 'fleecers', handcuffed the latter and we returned to the Police Station and booked our prisoners into cells.

This was very quickly proving to be a whole new way of life!

I was soon to discover that it was very important to have read the Police Station 'O.B.' (desk dairy) into which everything is recorded, plus the date, with the actual time of the report noted, before 'Mac' had perused it and made notations in the remarks column. He 'kept his finger on the pulse', nothing escaped his attention and woe betide anyone who, when questioned, did not know about an entry into the 'O.B.'. The next step was later that morning to re-read the 'O.B' to see if 'Mac' had made any entries that required immediate action. A common one was "What action here? See me."

One morning a European lady telephoned to report that her parrot had escaped. Mac made his usual notation "What action here?"

The Duty Officer, in a flippant mood, recorded beside Mac's entry "Police Airwing Informed."

Mac went berserk!

My first Friday morning arrived and there was an early mass exodus from the Mess heading for the parade ground, all wearing khaki shorts and a short-sleeved tunic top which had an open neck; not the ideal thing at this early hour, it was 'freezing'! I had been warned that if I chose to wear a vest underneath my tunic for a modicum of warmth, I must ensure that 'Mac' would not see it during his inspection, as a vest on these crisp, clear mornings, according to him, was only worn by 'poofs' and 'nancy boys'. I ensured that mine was well hidden.

We stood there at ease, all ranks waiting for 'Mac's arrival. I looked down at my shoes. My 'boy' had done a wonderful job, the toecaps were like black glass. My 'Sam Browne' belt was not quite in the same class but I hoped that it would pass inspection.

I could see 'Mac's' car arriving. Here we go... this was my first parade since leaving the Police School at Gilgil. The parade commander did a very smart 'about turn' and faced us.

"Parade, atten... shun!" We all came smartly to attention, not quite together and I was sure 'Mac' would not be pleased. The parade commander did another smart about turn and saluted, with 'Mac' returning the salute.

"Parade ready for inspection, Sir!"

Standing to attention it certainly was chilly, and I was more than glad that I had donned my 'nancy boy' vest, as I was very close to shivering.

It was a large parade, as all ranks from Constables upwards of Provincial, Divisional and Police Station staff were here. Due to the numbers and make up of the parade the sections not facing immediate inspection were ordered to "Stand at, ease!"

In this position, with my arms behind my back, I could at least press my bare forearms up against the rear of my tunic. Now it was our turn.

"Atten... shun!" Out of the corner of my eye I could see 'Mac' getting closer and closer. It was going to be a slow business. He stopped before one of my new colleagues.

"What is that underneath your tunic?"

"As it's so cold Sir, I put on a vest."

"I didn't ask for a weather report, I asked what is underneath your tunic!"

"Sir!"

"Typical 'Pioneer Corps!"

With these words he proceeded to tug at the vest top showing in the tunic's open neck and the end result looked like a rather tasteful ruff. Now it was my turn. I stared straight ahead and I hoped that my vest wasn't showing. He paused for several moments, his eyes scanning me from top to toe, grunted, then moved on. He hadn't seen it!

With the inspection completed, and with the early morning sun now providing some warmth, we turned into column of route and set off marching around the parade ground. It was good to be on the move and, strangely enough, to be marching like this was almost enjoyable and reminded me again of our Gilgil mornings some three years previously. Following the final "Parade, dis-miss!" we made our way back to the Mess for a very welcome breakfast.

I was soon to learn that every Friday morning was the day when 'Crime Branch' received back their pending case files from, you've guessed it, Mac. The procedure rarely altered, in either the method of delivery to our office, or, as I was quickly to discover, the written comments in red ink.

It was my first Friday morning in the Crime Branch office and I noted that everyone had the 'hunted look'. It was about 10.00am. Suddenly the door crashed open! There was Mac, his ginger moustache bristling and looking very red in the face!

"I have never read so much bullshit in all my life!"

With these words our pile of pending and unsolved case files was heaved into the air landing with a thud on the office floor, now followed by loose pieces of paper fluttering to the ground like a ticker tape welcome in New York. Everyone knelt on the floor searching for their files and trying to marry up the many pieces of loose paper. I picked up my first file. Scrawled across the cover in red ink was the word 'RUBBISH!' followed by, 'See Inside!' Inside were more caustic comments e.g. 'Investigate!' Another of my files had received similar treatment. This time the comment was "I DON'T BELIEVE IT!" I quickly learned to affix all papers into their respective files and that it was imperative to 'cross reference' every document.

During the following weeks Mac's comments on my files became more subdued in tone, but the method of delivery to our office hardly ever changed. His method of the Thursday evening scrutiny of our case files kept Mac au fait with local crime, plus our abilities, and without any doubt, it kept us 'on our toes'.

Working in a Crime Branch Section within this large and developing township, was, to me, an entirely new field of police work. I well remember my first ever case. It was a theft of a bicycle. (We all have to start somewhere.) I visited the scene, recorded statements, circulated the type of bicycle, the serial number of the bicycle, checked the records for known bicycle thieves and after two weeks was no further forward.

In the CID Section was a Chief Inspector, Giddy Singh.

"How is your first case coming along Mr Tompkins ?"

"Giddy, I've tried everything and drawn a blank."

"Then we'll solve it together tonight. I'll pick you up from the Mess at 8.00pm."

Our first 'port of call' was the local cinema bar. Giddy slapped some money on the bar counter.

"Two whiskies!" Giddy tasted his drink, 'pulled a face' and said, "Filth!" He leaned over the bar, then poured his whisky down the sink, quickly followed by mine.

"You scoundrel, you've been watering down the whisky!"

The Asian bartender turned white.

"Hand me that new bottle of 'Johnny Walker', yes that one."

Giddy studied the seal very carefully then handed back the bottle.

"Right, pour two whiskies for me and my friend Mr Tompkins."

We sat down and sipped our drinks. Giddy had his neat, mine was 'to the top' with soda water. We left the bar.

"What about the bicycle theft Giddy?"

"All in good time Mr Tompkins."

We visited several more bars. Some served 'good whisky', but those that didn't received 'the treatment'. As someone who doesn't drink very much I was finding the pace hard going, not to mention the seeing! I was glad I wasn't driving! All my semi-slurred requests regarding the bicycle met with the same reply.

"All in good time Mr Tompkins."

At about 11.00pm we again entered the cinema bar. Without being asked, the Asian barman removed a new bottle of 'Johnny Walker' from the shelf then showed the seal to Giddy. Giddy grunted his approval and the barman poured Giddy's drink. I put up my hand; I had had more than enough.

"Giddy, what about the bicycle?"

"Ah, the bicycle. Go outside. To the right of the door you will see a man. Tell him I sent you."

Just as Giddy had stated there was the man.

"Yes," he said he knew about the bicycle and gave me a name and address. Early next morning (with a 'thick head') I led the raid on the address given by the informer, recovering not just one bicycle but two!

The man subsequently pleaded guilty. So this was how detectives solved cases! Later I gave Giddy a bottle of 'Johnny Walker' with an intact seal.

Some weeks later Giddy asked me to assist him with applying a search warrant. The case involved theft of Government cement and Giddy had received information that a certain Asian's house contained incriminating evidence.

We arrived at the house and Giddy knocked on the door. It was opened by a smartly dressed Asian who looked shocked when he saw Giddy. Giddy explained our mission then produced the warrant. He told the man to sit in a chair and not to move.

"Right Mr Tompkins, you know what we are looking for. This man is hiding vital evidence and we will search this whole house, room by room, until we find it."

Giddy commenced to rake through drawers, emptying their contents onto the floor! He checked wardrobes, pockets of clothing, then throwing the garments onto the beds, searching on top of wardrobes, cupboards, under bedding, mattresses, the kitchen. Being new at house searches I was trying to be tidy... The place was starting to look as if it had been hit by a cyclone.

Suddenly Giddy shouted out "Got it!"

The man turned even paler and looked 'as sick as a parrot'. Giddy showed me some bank statements, plus numerous other papers.

"It's all here. Look at these payments, all gained from theft!" He turned to the Asian. "You are under arrest for conspiracy involved with the theft of Government cement. I must warn you that anything you do say will be taken down in writing and may be used in evidence. Do you wish to say anything?"

The Asian shook his head.

As we were leaving I said "Giddy, what about the mess?"

"Leave it. Let's go and place this man into custody."

Some weeks later our prisoner, together with three others, appeared in Court. The case lasted almost a week, and during one lunch-hour, the exhibits of Government cement – which had yet to be produced before the Court, had the Government seals removed by a person, or persons unknown. (Cement sacks are made from four to five layers of strong brown paper and only the top layer had been removed, most likely with a razor blade). The culprits had hoped that without the seals the prosecution could not prove that it was Government property, therefore, as a result there would be 'no case to answer'. What they had not realised was, that in order to maintain a 'chain of evidence', not only does the Police Officer make an entry into his notebook, but also initials and dates the exhibit. This act did not help their defence one iota. They all received the maximum sentence possible.

At night there had been a series of muggings of African drunks in the African area of town and we had not achieved any arrests, so I decided that I would act as a decoy and hoped that we could 'nab' the pair of villains responsible. I washed in plain hot water to eradicate any smell of soap or after-shave, blacked up my face, neck and the backs of my hands, and put on a scruffy, borrowed raincoat with a hat that could be pulled well down over my eyes. Up the left sleeve of the raincoat I slid an eighteen inch 'night stick' (truncheon) and had the raincoat splashed with some beer to give off the correct type of smell.

At the Police Station I met up with my Crime Branch team. There was much amusement at my appearance, and in particular my black face. They kept looking at it and turning away laughing.

Now for the serious part.

"Do we have nightsticks and handcuffs?"

"Ndiyo Effendi."

It was now just after 10.30pm, almost time to go.

"You two will tail me on the opposite side of the road, keeping back about fifty to sixty yards. You two will be on my side of the road and about a hundred yards behind me. I will act as if I'm drunk but, in order to avoid being spotted as a European, I will not talk to anyone. If they attempt to 'mug' me... come running!"

We were dropped near the road where most of the muggings had taken place and made our way to the area, splitting up as planned. It was Friday night and the road where we were heading had some street lights. I 'staggered' ahead with my head down in order to hide my face and soon I was passing several Africans. Some ignored me, but one playfully shoved me and told me to go home to my bed. I just grunted in reply. It was a very odd feeling to be in this situation. I continued down the road 'in my drunken state'. I passed another pair, could this be it? No, they just commented to themselves about how drunk I was. We stayed in the area until well after closing time. Our pair of villains failed to show. I was very disappointed; I was just dying to give them the shock of their lives!

Following our 'night out' the muggings ceased. We heard some weeks later that one of the African servants at the Mess had seen me disguised and that this had reached the ears of our two villains. I somehow doubt it, but whatever happened, they left the district.

An investigating officer dealing with an unexplained death has to attend the post-mortem to identify the body to the Government Pathologist and thus maintain a 'chain of evidence' should the investigation proceed to someone's trial. A post-mortem room is not the best place to spend the day; there is a strange smell in the air and on various slabs are bodies covered in white sheets. For anyone new to this experience it was not unknown for an attempt to be made to make the attending officer faint.

In this instance an African had died in suspicious circumstances and as one of the investigating officers I had to attend. I was invited to stand close in order to see and understand the procedure. The body was initially carefully examined all over, and notes were taken. Next an incision was made in the chest and a surgical instrument used to chomp through the sternum (breast bone), causing the rib cage to open. Soon various organs were being removed and examined. The Government Pathologist looked up from his examination of one of the organs.

"Come and take a close look at this liver, you might find it interesting." The liver was on a wooden tablet which was on a side table close to the dissecting slab. As I was standing there it was dissected. Luckily I was not squeamish and didn't faint. As this ploy had failed, I was asked to simply stand and observe if I wanted to. The examination of each organ continued, including the stomach and its contents. These two items were set aside for a more detailed analysis. I remained until the P.M. was completed. The sight didn't bother me, but the pervading smell remained with me for days.

Being a Police Officer means that at some stage in your career it will be your task to remove a dead body in order for a post-mortem to be conducted. Fresh bodies are easily handled, but bodies that have been exposed to the African sun for days on end are something else! We were called to a European farm to investigate a missing person report. One of the African staff had been missing for days and there was no apparent reason for his departure. He was married and his wife informed us that he was very fond of drink but, apart from arriving late at night the 'worse for wear', until now he had never failed to come home. Our team began their routine questions.

"Did he have any enemies?"

"No, he was well liked but was known to be a lazy worker."

"Did he owe anyone any money?"

"No."

Every routine question drew a blank.

"Where did he normally go to drink, and did he walk, or ride his bike?"

"He normally walked." His wife pointed out his usual route.

We decided to check this out.

About a mile or so from the farm in the corner of a field we came across the body of a male African. Two things drew our attention to it; the flies and the smell. The body was on its back and, due to decomposition, the stomach was very distended and the skin had turned a greeny black colour. Maggots were crawling from the nostrils, mouth and eye sockets. It was a disgusting sight. Two of our African staff turned away retching. Before even attempting to move the body it was important to make a detailed search in the immediate vicinity. The grass surrounding the body was reasonably long but there were no signs of a struggle and no signs of any possible weapon, e.g a small branch from a nearby tree. Looking more closely at the body there were no obvious signs of violence. His pockets contained money, so theft was ruled out. Having made a sketch of the area and recorded some notes, it was time to move the rotting corpse.

Having obtained a roughly constructed stretcher and some sacks our gruesome task commenced. The smell was horrendous and as soon as we attempted to move the corpse the scalp started to slough off the skull. Another of our African staff turned away, retching loudly as he did so. By now our open-backed vehicle had arrived and I sent the driver back to the farm for shovels. In its current state I had every reason to believe that the body would break up unless it was fully supported during the lift. With the shovels in position we managed to place the corpse on the 'stretcher' and place it into the rear of the vehicle. I pitied the Government Doctor having to carry out the Post Mortem.

It transpired that there were no signs of violence to the body but it did have an excessive measure of native alcohol in the stomach. There were no traces of poison. Further investigations failed to uncover any person, or persons, who had cause to kill the deceased so the case was closed as "Death due to exposure brought about by an excessive consumption of alcohol."

My list of new experiences was about to be increased. Early one afternoon an old European man was mugged. He told us that two African males had stolen his watch, a small amount of money and a cheque book. The attack had taken place on the edge of town and the complainant took us to where he was attacked. Here my Masai experience proved useful. I could detect scuff marks on the earth surface, which on closer examination revealed footprints and a distinct trail leading in the opposite direction from the town. I believed these to belong to the 'muggers'. We radioed in for a tracking dog.

I was surprised at the speed of the response as the dog arrived with its handler within ten minutes. It was a Doberman Pincer. I had never worked with police dogs before and I was to learn there were two types used by the Kenya Police; Dobermans for tracking and Alsatians for patrol work. Dobermans always appeared to me to be very ungainly as, when they are tracking, their rear legs appear to be out of proportion to their body.

The dog was on a thin rope about fifty feet long. The handler examined the scuff marks on the earth road, then pointed to one, and said to the dog "*Suk, suk.*" The dog sniffed it and we were off!

With the dog, nose constantly close to the ground, walking some thirty feet ahead of the handler and ourselves, twenty minutes later it stopped outside a hut door and barked. Inside were two men. The handler told them to come outside and sit on the ground. He then said to the dog "*Suk.*"

It sniffed both men, then went behind one of them, placed its forepaws on the man's shoulders and barked. This was one of the muggers!

Despite numerous tests conducted over many years the law still does not recognise the evidence given by a dog handler, therefore, if an arrest is made by this method, it must always be supported by additional 'hard evidence' when the case is presented before the Court.

I have little doubt that across the years many villains, having been traced by a police dog, have 'wriggled off the hook' when supporting evidence has not been forthcoming.

On another occasion we called for a tracking dog. It was at night and the dog soon picked up the scent and off we went. Soon we came near a petrol station. The dog stopped and sat down. The handler turned to us.

"The smell of petrol has destroyed his sense of smell. It's a pretty good bet that this person whom we are following is a real villain who knows how to get away from a tracking dog. I'll take him down the road for about a seventy yards or so, then perhaps he can pick up the scent again."

We followed at a distance. The dog handler stopped, lengthened the dog's rope and now said the now familiar words "*Suk-suk.*" The dog commenced to walk in a circle, then having completed it, sat down, shook its head and barked twice! It was almost as if it was saying, "Look, I've tried, but I can't find anything."

Thinking back over my initiation into Crime Branch, certain cases tend to stick in the mind, not always due to their complexity, but often due to the sheer satisfaction of solving them and arriving at a conclusion. One such case was the theft of an expensive Hasselblad camera from a photographic studio. The theft had occurred during the lunch break. There were no signs of a break-in so, taking the basic approach 'always start at base one', the question had to be asked and checked.

"Was it a 'put up job' to claim insurance?"

Whilst this was going on we checked their register of people who had attended the studio for portrait photography that morning. There was quite a cross section. The final two that morning were a European woman and a young male Sikh. The owner was adamant that only the missing camera had been used for all the photographs taken that morning. We carefully examined the studio. It was about fifteen feet by twelve. It had only one door with one window, the latter being 'blacked out'. There were no signs of a forced entry. Inside the studio were various reflector screens, high powered lamps, and in one corner a small curtained off area with a mirror that could be used if any 'sitter' wished to change into, for example, national dress, or adjust their hat etc. The ceiling was intact.

We now had three lines of enquiry: one, the insurance angle; two, someone had obtained a duplicate key; three, someone could have concealed themselves behind the curtain then left with the camera when the studio was closed during the lunch hour.

We questioned the owner very closely. Had he seen everyone leave the premises? Was it possible that someone could have obtained a duplicate key? The second question drew a blank; he always carried the keys with him on a special belt clip and never left them around the shop or the studio complex. As regards the first part of the question he had escorted the European lady to the front of the shop and had seen her leave. And the young Sikh? Yes, he was sure he had left. They had exited the studio together via the alley, he had entered the shop, realised he hadn't locked the studio, then returned, pulled the self-locking door to and heard the lock engage.

The insurance angle came to nought, as a search warrant revealed that the owner's bank account was in first class order. A check on the European woman revealed she was 'very well heeled', plus the fact she was not the last person to be photographed, so she could be ruled out. The young Sikh was employed as a junior clerk with one of the town's banks. We decided to 'check him out'.

We saw the bank manager in private. We asked him what comments if any would he make about our possible suspect.

"First class, diligent, very likeable and he's seldom off sick." Had any of the staff lost any personal items recently?

"It's funny you should ask that question. Within the building, one of the girls lost her purse containing about four hundred shillings (£20) in cash. Someone else discovered his 'Parker 51' fountain pen was missing. Also another member of staff found that his wallet had disappeared. It contained about the same sum of money as the girl's."

Had the bank manager reported these thefts?

"No, it's an internal matter and we do not like to get the police involved, it could give the bank a bad name."

Could we interview the three members of staff?

Their responses to our probing questions heightened our suspicions and we decided that we needed to check the house where the young Sikh lived. Having obtained his address we left and opted to intercept him just as he was about to enter his front door.

As it was late afternoon there wasn't time to obtain a search warrant, therefore, if we were of the opinion that the delay could result in a criminal act going undetected, we had to record the details and reason in our official police notebooks, date and time the entry and sign it. This gave us the legal right of entry which could, if need be, be challenged by a defending Counsel in court.

The young Sikh had not spotted us and we tailed him from work to his door. Just as he was about to open it, I tapped him on the shoulder. He quickly turned around and upon seeing us, turned several shades paler. I produced my police warrant card.

"We are investigating the theft of a Hasselblad camera from (shop's name). We have reason to believe that you have knowledge of this theft and the stolen camera may be concealed within your rooms, which we intend to search. I must warn you that anything you do say will be taken down in writing and may be used in evidence. Do you have anything to say?"

He just shook his head and was looking 'as sick as a parrot'.

"In your presence we are now going to search your rooms. Do you have any objection to this?"

He shook his head again. We didn't have to search, it was all on view. What did we find? The camera, a 'Parker 51' pen, a gold plated cigarette lighter plus an empty purse and wallet. He was cautioned and pleaded guilty 'on the spot'. We now commenced a thorough search, but nothing further was found. We took him to the Police Station, booked him in then had him placed into cells. He appeared in Court next morning and was remanded, at our request, pending further investigations, but nothing else was uncovered.

Later that week he pleaded guilty in Court and was placed on probation for two years. How did he steal the camera? When he left the studio with the owner and they entered the alley, he realised that the studio was not locked. As soon as the owner entered the shop part of the complex, he hurriedly turned around, entered the studio and hid behind the small curtained-off changing area. He heard the studio door lock engage, waited about fifteen minutes, removed the camera from its tripod, and then, having wiped every possible area clean of his fingerprints, exited with the camera concealed under his jacket, which he carried over his arm. And the other items? At the bank his clerical position allowed him free access to most of the work areas. As he walked around delivering files, it was not difficult when members of staff were deeply engrossed in their work to steal from desk tops, handbags and the inside pockets of men's jackets. He was obviously a very devious young man who had spent some time planning the theft of the camera. Add to this the thefts from his colleagues at the bank. In my opinion he should have 'gone over the wall'.

The next memorable case was the theft of two gold wristwatches; one a 'Rolex', the other an 'Omega'. It was a Saturday lunchtime. An Asian jeweller telephoned saying that he was holding five people in his shop and refusing to let them leave, as one of them was a thief.

We arrived to find two Asians, plus three Europeans, all very irate at being detained. The jeweller pointed out the glass showcase where the watches had been on display. He was adamant that the watches had been there in the show case when these five people entered the shop, as they had arrived within minutes of each other. Everyone gave a good reason to be in the shop, but there was a sixth person. As it was almost closing time an African cleaner was washing the floor, and behind the show case the floor was still semi-wet. My colleague emptied the bucket of dirty water. There, in the base of the bucket, were two gold wristwatches! We left with the thief, leaving the Asian jeweller apologising most profusely to his now somewhat placated customers.

I was not involved in the following case, but it highlights how observation can lead to uncovering other things. Two of my colleagues were entertaining their girlfriends to dinner in the local hotel. It had been an enjoyable evening and they called the waiter over and asked for the bill. This was in the days before credit cards had even been thought of, therefore payment would be in cash. The waiter presented the bill, then having checked it, they handed it back with a covering sum of money, plus a tip. The waiter was using a normal duplicate receipt pad with the top copy (which was handed to them) and the hotel's copy, separated by a sheet of carbon paper. One of my colleagues noticed that the carbon paper had some holes cut in it. Why was this? Then the 'the penny dropped'! It was a 'fiddle'! What the waiter was doing was simplicity itself. The carbon paper was correctly positioned within the receipt book, with the first hole positioned where the number of 'covers' had to be recorded. The second hole was positioned where the total cost was recorded. The diners received the top copy which contained the correct information. However, the hotel's copy at this stage was blank where both these pieces of information should have been transferred by the carbon paper. With the diners departed, all the waiter had to do was to slide the carbon paper to cover the 'covers' and cost information sections, then write onto the carbon paper lower figures. In this instance two covers instead of four, and only half of the actual sum of money received. He was arrested. Later the head waiter and chef were also implicated and charged.

Soon after becoming involved in normal police work I was in uniform on 999 duty. The vehicles were Peugeot station wagons, which looked very smart with their painted dark blue bodies, white roofs and Kenya Police crests on the two front doors, plus, as you would expect, blue flashing lights and VHF radio transmitters.

One evening whilst cruising around, we received an urgent call. There had been an attempted murder of a European woman at one of the local hotels. I was on call and sped to the scene in a 999 police vehicle with its blue light flashing. We were met at the entrance by an excited Assistant Manager.

"Thank God you're here! A man has tried to kill his wife with a cut-throat razor!"

"Is he still here?"

"Yes, that's him on the veranda."

A European male was sitting on the veranda rail, puffing furiously at a cigarette and looking down at the ground. The Assistant Manager was following close behind me, together with two African Constables. As I stopped the man looked up.

"You are under arrest," I said. "I have reason to believe that you have been involved in an attempted murder. I must warn you that anything you do say will be taken down in writing and may be used in evidence. Do you have anything to say?"

He scowled, said "F*** off!" and continued puffing on his cigarette.

As this type of response had not been covered at Police Training School I said, "Constable, this man is under arrest, keep him here." I then asked the Assistant Manager "Where is the woman who was involved?"

He led me to one of the bedrooms, the door was partly open and I could hear a woman sobbing inside. I knocked and entered. There sitting on the bed, holding her head in her hands and with hardly a stitch of clothing on, was a very attractive woman.

"I understand that someone attacked you. Is this correct?"

She nodded and continued to sob.

"Can you tell me anything about this and who it was?"

Between sobs she said, "It was my husband."

After a while she calmed down and covered herself with some bedding.

The story was this. They had been dressing for dinner and her husband had noticed some small bruises on her bottom. He had demanded to know how she had acquired them and then had accused her of having an affair. She denied this but he grabbed her by the throat, forced her onto the floor and reached for his cutthroat razor. Her screams had alerted the hotel staff and when they had opened the door with a pass key, he had the razor held close to her throat and was shouting "I'll kill you, you bitch!"

The staff had dragged him off and then called the police station. I examined her throat, there were no cut marks, only red marks where he must have pressed with his fingers. I arranged for her to be examined by the Government Doctor on call, recorded the names of witnesses and said I would return next day to take their statements. I took possession of the razor and booked my prisoner into cells.

I arrived at the hotel next morning to record witnesses statements and commenced with the complainant. She had partly regained her composure.

"I do not wish to press charges against my husband and I want him released."

I was dumbfounded!

"But he tried to kill you!"

"I suppose it was my fault. It was just a silly row that got out of hand. I don't wish to have him charged."

"But from what you told me last night he had the razor in his hand. You had marks on your throat. It was more than a 'silly row'."

"I've made up my mind, I do not want him charged, so will you please drop this case and release him."

I recorded her statement to this effect, had her sign it and he was released.

A few months later he assaulted her again, smashed some of her personal effects and slashed her clothing. Again the police were called and he was arrested, and again she refused to prefer charges. Her behaviour, to my mind, defied all logic.

One member of the Mess was a practical joker whose usual response when answering the mess telephone was "Headquarters, Bow Street Runners!" However, when attending a judicial function he 'overstepped the mark'. Mac was not amused and to our astonishment he dismissed the culprit from the Force under Section 13b 'Unlikely to become efficient'. Within less than twenty-four hours he was on his way back to England. Mac's action confirmed my first impressions – here was a 'no-nonsense tough cookie'.

On Saturday nights, as in most places, more alcohol was consumed than any other night of the week. To ensure the local licensing laws were obeyed Mac would prowl the town's more upmarket establishments in uniform, accompanied by two tall Inspectors. His favourite habit was to enter a bar dead on 11.00pm, whack his black and silver police cane onto a table and shout "Last drinks! This bar closes in fifteen minutes!" This rapid and unexpected arrival, accompanied by the crack of the cane onto a table, caused more than one client to spill their drink down his or her front. As this was a weekly sortie, it must have provided the local dry cleaners with a constant source of business. I cannot recall any establishment ever being charged with breaking the licensing laws, which is hardly surprising.

Within weeks of arriving at this new posting it was Christmas, then New Year. The local Country Club advertised the New Year's Eve Fancy Dress Ball. Five of my new colleagues would be off duty, so the six of us decided to go. We purchased tickets and were then faced with what to wear. After much discussion, which centred on our scant wardrobes, we opted to go as six Arabs. Our attire consisted of pyjama trousers with elastic bands around the ankles to give an authentic Arabian look, pyjama tops with the top two buttons undone, and dressing gowns, with gold painted daggers made from cardboard thrust behind each dressing gown's cord. We had white towels around our heads (worn Arab fashion) and for the final touch, a black police No.1 dress tie around each headpiece. Then, in order to add more authenticity, black shoe polish was used to simulate neat beards and moustaches. We looked a raffish bunch... Well we thought so!

Now, with many years of hindsight, I realise we must have looked like a scruffy bunch of refugees that even 'Oxfam' wouldn't deal with. However, we were full of the festive spirit, which, within reason, we had every intention of adding to.

We arrived at the Club brimming with enthusiasm, only to discover that nearly everyone else was resplendent in evening dress! A comment from one elegantly-attired male, looking like an 'Austin Reed' model as he passed us in reception was, "Good grief!"

The looks on the faces of the other guests carried the same message; we were *persona non grata*. I have to admit that standing at the bar ordering drinks dressed in pyjamas and dressing gown and looking an absolute 'wally' did feel rather strange.

Worse was to come. There were only ten other couples in fancy dress and it was very obvious that they had been to Nairobi to hire their attire. It was now time to judge the twenty-six of us. Beside this beautifully dressed opposition we looked even more ridiculous. As the band played we paraded around the floor looking for a crack in the floorboards to jump into. The competition was won by a scantily dressed couple, 'Samson and Delilah'. We were fully convinced the judges were biased due to the following facts: one, all the judges were male; two, 'Delilah' wore a diaphanous skirt with a slit almost to her hip with little, if anything, underneath; three, she exposed her navel; four, her deep cleavage could easily have accommodated four ballpoint pens! With the judging completed we left hurriedly for the Mess, changed into dinner jackets and arrived back just in time to welcome in the New Year normally attired.

A few weeks later I purchased a car from one of my new colleagues. It was a blue, four-seater Morgan with a leather strap across the bonnet and leather hip straps for the driver and the front seat passenger, which were necessary because, due to the very hard suspension, hitting a bump in the road at speed lifted both driver and passenger off their seats! It was a real 'get up and go' machine, but utterly impractical off tarmac roads. Not only did the dust pour in, but due to its low clearance (only four inches at the sump), it constantly touched down.

I had one very lucky escape. One morning on the way to work I sped down the main road into town and had to slow down when entering the thirty miles per hour zone and then decelerate even more to stop at the traffic lights. When I was down to about five miles an hour, the nearside wheel's steering rod sheared. I came to a shuddering halt with the offending wheel pointing at a right angle towards the pavement. I dread to think what might have happened at seventy miles an hour. I later sold the car to a local garage. The new owner lost control when descending the escarpment along the Nairobi-Nakuru road at speed, killing himself and his passenger.

Another of my colleagues, Neil, owned a rather unusual car; a 1923 Rolls-Royce that had been built as a hunting car. It was devoid of a roof, had a leather bench seat in the front, a huge brass and rubber horn and a 'split' windscreen to admit a cooling blast of air. The rear section was boarded, with clips to hold the hunting rifles. It was totally open to the elements and painted 'battleship grey'. Despite its age it could still produce a good turn of speed and, unlike my Morgan, it could go anywhere. I wonder if it still exists?

By today's standards it was very antiquated. It had to be started by heaving on the large brass starting handle that dangled at the base of the radiator, with the driver working the 'advance' and 'retard' levers attached to the steering wheel. This sometimes caused a loud backfire and at night a long tongue of flame could be seen erupting from the exhaust pipe – similar to the flame-gun on James Bond's Aston Martin! Another oddity was the clutch. Evidently, it was made of leather and the leather had to be kept moist. This was achieved by every five hundred miles pouring a quarter pint of engine oil down a large hole situated between the driver and his front seat passenger.

It was important not to exceed the 'stated dose'. To do so caused the clutch to spin and the car to remain where it was, with the friction so created causing a cloud of blue smoke to emanate from underneath the vehicle, some of which seeped into the front compartment, causing the driver and his passenger to rapidly evacuate their comfortable leather bench seat.

At the local European Hospital resided a large number of nurses from England, South Africa and even New Zealand and due to its capacity Neil's 'Rolls' was the favoured means of transport when we invited any of these girls for a night out.

One morning I was called to Mac's office. I couldn't think of anything I had done that might have justified this summons, but as it was Mac, I was expecting trouble. I knocked and entered.

"Sir, you wish to see me."

"Hmm. I suppose you have heard that Princess Margaret is going to pay us a visit?"

"Yes Sir, but I am not aware of the details."

"Well, when she does arrive, you and Assistant Superintendent Wallace are to be her bodyguards from the moment she arrives here, until the moment she leaves. You'll receive full details later."

I was stunned. What an honour! Selected to be one of Princess Margaret's bodyguards! 'Mac' was not known for 'dishing out' plaudits, but there was always a first time.

"Sir, why have I been selected?" (Perhaps he would say, "Because I see from your file you're a damn good pistol shot.")

"I can't spare anyone else. Oh, and you'll need a suit."

I was dismissed.

"Thank you Sir."

"Don't thank me. You could be shot."

When I received the briefing I understood Mac's final comment. In the event of an attempted assassination we were to place ourselves between the attacker and the Princess. If we had to open fire we were to ensure that no member of the public was shot and finally, we were not to look at the Princess but to watch the crowd at all times. [4]

The day duly arrived.

Wearing my best suit with my Smith & Wesson .38 revolver in a shoulder holster, we met the diminutive figure of the Princess as she alighted from her car. Then, with us walking ahead, her entourage made its way to the dais where she would deliver her speech. Her private detective walked directly behind her and sat behind her with the local dignitaries. We stood in front of the dais on either side, as ordered, scanning the multi-racial crowd.

---

[4] Security ahead of any Royal visit has to be seen to be believed. Every inch of the route is inspected. Bridges are checked, culverts are checked, the microphones are checked, and ahead of the Royal personage someone is trying doors, beds, toilets, cupboards, everything that might be touched, used, or walked on. Then each area is sealed off.

The day passed without incident and Princess Margaret departed.

If we had been expecting a 'thank you' or even a congratulatory letter for being prepared to 'lay our lives on the line', we were to be disappointed. It was just considered 'part of the job'.

At the Mess, Sunday lunch was always an excellent curry. Anyone off duty would normally have a pre-lunch 'snifter' at the bar then, following lunch, about two hours of 'Egyptian PT' (asleep on the bed). On this particular Sunday after lunch I was challenged to a game of table tennis (I suspect the challenger knew he would win). Having just returned a serve, the swing doors crashed open! There stood Mac in uniform, hands on hips, red in the face, moustache bristling. He was not looking very pleased.

"Where's the Traffic Officer?"

"I have no idea Sir, but I'll try and find him."

I found the 'culprit' on his bed, fast asleep. I shook him violently.

"Quick! Mac's in the Mess breathing fire and brimstone. Get moving there's been an accident!"

Our Traffic Officer was fully dressed and very bleary eyed.

"I'm on call, but no one has told me about an accident."

"Have you had a drink at lunch-time?"

"Of course not. I'm on call."

"Well, you're on call now, get moving, Mac's waiting."

Grabbing his white covered cap our T.O., still half asleep, went outside and evidently sat in Mac's brand new Jaguar car.

"I've found the Traffic Officer Sir. He's waiting for you outside."

The sight of his T.O. having the effrontery to sit in his car without being asked raised Mac's already high blood pressure by at least ten points.

"What the hell are you doing in my car? Out! Out!"

"But I thought you wanted me, Sir."

In a voice brimming with menace Mac replied, "I do not want you now, but I will tomorrow morning! You are wanted at the scene of an accident!"

With this, Mac slammed the passenger door shut, slammed the car into reverse gear and hooked his rear bumper onto a large stone on the rockery! He now slammed it into first and revved the engine. The rear wheels spun and the car stayed where it was. He got out, kicked the wheel and shouted, "Don't just stand there … do something!"

Five of us heaved on the rear bumper as if our lives depended on it. With his 'Jag' released, Mac made off down the drive under full power, the rear end of the car snaking and raising a huge cloud of dust! In case he was heading for the Police Station, I decided I had better warn the Duty Officer that Mac was 'on the warpath'.

By this time Mac could not have been gone for more than five minutes. I picked up the Mess phone and asked switchboard to connect me to the Duty Officer.

I heard a 'click' as the phone connected.

"For God's sake ensure everything is OK. Mac's been here and he's breathing fire and brimstone!"

My one-way conversation was cut short by Mac's voice on the other end of the phone.

"Who is making this call to the Duty Officer?"

I very nearly dropped the phone! He'd been gone only minutes! I quickly put the phone down and spent the rest of Sunday wondering if he had recognised my voice.

I am not sure if the following Friday morning Mac's blood pressure was still high, but the way his car swept onto a corner of the parade ground and the way he slammed the driver's door did not augur well. Each section he inspected took longer than usual before, at long last, it was our turn. One of my colleagues had been nurturing his first attempt at a moustache for about two weeks, although compared to Mac's it was pathetic. Mac paused before this hirsute offering.

"What is that underneath your nose?"

"It's a moustache Sir."

Mac scowled.

"Either grow a moustache or shave it off!"

He took just two paces, turned around and said, "Shave it off!"

Worse was to come. Mac addressed the whole parade. Never in his whole career had he seen such a scruffy bunch. We lacked crispness, vitality, and our drill was dreadful. As a result we were going to march around the parade ground in 'double time'.

On the order we turned into column of route. Then, on the order "double quick... march!" we set off on a circuit of the parade ground.

We halted. Mac was not satisfied. We would now *run* around the parade ground! This we proceeded to do. One of my colleagues' hat fell off and was trampled into the dust by the following masses of hobnailed boots. Finally we were ordered to halt, then ordered to turn into line and, thankfully, dismissed. At the Mess there was a rush for the showers as everyone was covered in sweat and ochre red dust.

What a start to a Friday!

One afternoon Mac was conducting a group of Senior Army Officers on a tour of inspection. I had just arrived in the CID office with a case file. Their European secretary had just returned from lunch with a small-sized paper bag with the name of a local ladies' dress shop stamped on it. At the time of my arrival Bob with his colleagues were questioning her as to what was in the bag. She was blushing and said, "It's very personal and nothing to do with you men, so don't ask."

They continued to ask what it was.

"Damn you. This is all it is."

She held up a pair of pink ladies knickers.

At this very instant Mac was passing the window with his army guests, who must have seen the garment on display. Mac opened the office door and shouted "Put those back on at once!"

The poor girl went scarlet. It was the first time I realised he had a sense of humour.

The phone on my desk jangled. It was Mac's secretary.

"Are you free?"

"Yes, I'm just updating some case files."

"Excellent, you are wanted."

The 'phone 'clicked' and went dead. I hoped it was a similar summons to the Princess Margaret episode. I knocked on 'Mac's' door and entered.

"Sir, you wish to see me?"

Mac sat behind his desk with one eye partly closed, giving me his usual quizzical look.

"Hmm. Evidently they want to make you into a Police Officer."

"Sir?"

"You're off to the Police Training School at Kiganjo. You leave this weekend. My secretary will give you the details."

I was dismissed.

Back at the Mess I packed all my gear and was assured my room would be kept vacant pending my return. That weekend I set off to drive to Kiganjo, some miles North of Nyeri on the Nyeri-Nanyuki road and not so many miles from the famous Treetops Hotel.

The Mess at Kiganjo was excellent and run by a very effective European manageress. The food was good and varied and my new colleagues, some fifteen in number, were very pleasant and there was a good community spirit, rather like a bunch of new schoolboys on the first day of term.

We attended lectures, sat various tests and went onto the firing range to learn the use of various weapons. We fired and experienced tear gas, had our powers of observation put to the test, learned more about the law and then, of course, there was the inevitable drill on the square. This consisted of being some ten paces apart from your other colleagues, and shouting commands to your 'opposite number' some thirty-five yards away on the other side of the square. As everyone was giving different commands it was very noisy, sometimes confusing, and everyone soon developed a hoarse voice. But it worked! To this day I can still produce a 'parade-ground' voice.

There was trout fishing locally and on most Sundays this was a popular form of relaxation. Our catch was handed over to the Mess cook and as we normally caught our quota, from time to time, trout would appear on the menu. It was an enjoyable time.

Our time to depart was only two weeks away and we concentrated on the final passing out parade that would consist of (all ranks) about two hundred and fifty men, with the Kenya Police No.1 band in attendance. The usual dignitaries and the Governor would be there.

I am sure it never occurs to the average citizen how 250 men, all setting off at different intervals, can march in step. It's not easy to achieve. The next requirement is to have equal gaps between each column of men. This is relatively easy. If the gap is to be twenty paces, then it is simply a matter of observing the column ahead of you setting off, counting to nineteen paces, then giving the order "quick march!" as their next pace with their left foot 'hits' the ground. This latter item is the difficult part. Get the order out of sequence with the column in front and there is chaos. Two things can occur: one, your column is out of step with the entire parade or two, you realise that you have made a mistake and you try to correct it by shouting "Wait!" Then all your men 'cannon' into each other because you have already given the order to "quick march!"

I was chosen to lead our column and thus to give the order to march. On the day we had a Senior Officer heading our column with white gloves and drawn sword. The order to march was still my responsibility. We turned into column of route and each column stepped off. Now it was our turn. I counted the paces, gave the order "By the left… quick march!" It was 'spot on', except the Senior Officer leading our column was out of step! There is nothing more difficult than to have someone ahead of you out of step; it can easily develop into everyone doing a 'shuffle'. I had to really concentrate and I dared not look at his feet! We passed the saluting base, I gave the order "Eyes right" – he saluted with his sword and was still out of step as I gave the order "Eyes front!" We marched off the parade ground to the 'thump thump' of the Police band.

When the parade was finished we retired to the Mess to meet the various guests, make polite conversation and consume a limited quantity of alcohol. Following this final episode, it was time to pack and return to our respective Divisions.

It was good to be back 'home'. We enjoyed our work, had a very good social life and, thanks to the local European Hospital, a plentiful supply of female company. I was given the job of 'Entertainment Officer' and soon was able to organise various Mess functions to which everyone could invite their friends.

On one occasion I organised an 'Oriental Night' and had rounded-up some volunteers to make up a punch with which to greet the guests. We called it 'Canal No.5' and it was quite a brew! Charles, one of my colleagues, suitably attired in Arab dress (which was a five hundred percent improvement on our New Year fiasco), sat at the entrance to issue this heady mixture. Everything was organised and we had large numbers attending. To our amazement most guests thought that the punch was a joke, laughed at being offered a 'snifter' of 'Canal No.5' and went straight into the Mess to join in the jollifications. The mixture had not been cheap and it was not until midnight that the word spread that available by the entrance was a most fantastic cocktail! The lot 'disappeared' in minutes!

These special Mess nights were very good for public relations and became very popular. I always carried some blank invitation cards with me and issued these whenever the opportunity presented itself.

Another popular function that we had was a nostalgic 'Fish & Chips Night'. The Mess cooks excelled themselves, and to add to the image each packet was wrapped in greaseproof and newspaper, with salt and vinegar also available. It was a pity it had to be lake fish, but to have transported sea fish from Mombasa was not practical due to the distance and high cost.

During one of our special Mess nights I was outside greeting the guests as they arrived. A car had parked where directed by the Constable on duty. As the driver and his female passenger alighted, in the gloom he appeared to have fallen down. Surely he wasn't drunk when attending a Police Mess function? Then I heard him shouting.

"Help, help, I've fallen down a hole!"

The Mess had been in existence for many years and, unbeknown to us, the area of this rarely used parking lot was once the site of a number of pit latrines, long since disused. Our guest was now dangling over an unthinkable situation! Thank goodness he hadn't plunged down to the bottom! He was retrieved from a 'fate worse than death' and apart from having earth all over his dinner jacket and trousers, he was unharmed. We apologised, brushed him down, and offered to pay his dry-cleaning bill. Despite his soiled appearance he entered the Mess and, upon leaving some hours later, thanked us for a very enjoyable evening.

About a week later I was involved in a special investigation involving diamond smuggling. I was told that I would be joining a Chief Inspector to investigate how diamonds were being smuggled from the Congo and on to India. We were to meet, as if by accident, a Goan informer in a restaurant, as he had some very 'hot' information. Evidently he was overly fond of whisky. The objective was to ply him with his favourite drink to make him 'friendly' and then obtain the information.

As arranged, we 'bumped into him' in the bar section of the restaurant.

"Have a drink – and how are things with you?"

"Thank you, I'll have a large whisky."

We all had large whiskies. We sipped ours but he obviously 'got the message' that it was a night out and that we were paying, and downed his double in minutes.

"Care for another?"

"Yes please, another double bartender and one each for my friends here."

My colleague paid for the drinks and enquired, "Would you care to eat?"

"That's very kind of you. Yes I fancy a good curry."

Beside our table was a large potted plant, which proved more than convenient as will become apparent. I was now carrying one double whisky and another glass with almost a double, and we needed to stay sober. When our 'guest' wasn't looking, I poured the full double onto the side of the plant and prayed that it wouldn't reach the roots too quickly and make the foliage collapse before our departure.

Throughout the meal it 'drank' three more doubles, and our 'guest', started to appear slightly 'the worse for wear'. The situation reminded me of one of the old Hollywood movies with the villain plying the damsel with drink and pouring his champagne onto a large fern beside their table. My colleague had also been passing me one or two of his glasses. I knew it was a big plant and maybe it had quite a thirst, but these were 'doubles'! Just how much could it take?

The time to obtain the information now seemed ripe. My colleague leaned across the table and said in a very quiet voice, "We hear you have friends who deal in diamonds."

Our guest said in a loud, slurred voice, "Diamonds!"

Several people on nearby tables looked at us, then resumed eating.

"Not so loud. All we want to know is how and where?"

To our utter surprise our 'guest' lurched to his feet and shouted "Diamonds! So that's what you want to know about! Diamonds! I'll tell you about diamonds!" He then collapsed into his chair and slumped onto the table, 'out for the count'. We took him home and left him on the doorstep, still muttering about diamonds and double whiskies.

Soon after this I was on the move again. This time I was being transferred to another Division very close to the Uganda border and in the heart of a European farming area. It would prove to be another very pleasant posting with plenty of variation. I said goodbye to all my new friends, packed the car and set off towards a whole host of new experiences.

About three years later I was to meet Mac again when he was touring one of his Divisions. Wherever he went, everyone 'was on tenterhooks'. On this particular day he asked an Inspector for a stone, as he wished to check the pit latrines.

"A stone Sir?"

"Don't you know what a stone is?"

"Yes Sir."

"Then bring me a stone."

The stone was duly produced.

Mac now produced a stopwatch, studied it intently, dropped the stone down the hole and clicked the button on the watch before declaring, "Fill this one in and dig a new one!"

My final contact with Mac was when I was on what was to prove, my final home leave. Talk of Kenyan Independence was in the air and it was highly likely that this would take place before my due date for return to duty. Mac sent me a personal handwritten letter saying that, with the declaration of Independence, he would understand that as I had a wife and young child, I may not wish to return to Kenya, but if I did return I would be promoted and he would be delighted to have me in his command. Whatever would be my ultimate decision he wished me well for the future.

Soon after Kenya's Independence Mac transferred to another Colonial Police Force and I was very saddened to hear some years later that he had died. There are very few Mac's in this world and his early passing was a great loss.

8   'Routine' investigations

The 'rains' had yet to arrive so my drive to my new posting was uneventful. Once the rains arrived, the usual earth main roads 'up country' could turn into quagmires and it was not uncommon to see several stranded motorists and lorries in the ditch, or crabbed sideways where they had failed to 'make it' up a steep incline. I was enjoying the drive and en route I had crossed the equator at close to nine thousand feet. All my older colleagues had told me how lucky I was to be posted 'up country'.

"There are bags of European farmer's daughters. Some have all the luck!" Little did I realise, as I drove along this earth road, leaving a dust trail in my wake, that before my next leave I would meet my future wife. At this stage of my life, marriage had never entered my head; I was happy to be 'footloose and fancy free'.

At this new posting I was to experience a wide variety of police work, meet some interesting colonial characters and become involved in prosecutions. Being a smaller Divisional unit, apart from CID, Special Branch and Prosecutions, there was no specialisation.

I arrived at Divisional Headquarters and met my new boss, who expressed disappointment at my stature; he needed an 'anchor man' for his prize winning tug-of-war team and had been hoping for someone six-feet-six and built like an elephant.

My response, which with hindsight was somewhat flippant, was, "It depends, Sir, whether you need quality or quantity."

I was directed to the Police Mess, which was much smaller than my previous abode and it was very obvious that the decor was in need of a 'facelift'.

It was about four thirty when I arrived at the Mess to find three of my new colleagues having afternoon tea. After the usual introductions and handshakes I naturally asked what was it like being posted into such a pleasant location.

"It's wonderful. Bags going on, lots of European girls and the farmers are so friendly around here. I bet within a few days one will invite you out for dinner."

It sounded too good to be true.

"Surely not without having met me?"

"You wait and see."

The next morning I reported to Police Headquarters and the day was spent mostly settling in and studying the odd case file. I returned to the Mess around 4.30pm for tea. I had just sat down when I heard a female voice outside saying "Can you direct me to Inspector Tompkins please."

Who could this be? The lady, well dressed and of middle years, entered the Mess and we were introduced.

"Inspector, if you are not busy tomorrow evening, could you join us for dinner? Say about seven thirty for eight?" She gave me directions to the farm and left. I was stunned! So it was true, the 'locals' were very friendly. This was a posting 'in a million'!

The following evening I 'spruced myself up' and wearing my police blazer, well pressed white shirt, police tie, 'knife edged' grey trousers and highly polished brogue shoes, set off in my Volkswagen for the farm. I arrived, to be met by the hostess, who directed me into a very pleasant and spacious lounge. There, standing to greet me, were two very large and 'gawky' girls. The smallest of the pair was about six feet one and towered above me by several inches. Both were in their early twenties. I was asked to sit on the settee and within seconds, had a daughter on either side of me. I felt like a bush between two pine trees!

Their Mother explained that she was now a widow and ran the farm with her two daughters. Did I like farming? I stated that I knew nothing about farming, to be informed that it was not very difficult, all it required was common sense and, as I must realise, really it was a man's world. I was beginning to acquire the distinct impression that this dinner date had matrimonial overtones!

We made polite conversation until dinner was served. The food was excellent but facing me across the table and giving me flirtatious smiles throughout the whole meal, 'Tall' and 'Very Tall' vied for my attention. When coffee was finished I made the excuse that I had to return to the Mess due to some early morning activity. The word that kept flashing across my mind was 'ESCAPE'!

Back at the Mess I was met with broad grins and asked how I had enjoyed my evening with the lady and her daughters? I politely refused all future invitations to the farm and during my stay in the Mess saw the lady appear every time we had a new arrival. She was very determined to find a son-in-law, if not two!

Some months later I had another 'close call'. Not far from the Mess lived a European family who owned a small business in town. As we lived close by we often bumped into them and it was during one such meeting that one of my colleagues and I were invited to tea. Their lounge was very English with chintz covers and curtains, bowls of roses and mahogany furniture. Sitting in an armchair by the window was a young woman we had not seen before. We were introduced. It was the local lady's sister, on a visit from England. I quickly assessed that she must be somewhat older than me, in her late twenties or early thirties. Tea was served and featured an excellent assortment of cakes, ranging from chocolate éclairs filled with whipped cream to delicious home-made fruitcake – somewhat more upmarket than our Mess teas, which normally consisted of assorted sandwiches and biscuits. Following tea we made the usual polite conversation and left.

A week later the invitation was repeated, which we accepted and, during tea we were asked if we would care to join them for dinner one evening. We had 'safety in numbers' so had no hesitation in accepting. It was an excellent and memorable meal. Following this I invited the sister out to one of the local country clubs to see a Jacques Tati film and, on another occasion, to dinner.

A few days after this final excursion, I received a telephone call asking if I would call at their house to collect some home-made cakes for the Mess. When I arrived at the house, everyone was out except the sister from England and an aunt, who quickly excused herself and left the room. I accepted the parcel and said that I had better say goodbye to her aunt. I went into the next room where the aunt was stitching some very elegant yellow silk lampshades. She showed one to me saying "These will look very elegant in my niece's and your bedroom."

My heart nearly stopped! All contact ceased and their displeasure was very apparent. Whenever I met a member of their family from then on, I was snubbed.

One Saturday lunchtime we received a call from the Post Office. They could not resolve a bookkeeping anomaly and could someone please come. On arrival we were shown into the Post Master's office. Inside were an Asian postal clerk and an African male. I asked the Post Master why we had been called.

"This man (he pointed to the African) regularly comes in here to make deposits into his Post Office savings book. He came in today and my clerk here noted that following the last deposit made by this man, my clerk had omitted to stamp the savings book with our official date stamp. As the date on the stamp cannot be altered without my authority, he produced the pass book to show me his error and asked me to alter the date."

"So why have you called us?"

The Post Master produced the savings book.

"Here on the left of this page are my clerk's entries, giving the amount of money paid in, then his signature here, and on the right hand side are the blank circles where the date stamps are placed. As you can see, the number of handwritten entries is correct, but they do not match the number of date stamps. One is missing."

I turned to the clerk.

"Are all these amounts of money and these signatures your writing?"

"Yes Sir, without any question of doubt."

I turned to the Post Master.

"So what is preventing you from agreeing to have your clerk here stamp the book?"

"The ink of the last entry is a slightly different colour and we do not have any pens here with that slightly darker ink."

Was this 'a storm in a teacup'? I turned to the African and spoke to him in Kiswahili.

"What do you have to say about this?"

He replied in excellent English.

"I do not know what this trouble is all about. I came here as usual to make a deposit in my savings book. This gentleman here (pointing to the clerk) said he was sorry as he had forgotten to stamp the book when I last made a deposit and he would see the Post Master to obtain authority to stamp it. I hadn't noticed the error, but he did. All I want to do is to have the mistake corrected so that I can leave."

I looked at the clerk; there wasn't a trace of fear on his face.

"You are positive that all these entries are your writing?"

"Yes Sir, as I have told you. It is all my writing."

"So how do you account for this last entry being in a slightly darker ink?"

"I cannot explain it, but it is my writing."

I examined the savings book very closely checking through the previous pages. Sure enough, all the ink entries were the same colour, except the last one. Something was amiss, or was the Post Master being overly pedantic? The sum involved, two hundred shillings (£10), although 'not a fortune' was not an insignificant amount of money, though not out of line with some of the previous deposits. I looked at the African; he too showed no signs of any fear. Was he in collusion with the clerk? I decided to carry out a search of his house. I took out my police notebook and made the entry giving me the right of search, then told the African what I was doing and the reason. For the first time I saw a tiny flicker of fear on his face.

At his house we found two school exercise books filled with entries trying to copy the Asian clerk's writing. The final entries, even I would have agreed, were the clerk's. He was cautioned, arrested and charged in Court the following Monday and sentenced one week later. He had almost 'pulled it off'.

On another occasion the local CID was called to investigate a case of demanding money with menaces. A European family had received a letter made up of cuttings from English newspapers threatening that unless the sum of four thousand shillings (£200) was deposited at a specified location, something dreadful would happen to them. It also said that if the police were informed, immediate retribution would follow. However, they did inform the police and a dummy parcel was duly placed at the designated spot on the date and time demanded and an ambush prepared. Five minutes after the trap was set, a fourteen year old European boy arrived on a bicycle, looked around, then went straight to 'the spot' and picked up the parcel. He was immediately arrested, taken to the Police Station and charged. His parents were called to the Police Station and he was placed into their custody on a two thousand shillings (£100) bail. He appeared in Court the following morning, pleaded guilty and was sentenced (subject to a medical examination) to five strokes of the cane, which he received.

So ended a budding criminal career (or at least I hope so).

My new posting involved a wide variety of police duties and I sometimes felt we should erect a sign outside the Police Station stating, 'You Name It; We Do It'.

Late one afternoon we received a telephone call from a very worried European woman saying that her husband had gone off to shoot guinea fowl and despite having said that he would return for afternoon tea, he was now long overdue. Could we please come and try to find him? We duly arrived and she pointed in the general direction that he had taken. We fanned out and commenced our search. If we'd had a tracker dog we would have found him much sooner. His body was slumped over a wire fence. Protruding in front of him was the butt of a shotgun with the barrel pointing towards his body. We examined the area very carefully; there were no other tracks in the grass. Viewed from his right side he appeared to be normal, but the shotgun had discharged, blowing most of the left side of his face away. It was obvious what had happened, he had failed to follow the usual safety rules when carrying a shotgun or rifle across a fence. He had kept it loaded and placed the butt through the fence with the barrel pointing towards himself. A tragic accident that could have been easily avoided.

I felt very sorry for his wife who, when she saw us approaching with a stretcher with her husband covered with a blanket, became very distraught. We advised her to remember him as he was. In her grief I could understand why she wanted to see him, but I believed that had she done so, she would never have eradicated the sight from her mind. Prior to the Inquest the shotgun was examined and it was discovered that it had a faulty safety catch; later it was destroyed.

Perhaps the most tragic case was that of a young Asian boy who fell in love with a girl from a different and higher caste. When they found out, her family forbade her ever to see him again. His reaction was to lock himself into the outside toilet, pour a gallon of petrol over himself and ignite it.[5] His screams alerted his family, who broke down the door and extinguished the flames, but he had suffered in the region of 75% burns and the doctors at the hospital rated his chances of survival at close to

---

[5] For some reason unknown to me at the time, Asians often chose to commit suicide by this horrible and painful method.

nil. His face and body were so badly burned that, despite drugs, he must have been in terrible agony. He died later that same day; such a tragic waste of a young life.

Luckily, not every incident had a tragic ending...

A favourite 'watering hole' for a small minority of the local European male community was the 'Theatre Bar' – a misnomer if ever there was one, as the local theatre was at least half a mile away. It was owned and run by a gentleman of Irish extraction who was not averse to disregarding the laws regarding opening hours. Having had several warnings, apparently ignored, the Superintendent decided to raid the place on a Saturday night, well after closing time.

A group of six police, led by the Superintendent, pushed open the door to find the party in full swing. Caught in the act... or so we thought, but the bar-owner exclaimed, "Thank God you've arrived Superintendent! I have asked these people to leave and they have refused."

This was not what we had expected!

"Are you telling me that as owner of the licence you have asked all these people to leave, and they have refused. Is that correct?"

"Yes Superintendent."

"Right, everyone here is under arrest!"

Names and addresses were taken and the 'crocodile' of prisoners, numbering some twelve European males, made its way to the Police Station. All were bailed to appear at Court on Monday morning to answer the charges. On Monday morning they all appeared and due to the large number some had to stand outside the dock. They all pleaded guilty and were fined four hundred shillings (£20) each. Outside the Court a certain Irish bar owner was seen handing out a pile of one hundred shilling notes to his best customers!

One of the number receiving four hundred shillings was an individual who, even during daylight hours, appeared to be 'under the influence'. Popular rumour had it that he was a 'black sheep of the family' and had been 'shipped out to Kenya', but he was never a cause of trouble and was always a polite, harmless individual. He lived some miles outside town and from time to time, especially Saturdays, drove into town in the morning to pick up essential supplies. On this particular day he drove in his Morris van, leaning his .22 rifle against the passenger seat for safekeeping.

He parked outside the local bookshop and, overlooking that he had left his rifle behind, went off to visit the various *dukas* (shops). At this time the law regarding the security of firearms was very strict and loss of a firearm earned an automatic twelve months imprisonment. A certain Irish bar owner was also out shopping. Seeing one of his drinking customer's cars he sauntered over and on looking inside saw the rifle. The van was unlocked. What a superb joke to play! Remove the rifle and then hand it back when his customer arrived at the bar for his usual Saturday night 'entertainment'. What a laugh!

Returning to his van the customer was horrified to note that the rifle was missing! Despite realising the consequences, he reported immediately to the Police Station. Panic stations! Every department was alerted: Traffic, Crime Branch, CID, every beat patrol and even Special Branch. The hunt was on!

Within ten minutes we had identified the individual responsible. A certain Irish bar owner was seen to have removed the rifle. A visit to his bar found it locked. It was possible that the bar owner, who had a property some miles outside of town, could be found there. A vehicle was despatched with the Officer in Charge Police Station on board. Arriving at the house – by now it was around 2.30pm – the 'thief' was discovered on the veranda fast asleep in a chair with the rifle beside him. Tiptoeing onto the veranda, the Police Officer removed the rifle and handed it to the Police driver. He now returned and shook the recumbent figure. After a few seconds our 'thief' was awake.

"Mr 'X', I am the officer investigating the theft of a firearm from one Mr 'Y'. I have reason to believe that you have knowledge of this. I must warn you that anything you do say will be taken down in writing and may be used in evidence."

Our bar owner was now wide awake!

"There's no need for all that, it was a joke. Here it is… Oh my God! It's been nicked!" He visibly paled and sat heavily into the chair. "I'll be imprisoned. Help me."

On Monday he pleaded guilty to a minor offence and was 'relieved' of four hundred shillings.

The Almighty moves in mysterious ways!

The 'regulars' at the 'Theatre Bar' found that having to adhere to the law with regard to licensing hours was impinging on their lunchtime and nocturnal drinking. This resulted in their wondering if the Assistant Superintendent had a known father and then deciding he should be told how they felt about him and the law. With courage bolstered by many a pink gin, one of them volunteered to do just this. He made his unsteady progress towards Divisional Police Headquarters and encountered the Assistant Superintendent on the steps.

Trying to focus, he delivered his slurred speech.

"You Sir... are a bastard... a scoundrel... who hates... hates... a man... having a drink!" His voice tailed off and he stood there, swaying slightly in the hot afternoon sunshine.

At this juncture two Police Inspectors arrived.

The ASP's voice was like ice.

"This man is under arrest and is to be charged with being drunk and disorderly!"

Our orator was whisked off to the cells and released on bail when he was sober. On the Monday he pleaded guilty and was fined five hundred shillings. Not surprisingly, there were no more volunteers to tell the ASP that he was spoiling their fun.

Another function that the police performed in 'up country' areas was to assist, if needs be, the local Fire Brigade. On one occasion an Asian duka caught fire. When the Brigade arrived, the owner was heard to say "Don't touch, everything's insured!"

The blaze had started beside a stack of full kerosene tins, a fact which, along with his comments, led the CID to investigate and he was later charged and convicted of arson and attempted fraud.

However, that was in the immediate future.

We arrived at the scene of the above fire to assist, not only in crowd control, but also in manning a hose. The Superintendent 'threw himself' into this new role with gusto, seized a fire hose that was at full pressure and with great difficulty climbed a ladder, with the hose acting like some live giant snake that was determined to break from his clutches. Somehow he made it onto the roof. Just as he was about to direct this powerful jet onto the fire someone down below turned it off! The air was 'blue'! It reminded me of the 'Keystone Cops'. My colleague and I also became involved and once on the roof we spotted a looter in the rear yard of the shop. We shouted for the hose to be turned on and hit the escaping looter right between the shoulder blades as he tried to scramble over the wall. We then washed him into a corner of the yard. Every time he tried to escape, the deluge of water knocked him down. It was our easiest arrest ever.

You may recall that when I arrived at this new posting I discovered that my new boss was 'mad keen' to maintain the reputation of his prize-winning tug-of-war team. As a result they held practice sessions once a week in front of the Mess, with the Assistant Superintendent (ASP) joining in and supervising the training. This involved pulling a Police three ton truck up the slope of the drive, numerous press-ups, plus squats with large logs on their shoulders. If any member managed twenty five squats, the ASP would manage twenty six. One week the team decided to really put him to the test. His car had a very distinctive exhaust note. Hearing his car approaching the Mess, a member of the team seized a log and did about five squats. As the ASP stopped he threw himself onto the grass 'gasping' for breath.

"How many did you manage Lapham?"

"Thirty-five Sir."

"Give me that log!"

By the time he reached twenty-eight the veins were standing out on his forehead and his arms were shaking. Should we stop him? With a struggle he continued

"Thirty six!" He threw himself onto the grass as if gasping his last! We thought he was going to have a heart attack! Those 'thirty-five' squats to this day have remained a closely guarded secret.

Government employees at any level were not allowed to receive gifts from the general public. It was almost Christmas and a colleague and I had cause to call at the local 'Public Works Department'. In the main office were five Sikhs who I recognised as local contractors. Each one was carrying a large cardboard box covered in Christmas wrapping paper and from one of the boxes protruded the head of a bottle of champagne. Talking to them as we entered was the European responsible for issuing contracts. They all looked shocked, particularly the European, but he exhibited some of the quickest thinking 'on the spot' that I ever witnessed when he said, "There we are gentlemen, it's my method of thanking you for all you good work throughout the year. Thank you for your support and I hope that you enjoy your presents."

The five Sikhs left the office with strained looks on their faces. Their expansive 'benefactor' now turned to us.

"Well gentlemen, what can I do for you?"

I couldn't resist saying, "You must have spent quite a considerable sum for your contractors' presents."

Looking very strained, he said "Well, it's important that we obtain and maintain quality workmanship."

The next fire we attended was totally without humour of any kind. It was Christmas Day and I was off duty. My wife and I had joined a senior colleague and his wife for a very enjoyable lunch and we were in the garden relaxing. It was about 2.30pm and all was quiet. Suddenly the riot siren sounded! The standing instruction was that whatever you were doing or wearing you had to report to the Police Station immediately! We set off at speed. At the Police Station members of staff were arriving in all states of dress, from normal uniform, to vest and shorts and some were in civilian clothing. Evidently there was a fire in the African section of town and the Fire Brigade was on its way to the scene. The police party, consisting of some thirty other ranks with just we two Europeans, set off to assist in a three-ton open-sided police lorry and a Land Rover equipped with a VHF radio.

Arriving at the scene we discovered that several huts with thatched roofs were on fire and that the wind was causing the flames to jump from hut to hut. The crowd, some two hundred strong, had seized the hose from the Fire Brigade and were directing the jet into the air and laughing. It appeared that they were all drunk! An old woman, also under the influence, staggered towards us screaming that there was a child in one of the blazing huts.

"Which hut is it?"

"*Shauri yako!*" (that's your problem), she shouted and staggered away, cackling with drunken laughter. Despite her state, we could not ignore what she had said. Bending very low to minimise the heat, two of us commenced checking the blazing huts by kicking open the doors. Despite the intense searing heat it had to be done. Every hut was empty.

By now we had managed to take the hose from the crowd without any problem. Suddenly I saw an African with a piece of wood in his hand about three feet long, and through its end protruded a six inch nail. My colleague had his back to him and just as the man raised this weapon to strike I shouted "Derek, behind you look out!" He quickly turned and managed to knock the man to the ground and two of our party handcuffed him. At this the crowd went berserk! Screaming and shouting they attacked us. Thank God they weren't armed. All we had was what we stood up in. We stood back to back, fighting for our lives. There were no 'Queensbury Rules', it was fight or be killed. I can recall even punching women in the face as they were trying to grab us and pull us into the crowd. Derek shouted "Try and get to the vehicles!" We just made it. Some of the crowd now seized the sides of the vehicles with the intention of turning them over and others tried to clamber over the sides. We were punching, stamping on fingers as they tried to grasp the sides of the vehicles to prevent our escape. We could not go until we were sure that everyone of our party was safely aboard the vehicles. Derek shouted "Go, go!" I was in the lead vehicle and as we were moving off the crowd started tipping our Land Rover but had to let go as it gathered speed. My colleague radioed ahead for full riot equipment to be made ready. It had been a very close thing and luckily no one had been killed or seriously injured.

It was something I do not wish to live through again. What saved us was discipline, a common spirit, plus the boost of adrenaline that fear can generate. Had we been fewer in numbers and had the crowd not been drunk and unarmed (instead of carrying pangas (machetes) as Africans often did), some, if not all of us, would have been killed.

We returned to the scene fully equipped and went into the full riot drill. Steel helmets on, shields held in front of the chest, riot batons resting on the right shoulder and standing at the 'at ease' position. Four rows of ten men, one behind the other with an NCO in the centre of each row, tear gas ready at the rear. The crowd, which had been 'full of fight' not fifteen minutes before, just 'melted away'.

Houses situated on the outskirts of the township did not have flush sanitation. Toilets were situated in the gardens, away from the houses and consisted of various structures, but with one common denominator; a wooden floor placed above the 'long drop'. Under normal conditions this would be perfectly safe. However, in East Africa there are insects called white ants which love to eat wood and as a consequence, from time to time some poor soul would enter the toilet and find themselves plunging down into a very unpleasant situation. Police Station files contained scores of letters written over the years from grateful members of a multi-racial public who had been rescued from a 'fate worse than death'. Fortunately, I was lucky and every time a report of this nature came in I had just gone off duty. Thank goodness!

A couple who owned a farm some miles outside of town had a 'his' and 'hers' long-drop. Neither structure had a door; they were built near the edge of a small cliff that faced out over Africa. In order to avoid descending unexpectedly down the abyss, dangling from the roof of each structure was a thick rope, knotted at the users end, which was grasped very firmly whilst inside. I leave the remaining picture to the reader's imagination!

One night a beat patrol in town reported they had discovered the security netting at the rear of a chemist's shop had been disturbed and they believed the intruder was still on the premises. Within minutes the building was surrounded and my colleague Derek, armed with his police revolver, entered the building. Suddenly from inside there was a terrific scream and he emerged with a small African boy no more than nine years of age. The front of his shirt above the waistband of his shorts was bulging with loot and contained at least a hundred 'gold' plated lipsticks. We were to discover that his name was Ernest. How had he managed to pull the security netting off the window?

"It was easy. In the yard was a long metal pole. I put one end just under the mesh and heaved."

Had Ernest been studying physics? And why lipsticks?

"Being gold they were obviously worth a lot of money."

We were to encounter Ernest again.

Being night Duty Officer was never a quiet affair; anything could happen. I was in the office thinking that apart from two drunks, as it was just past midnight, this could be my lucky night. Suddenly there was a sound of running feet and one of the beat Constables ran into my office accompanied by a night-watchman whom I recognised as the man who guarded one of the local shops. From the expression on the night-watchman's face I could see he was very upset. The Constable quickly gave his report.

"Effendi, a European man exposed himself and attempted to indecently assault this man. He pushed him off and chased him to the hotel." The night-watchman now added his words saying how disgusted he was and produced two hundred shillings (£10), consisting of two one hundred shilling notes which were folded not in half but slightly off centre and at an angle.

"Could he recognise this man?"

"Ndiyo Effendi, I chased him into the hotel right to his bedroom door. I can take you to his room."

Donning my police hat I followed the night-watchman who led us unerringly up to the hotel's first floor, stopping outside one of the rooms. I put my finger to my lips, cautioning them to keep quiet. I knocked on the door. Silence. I knocked again even louder.

From inside the room someone said "Shhh!"

I knocked again. This time the response was an even louder 'Shhh!'

I said, "I am a Police Officer and I want you to open this door."

There was a considerable delay. The door was eventually opened by a European male dressed in pyjamas.

Immediately the night-watchman said, "This is the man!"

I said "I have reason to believe that you have been involved in an indecent act or assault. I must warn you that anything you do say will be taken down in writing and may be used in evidence. I now wish to enter this room."

His response to this was, "I am an army officer and I have no idea what this is all about. Following dinner I had a drink at the bar and then came to my room."

"How long ago was this?"

"Oh, at least an hour and a half, maybe two hours."

His shoes were beside the bed; I felt the insides, they were still warm.

"How do you account for the fact the insides of your shoes are still warm?" He shrugged his shoulders. I noted his jacket was thrown over a chair; I felt the armpits, they were also warm.

"Can I see your wallet?" He produced it, and when I opened it the notes inside were folded in exactly the same way as those produced by the night-watchman. The notes were not new and therefore there was no chance of having consecutive serial numbers. I was more than convinced he had committed the offence.

"I want you to get dressed and I am arresting you for an alleged indecent assault on this night-watchman. Once again I must warn you that anything you do say will be taken down in writing and may be used in evidence. Do you have anything to say?"

My suspect was looking very stressed.

"I am an army officer and I insist that I am allowed to telephone the army authorities. I know nothing about this incident and I wish to stress that I have never met this man, or offered him money."

I took possession of his wallet and issued him with a page torn from my police notebook as a receipt for its contents.

At the Police Station he was allowed to make his phone call and he was bailed to appear the following morning. I recorded the night-watchman's statement, plus my own and made a full report in my police notebook and the Police Station O.B. (charge office desk diary).

Next morning he duly appeared along with two senior army personnel. They said as it was an army matter they would now handle the investigation. They insisted on an identification parade, at which, as expected, the night watchman immediately identified the army officer. I handed over all the evidence and statements. They left with the accused and I never did hear of the outcome. Had he been charged in a civil court I am positive we could have achieved a conviction.

One Saturday morning I was finalising some routine paperwork when Corporal James from Crime Branch knocked on my office door and said that an African woman wished to speak to me. She entered with a small boy aged about six. Evidently the reason for her visit was to scare the boy into staying out of trouble.

"He's been very naughty and sometimes steals some of my money. Other days he doesn't go to school, and I've told him that if this continues the police will come and lock him up in prison."

This was something that I had never been faced with before, so I talked to the boy at some length. All the time he kept his eyes to the ground and I could see tears on his cheeks.

"Will you show him where bad people go?"

Accompanied by the mother I showed the boy an empty cell and then closed the door for a few seconds then let him out.

"Well, did you like it in there?" the woman asked.

The little boy, still with downcast eyes, shook his head.

His mother grabbed him by the shoulder.

"If I have any more trouble from you I am bringing you back here, and this man will lock you up!" She gave her son a quick 'clout' behind the ear, thanked me and left.

If only all mothers were like this!

A European lady called at the Police Station looking very distressed and asking to see someone in private. She had with her a letter addressed to her son, who was at boarding school in Nairobi. The letter was from a European male and the content suggested that she had been right to bring this to our notice. The boy, and later it was discovered several of his friends, had been receiving lavish gifts from this man whom it was discovered was a 'well heeled' civilian working in one of the Police Departments in Nairobi. As a result of further investigations, he was arrested and charged with indecent conduct against young boys. He pleaded guilty and received a heavy prison sentence.

As you will have noted, life was never dull. For example, at one of my postings, it was about 10.00pm one night when we received a telephone call from a local hotel manager. He had locked himself in his room and had armed himself with a pistol. The Mau-Mau had come to get him! He needed protection and could we come quickly! The Mau-Mau campaign had ended over a year before, so what was going on?

On arrival at the hotel a member of staff led us to the manager's ground floor apartment. Having ascertained it was the police a very nervous manger let us in and quickly bolted the door again.

"Look what I found when I came off duty." He led us into the bed-room. On top of the bed were his pyjamas. Passing through each leg of the trousers was a banana leaf. Another leaf was threaded through the jacket sleeves. Placed on top of the pyjama jacket was a small pile of raw meat, and on top of the meat a live bullet. His hands were shaking as he pointed out the scene. Had he touched anything?

"No, just the door handle and the handle of the drawer where I keep my automatic pistol."

On returning to his room he had unlocked the door, and when first entering the bedroom, he had noticed first the bed, and then that the window was broken and open. This was the obvious point of entry. We sealed off the room and had him placed into one of the hotel bedrooms, together with his wife, and provided an armed police guard.

In the morning investigations began. As expected, the banana leaves came from the hotel grounds and the meat was identified as veal. This had been one of the dishes on the hotel menu the night before and was pronounced by the chef as scraps of fat and skin that had been cut off and discarded. The bullet was the same make and calibre as the manager's automatic and when we checked, one of his bullets was missing. This looked like an inside job, perhaps organised by one of the African staff with a grudge. There was to be another surprise. The broken window glass was on the ground outside the window and there were signs of disturbed ground directly below the window where it had been lightly dug over.

More pointers to an 'inside job'.

When questioning members of the hotel staff it transpired that the manager and his wife slept in separate rooms and had done so for at least a year or more. They were not aware of anyone with a grudge. There had not been any disagreements and no one had left recently.

The comment about the domestic sleeping arrangements was interesting. The ground floor of the apartment had highly polished floors, and when dusted with white fingerprint powder, shoe prints with a faint criss-cross pattern could easily be seen in both rooms used by the husband and wife. Dusting the window had drawn a blank. Questioning their maid very closely revealed that the wife never normally entered the manager's room and of late, there had been many rows. This was very interesting, as, due to 'intelligence', we knew that the manager favoured 'ladies of the night' and often returned to the hotel very late. We decided to take a close look at the manager's wife's room. Her slippers had a small criss-cross pattern on the soles and in the bookcase in her room were several books about Mau-Mau. When questioned, she stated she was often in her husband's room and they slept apart as he snored very loudly and disturbed her sleep. This statement was at variance with the maid's report. During her interview I noticed that the manager's wife was smoking in a very stressed manner. It could have been a normal nervous reaction, but our approach had been friendly and relaxed. Was she hiding something? Was it possible that this inside job was more inside than at first realised? I decided to 'bite the bullet' and requested that she came to see me at the Police Station.

On her arrival I could see that she was flustered and had difficulty in breathing normally. I set out the facts and stated that in our opinion it was an inside job. I now added that I believed she knew more about this case than she had admitted and cautioned her. To say she was indignant was an understatement! I was to be sued for defamation of character, she would write to the Commissioner of Police. I looked her straight in the eye and repeated my assertion. She collapsed in tears and all was revealed.

Like us, she was aware of the husband's preference for 'ladies of the night' and, as a result she had refused to sleep with him due to possible infection; also they had had many rows over his behaviour. She had decided to 'scare him to death' as a method of keeping him away from African prostitutes, hence the 'Mau-Mau warning'. I told her that she would not be charged, but we would need to inform her husband of the result of our investigations. After that it was up to them to sort out their domestic affairs. Having dried her tears and gained her composure she asked me if the information would become public knowledge. I assured her that nothing would be given to the local press and as far as we were concerned the case was closed.

Some two months later I had cause to visit the hotel and the manager's wife asked to see me in private. Once we were alone she said

"What would it take for you to destroy my case file?"

"Repeat that again and you are under arrest for attempting to bribe a Police Officer!" I replied.

Her tan turned several shades paler and she swept out of the room. For my own security I reported and logged the incident. The matter was closed.

Saturday nights produced the usual crop of drunks, the 'odd' assault and sometimes a stabbing. The worst time was the end of the month, as this was when the locals were paid, causing 'the beer to flow like water'. In order to keep crime caused by drink to a minimum, a party of four Constables, plus an Officer in Charge and a driver would tour all the African bars on a constant 'round robin'. Each bar would be packed to capacity and to enter and maintain control required humour and tact. My usual ploy was to approach any drunk and say with a broad smile, "Good evening friend, where are you sleeping tonight?"

The drunk would try to stop swaying about and try to focus on my face.

"I'm... j-just enjoying myself... and then... then I'm going home."

"I've been told you would prefer King George's Hotel (an African term for the Police Station cells) and we've a *kitanda* (bed) just for you."

This approach always caused a laugh with the patrons and ensured that we remained in control. To have been 'heavy handed' would be asking for trouble. The drunk would still be trying to focus.

"Thank... thank... you Effendi, but... but... I will be going home."

"Now?"

"Yes... now... Effendi." .

He would start to make his unsteady way to the door. I would then say to the barman, "When I return here, if he's still here and has been served more drink, you will be charged. Understood?"

The barman knew full well that in an hour or so we would be back again. Once outside, the drunk was offered the choice, go home or be 'nicked'. Any argument and he was arrested. We maintained these patrols until closing time and stood down around midnight. As these bar patrols were a constant Saturday night feature, it kept drunkenness within reasonable limits.

Employed by one of the local garages was a middle-aged South African mechanic who was very mild mannered and when spoken to by anyone in authority always removed his hat and held it over his heart. Imagine our surprise when one night we received a call from the local hotel saying 'our' mechanic was spoiling for a fight! When we arrived he was on the steps of the hotel, obviously drunk and trying to adopt a boxing pose and inviting all and sundry to take him on. We grabbed him by either arm and marched him backwards down the steps. He did not resist, but kept up his dialogue to take on all-comers.

At the Police Station he said "Look... look... at this war wound." He tried to raise one of his legs and crashed to the floor! We picked him up.

"And... and... this leg!" Before we could grab him he fell down again! That night the cells were full to overflowing. What were we going to do with him? Evidently he had a very fierce Afrikaans wife who was somewhat bigger than he was. We decided to take him home, knowing full well that she would deal with him!

Our police vehicle stopped outside his house. On trying to alight he fell into the drainage ditch! Derek and I hauled him out. He then collided with the stay wire of a telegraph pole. We each held an arm to prevent him injuring himself further and deposited him on the doorstep into the arms of his very 'beefy' wife. Next day he appeared at the Police Station his normal subservient self, very apologetic and saying he would never do it again. He appeared in Court, was fined, and from that day on 'stayed on the straight and narrow'. Upon reflection, perhaps this was due more to his wife than the fine and fear of the law.

Another night our mobile patrol came across a car parked at the side of the road. Inside slumped over the wheel was a Catholic priest. I opened the driver's door and shone a torch on him. He smelled of drink.

"Are you all right Father?"

"Yes... yes Officer... I'm quite... quite all right." His speech was slurred and I ordered him out of the car. He was very unsteady on his feet and I told him that he was under arrest for being drunk in charge of a vehicle. He was taken to the Police Station and booked. Still speaking in a slurred voice he asked to make a phone call. This was allowed. In the interim period a call was made to request the Government Doctor to examine the priest. All attempts to raise him failed. Within ten minutes another Catholic priest arrived. His opening statement amazed me.

"Officer, the Father here has been working very hard and he's totally exhausted so with your permission I'll take him home."

I looked the priest straight in the eyes.

"Look at him, he smells of drink, he's unsteady on his feet and he is finding it difficult to talk to you... he's under the influence of drink!"

"No, no," came the reply, "The poor man's exhausted."

The priest was charged and at his colleague's request I released the culprit into his custody. This action did not assist our case. The accused duly appeared in Court and swore on the Bible that he was exhausted. His colleague also swore on the Bible that his colleague was exhausted and that they had only consumed one small beer. We lost the case.

By now I was in charge of the Mess. I had had the lounge and bar areas completely redecorated, all the easy chairs had been recovered, we had new curtains, plus a new coffee table; a vast improvement on its original 'scruffy' appearance. In addition, as the mess was quite small, my duties also included catering which included the weekly menus.

In any Police Mess there had to be organisation to ensure that Mess bills were paid, suppliers' invoices and wages paid on time; food and drink ordered. We normally either volunteered for the job, or it was by rota. As I was dissatisfied with the current standards, I had volunteered.

I arrived back at the Mess one evening to be met by the cook. He could not produce dinner.

"Why not?"

Evidently the Superintendent had called, saying that he and his wife had some guests arriving very unexpectedly for dinner and, as the shops were closed, could the Mess assist? Without my authority, one of my colleagues, Phillip, had given away the chickens that were for our dinner. I was furious!

"Where was Bwana Phillip?"

"On duty Effendi."

"And what time is he expected back for dinner?"

"About half past eight Effendi."

"Right, you and the kitchen staff take the night off. We will have dinner at the hotel."

Evidently, Phillip arrived expectantly to be greeted by an empty dining room and no dinner. Tough!

Being in charge of catering was a thankless task, particularly where complaints were concerned. Sunday lunchtime was by tradition a 'Madras' curry, made with chicken, and served with rice, chopped fresh pineapple, banana, tomato, orange, coconut and popadoms. One Inspector always complained that the curry was "only fit for women!" As this was a constant weekly 'bind' and no one else complained, I decided that I had had enough. From the local *duka* I purchased some ground hot red peppers.

On Sunday morning I told the cook that about an hour before serving lunch he was to remove a portion of curry into a separate saucepan and then to add some of the ground hot red pepper. This special curry was to be served to this specific Inspector and no one else. Just before Sunday lunch I entered the kitchen and asked the cook how much of the ground red peppers he had added to the special curry?

"*Tatu Effendi.*" (Three Sir).

"Add three more." I told him.

I tasted the result and was very thankful that it would not be my stomach on the receiving end! We all sat down for curry lunch. The complainant took his usual seat.

"I hope it's more like a curry today, not the usual mild stuff."

I felt benign. "No, I've spoken to the cook and I am sure that this will be ideal for your palate."

He rubbed his hands in anticipation as the special curry was set before him. Helping himself to the plethora of side dishes and a popadom he took his first mouthful. His expression immediately changed.

"Bloody hell! His eyes were watering and he commenced to drink a glass of iced water.

"I told you that you would like it."

"Like it? It's like eating liquid fire!"

"Perhaps you would like some of our normal curry?" He pushed his plate away and was served with our curry. He took a mouthful.

"Hmm, this is all right, but that other one, it was a killer!"

From that day forth all 'curry complaints' ceased.

One of the standard duties was traffic. The appearance of the Traffic Officer at the top of the High Street was sufficient to cause many of the shops to empty of customers as they hurried to their cars and drove away, only to be greeted by road blocks situated on the main exit roads. There were always the usual offences of expired road fund licences (which often resulted in discovering expired insurances) and faulty hand brakes etc, to name but a few. At the road blocks when checking the latter item it was necessary to look inside the vehicle, as putting the right shoe on the foot brake by the driver to avoid detection of a non-existent handbrake, when the vehicle was being pushed from behind (as a simple hand brake test) was par for the course. Some vehicles that had faulty foot brakes were towed to the Police Pound for a thorough inspection. One such car having been towed away, the irate owner arrived with his lawyer who demanded the release of the vehicle. His attitude was hostile to say the least. The lawyer's car was parked just outside the Police Station, so I had it inspected. As a result his car was also towed away to the Pound. Later both he and his client pleaded guilty to a series of offences relating to unroadworthy vehicles.

Another task was taking driving tests. These were always conducted on a Friday and following my first exposure to this task, I decided that I needed to increase my life insurance cover! Having had to grab the steering wheel to avoid a collision, been bumped up the kerb, going into reverse when I expected to go forward and had a European lady burst into tears when she made a minor mistake, I suddenly became aware why there was never a rush by my colleagues to carry out this task. The second Friday was no better. It commenced with a middle aged Asian gentleman saying I should excuse his driving as he was about to have a heart attack! So was I! I had visions of never, ever reaching the ripe old age of twenty seven, and my birthday was only two weeks away. Something had to be done!

With the Assistant Superintendent's permission I had a curving 'roadway' outlined with white wooden pegs next to Headquarters and off the public roads. If the person to be tested could not reverse along its twenty yard length, there was no way I was going to let them take me onto the public highway! It worked 'like a charm'. I was to discover that if they could reverse, then, normally, I was safe and the examinee usually passed. My 'roadway' proved to be quite a crowd puller, as it was not unknown for vehicles to hook themselves onto the white pegs and become stuck with their wheels off the ground, or to hook their rear bumper onto a peg and then lurch forward, ripping the peg out of the ground. The mainly African crowd loved it, and every Friday without fail would gather to watch the 'sport', which came in handy as there was never a shortage of willing hands to lift and unhook the impaled vehicles.

One Friday morning, just prior to testing, I was sifting through the applications. I could hardly believe my eyes. Someone was bringing a huge road grader! This vehicle was in common use throughout East Africa. As most of the main road routes were earth, the graders were used to skim the surface of the road to remove the corrugations caused by rainwater. Painted yellow, they had a high cab, with very large, deeply-cleated rear wheels, with two smaller wheels at the front, where there was also a large steel blade about twelve feet across that could be raised, lowered and angled. Where could I safely test a grader? Our parade ground was made of hard-packed earth and could do with some grading... I set up some empty oil drums and some white pegs. The grader duly arrived with its normal driver, after which the African examinee and I climbed aboard. At my request he started the engine. At first I asked him to operate all the controls; he did so perfectly. Next I told him to lower the blade and to stop just before the oil drums. Again perfect. Now he was to reverse for fifty yards with the blade raised, then stop and head for the oil drums at full speed and apply the brakes when I raised my hand. I left it as late as possible and he also passed this test. At the end of the test we had only graded an area some ninety feet by twelve, but I was more than confident that this man could handle the huge machine with perfect safety and congratulated him on his skill. Later I was to use the same location and method for another would be grader driver, who, due partly to nerves but more to inability, failed my improvised test.

Living within the township was a charming old European lady who at one time had been a nurse in a leper colony. She now ran a small guest house and had 'under her wing' a number of orphan African children. She would drive into town in a large old 'Ford' car, always with a crowd of African children in the rear. She was very well known and waved in greeting as she proceeded down the High Street. Under normal circumstances this would be an acceptable thing to do, but on one occasion while waving her attention was diverted and she struck three parked cars! She was charged with 'driving without due care and attention' and the insurance companies sorted out the various claims. Two weeks later another two cars were hit! For her own and public safety, her driving licence had to be revoked.

She told the Superintendent that he was a "cruel, cruel man to treat an old lady like this." One had to feel a degree of sympathy, considering her background and age, but it would have been irresponsible to let her retain her licence.

Not all traffic duties were pleasant. One night we were called to an accident between a Land Rover and an African cyclist. Both were approaching a small hump-back bridge from opposite directions and both approaches to the bridge were downhill. The cyclist was without lights and they met head-on at the centre of the bridge. When we arrived the driver of the Land Rover was kneeling beside the cyclist and had covered him with his jacket. We carried a medical kit and I was qualified in first aid. I lifted the jacket, the cyclist was still alive but at least a three foot length of his intestine was wrapped around the smashed front wheel of his bicycle. We didn't have any morphia and I hoped that the shock had deadened the pain. Being as careful as possible, I removed the intestine from the wheel and placed it onto his stomach and covered it in a large wound dressing soaked in saline solution. I used our VHF radio and told the Police Station to alert the hospital and gave details of the cyclist's injuries. It took us over half an hour to reach the hospital and he was still alive as we passed through the entrance. Sadly, he died some moments later.

It was about this time that a new crime 'reared its ugly head'. It started in Nairobi. If a European, or Asian, was involved in a traffic accident with an African cyclist, irrespective of guilt, they would be dragged from their car by a very hostile crowd and badly beaten. I seem to recall that one driver was killed. In our area we had not had any incidents of this nature until late one afternoon when I was in my office studying a case file. A Constable rushed into my office.

"Effendi, come quickly a crowd are killing an Asian!"

He had just returned from prisoner escort duty and handed me a rifle and five rounds of ammunition. We ran some two hundred yards to where a crowd of about a hundred Africans were gathered and as we drew closer, above the noise of the crowd I could hear screams. We pushed our way into the centre, knowing that despite the fact there were only two of us, I had to seize control. There on the ground was an Asian male covered in dust with blood on his face.

I put on the sternest look that I could muster and shouted "If anyone hits this man again I will shoot them!"

It was pure bluff, but it worked. The crowd started to ease back. I turned to the nearest African and said in a fierce voice, "Did you do this?"

"No Effendi, it wasn't me."

I turned to the next one.

"Did you beat this man?"

"No Effendi, I didn't hit him."

"Then who did? Was it you?" I turned and faced another man.

"No Effendi."

"Who witnessed this accident?"

No one came forward.

"Where is the cyclist?"

"It's me Effendi." He came forward from the body of the crowd pushing a bicycle which had twisted handlebars. Apart from the damage to his bicycle he appeared to be uninjured. I tested the brakes, they were non-existent.

"You haven't any brakes! So how can you stop?"

The cyclist avoided eye contact and a lot of heads were nodding in the crowd. I was now in control.

With the Constable looking after the Asian I started his car, ordered the crowd to stand back and did a short run then applied the brakes, they were not very effective. I alighted and told the Asian his brakes were faulty. More nods from the crowd. Again I asked for witnesses to the accident and the beating, no one came forward. By this time 'backup' had arrived from the Police Station. I told the crowd that as both parties had defective brakes I was arresting both of them. It was 'the judgement of Solomon'. The crowd nodded in agreement and I told them to disperse.

It was at this juncture that I breathed a 'sigh of relief'. Phew!

The Asian was sent to the Government doctor for examination. Apart from multiple bruises and a suspected cracked rib, he was in one piece. The African cyclist was uninjured, but despite this he too was sent for a check-up. Both the Asian and the cyclist were later charged with having transport with defective brakes, and we never did manage to deduce who was responsible for the accident, or who was responsible for the assault.

Sometimes I considered our function to be 'You name it, we can do it'. We received a phone call from a European lady saying that one of her cows had gone berserk and had almost killed two of her staff. Could we come quickly!

Had she called the vet? We asked.

"Yes, but he was away for the day."

Couldn't her husband deal with it? We suggested.

"No he's also away."

How did she know that the cow was deranged?

"It's charging anyone who goes near it, and its eyes look peculiar and its salivating, Please come as soon as you can!"

I withdrew a rifle and ten rounds of ammunition from the armoury and set off for the farm.

On arrival we were met by a very agitated lady.

"It's over here in this field."

There was the cow. On seeing me it charged straight at the gate, hitting it with a loud crash! Then retreated and charged again. I loaded the rifle and aimed at the point where two imaginary diagonal lines from each horn to eye cross. It was a perfect shot and should have killed the cow instantly. It didn't. It shook it's head and staggered towards the gate again with its horns lowered. I fired a second shot. It was still standing! The third shot knocked it back onto its haunches and it was dead. I told the lady that she must inform the Government vet and that the carcass was not to be disposed of until he had carried out a post mortem.

As you will have noticed, the word 'routine' is a misnomer when dealing with police matters. One night a report was received from the African Hospital that there were noises coming from inside the mortuary. Arriving as soon as possible the police found a small number of staff had gathered by the mortuary entrance and from inside could be heard the occasional moan.

Had they checked the cause?

The shaking heads conveyed the silent message "not bloody likely!"

Had they called the Duty Doctor?

Again a shake of heads.

Inside on a slab was a body covered in a sheet from under which emanated the odd moan. The man was alive! He was rushed into the hospital and enquiries began. Evidently an unqualified African nurse, without authority and just before going off duty, had decided that this patient had died and that the 'body' should be removed to the mortuary. The poor man died shortly afterwards from (mainly) hypothermia. The subsequent inquest led to more stringent checks being imposed to avoid a repetition of this tragedy.

The African Hospital was to be our destination on another occasion. A report was received that an unqualified African male nurse was giving illegal injections and charging ten shillings a time. As any qualified person trained to use a hypodermic syringe will tell you, if air is accidentally injected into a person, death soon follows. Something had to be done. The 'nurse' had 'set up shop' in a disused store on the edge of the hospital grounds and normally opened for business at dusk. The police party were nearby in hiding. The 'nurse' was seen to enter the store and exit again with three wooden boxes which he placed just below a window, two stacked on top of each other and the third in front of the first pair, forming a kind of step. At the time it was noted that the metal-framed window had a broken pane. This would prove to be significant. Soon after dusk people were seen arriving and forming a small queue by the 'steps'. One by one the male and female 'patients' reversed up the steps and were seen to either drop their trousers or lift their skirts, placing their rumps to the window. Having descended and adjusted their dress they then handed something through the broken pane. As each 'patient' departed they were grabbed by the police and questioned. The story was basically the same. They all professed to have various illnesses and had just had a special injection that was far more powerful than anything the hospital could provide. The price was ten shillings. The police party swooped.

Our 'nurse', as it transpired, was not giving injections, but simply rubbing his victims' bare posteriors with methylated spirit, pricking them with a pin, rubbing again with methylated spirit and pocketing ten shillings from each grateful patient! He pleaded guilty to 'obtaining money by false pretences' and received six months imprisonment.

When foot and mouth was discovered in the area, unlike the UK the cattle were not slaughtered but given injections and the infected area cordoned off. Vehicles had to stop to have the undersides sprayed with disinfectant, and the tyres had to run the full length of a bed of straw soaked in the same solution. Every passenger had to alight and stamp his or her feet in the disinfectant soaked straw. This procedure would be repeated at the entrance to any infected farm. Who would believe that these precautions would present a money making opportunity...

Some months after the 'injections' incident we were called to the African Hospital yet again. Two people had been brought in suffering from shortage of breath and carrying on their clothing a very strange odour that could not be identified.

When we questioned them, all was revealed. At the time there was foot and mouth in the area and all roads and footpaths into the area were manned by the Veterinary Department. Everyone either entering by vehicle, bicycle, or on foot had to stamp their feet on straw soaked in some special chemical, and vehicle and bicycle tyres had to be sprayed with the same solution. It transpired that in yet another case of obtaining money by false pretences, two African Veterinary Scouts manning a footpath had been illegally charging everyone two shillings to pass into town. On their backs they carried tanks of disinfectant solution, attached to which was a nozzle that despatched a fine spray with which they could keep the straw moist and spray bicycles. Evidently, they had given the pair now in hospital an 'extra dose' by spraying them from head to foot, causing them to breathe in a quantity of the spray.

In East Africa there are two types of doctors; the medically qualified and witch-doctors. The latter are simply rogues living on ignorant superstition. One such person was Saa Sita (translated this means Twelve o'clock). His *modus operandi* was to use a cow horn with a small hole drilled into the tip. His 'patient' would arrive suffering, for example, with a headache.

"No problem, where does it hurt?"

The area of pain would be identified and Saa Sita would make a small incision with an unsterilised razor blade. Then, placing the cow horn over the cut, he would mutter all kinds of incantations, pausing only to suck and suck at the tip of the horn. Suddenly he would remove the horn and blow very hard into the tip. There on the floor was a scrap of human hair bound with a small piece of wire with some blood (from the wound) on it. The result: one grateful 'patient' with a cured headache and Saa Sita now ten shillings richer. Why go to hospital when you could have such first class treatment from Saa Sita?

He and all the others operated on 'mind over matter'. If he placed a curse on someone and they heard about it (and the person paying for the curse would ensure that they did), they simply died. Nothing could convince them that it was a 'load of rubbish'. In summary, witchdoctors were best described as 'con-men' with an understanding of human psychology. Saa Sita was arrested and charged with obtaining money by deception. It will not surprise you that he pleaded guilty.

I recall during my early days being called to a European farm where the store had been broken into and several sacks of maize stolen. I went there with a Corporal from Crime Branch. Before we arrived he said "Effendi, look for the man with something in his mouth." We questioned the farm labourers and sure enough there, almost as if he had a large sweet in his mouth, was one with a bulging cheek. The Corporal walked behind him and gave him a hard slap on his back. From his mouth out popped a piece of leather stitched on all sides with a slight bulge in the centre. It was a witchdoctor's *dawa* (medicine) to save the thief from arrest. He confessed 'on the spot' and the maize was recovered. We later arrested the witchdoctor for being an accessory. He also pleaded guilty.

Witchdoctors also applied basic psychology to find a thief. There were normally two methods; one used dry maize flour and the other a knife heated in a fire. Suitably dressed in skins, with the odd bone dangling here and there, the witchdoctor would have all the suspects lined up. Then, drawing circles and shapes in the earth with a pointed stick and studying these drawings very intently, he would commence to walk down the line of people, asking each in turn to put their tongue out. As we all know, when we are really frightened it is difficult to salivate. Therefore, using either method, the thief would reveal himself by not being able to swallow the dry maize flour or by his tongue being burned by the very hot knife. Normally they would confess before either of these things happened. You may have heard many stories about witchdoctors, but believe me, their 'magic' simply doesn't exist.

It was Saturday lunchtime and I was looking forward to a duty free weekend. Just as I was leaving a report came in; a European female had been indecently assaulted at the nearby hotel. I walked to the hotel and entered by the side door. Now let me digress slightly. My height is five feet eight and a half inches, the minimum height for the Kenya Police. As I entered the hotel I was instantly grabbed by a huge European male and lifted completely off my feet! The peak of my hat finished up above my right ear and my uniform jacket half way up my chest. His face was now about an inch away from mine.

"Are you looking for me?"

His breath was fetid and smelled strongly of drink. I surmised that for me to say "you are under arrest" was not ideal in the current situation! The best I could manage, and hopefully avoid annihilation, was, "It depends what you've been up to."

He put me down and repositioned my hat. I realised that I would have to call for reinforcements. I asked to use the phone. Soon help was on its way...

The girl who alleged she had been assaulted was the hotel receptionist and she was obviously very upset. That day she had been wearing a low-cut Spanish-type blouse and when leaning forward across the reception desk, had revealed somewhat more than when in the vertical position. In order to ascertain the true extent of this exposure, a European male had put his hand down the front of her blouse. Who and where was this man? You've guessed it! It was the 'giant' who had 'greeted' me at the side door. It took five of us to get him through the hotel entrance and the idea of using a car to take him to the Police Station was ridiculous! The easiest method was in the back of a Land Rover.

We called the Government Doctor to examine him but he was very busy. Could we bring this man to the hospital? Another struggle ensued as we entered the hospital. At this stage our prisoner was handcuffed with his hands behind his back. The doctor refused to examine a man in handcuffs and despite the fact that we went to great lengths to explain just how long it had taken to put them on, they had to come off.

This was not a good idea!

At this juncture the prisoner was on the floor with five of us holding him down. I had visions of a Spanish fighting bull as it enters the ring looking for trouble and hopping mad! I was not wrong; once released he stood up and crashed through the swing doors, making his way at speed towards the first ward. With us in hot pursuit he crashed through the doors of the maternity ward amidst screams from mothers and mothers to be. He was brought down by one of my colleagues with a rugby tackle and 'battle' commenced all over again, to a chorus of screams from at least twenty agitated females.

It was utter chaos!

Back at the Police Station he spent the weekend in the cells and was taken to Court on Monday morning a changed man. Docile and very apologetic he pleaded guilty to the two charges. The hospital matron was called to give her version of events and our 'giant' received six months imprisonment.

So much for my off-duty weekend!

The standard practice with regard to vacating a hotel room has changed very little across the years. Some establishments insist that guests leave by 11.00am and others twelve noon. One European-run hotel had the 11.00am rule. From 10.00am onwards the cleaning ladies had tried to gain access to one of the rooms without success and obeyed the 'Do Not Disturb' notice hanging on the door handle. Just before mid-day they alerted the hotel manger who, having banged on the door and received no response, used his pass key to gain entry. The door had been jammed with some heavy object and would only partly open. Nothing could be seen through the narrow gap and we were called to assist.

Two of us, plus the manager, succeeded in forcing open the door. Slouched on the bed, fully clothed was a European man holding a part filled bottle of brandy. On the floor were five empty bottles and in an open suitcase beside the bed another six full bottles. He was unshaven, had yellow 'crusts' around his eyes and the room stank of brandy and human body odour. In basic terms, he was in one hell of a state! He was incapable of speech. We had to get him to hospital where they used a stomach pump and managed to save his life. The doctor said that in another few hours he would have died from alcoholic poisoning. He was later charged with being drunk and incapable. As it was a tragic case, he received a '36.1', which meant that he was convicted, but without fine or imprisonment.

Some two weeks later I was driving towards the Police Station and noticed a Morris van coming towards me in a series of lurches. My initial suspicion was that the driver had a problem with his clutch or that the engine was suffering from fuel starvation, but as I drove past I saw that the driver was slumped over the wheel and I recognised him as our '36.1' client. I stopped my car, rapidly reversed, jumped out and ran after him. As he was going so slowly, I soon caught up with the vehicle, reached inside, switched off the ignition and removed the key.

I opened his door, saying, "You are under arrest and I want you to get of out this van."

He looked at me all bleary-eyed and muttered some obscenity. I grabbed him and pulled him onto the road and, as he was struggling, I rolled him onto his face and put an arm lock on. Reinforcements soon arrived and he was placed in the cells. At court next morning there was no repeat of the 36.1 – he received six months imprisonment, which I hoped would 'dry him out' but I had very little doubt that he would 'not make old bones' and that at some point in the not too distant future, his drinking would kill him.

Drink was the root cause of most African assaults, however, the following case was pre-meditated murder...

Two African members of the Investigation Team arrested a well-known villain for burglary. It was at night and they made two major errors that would result in one of them being killed.

1. they failed to search the man, and
2. two, didn't handcuff him to one of themselves.

As they and their prisoner made their way on foot along a dirt road back to the Police Station, they were overtaken by a bus. They parted company; one detective staying with the arrested man, the other going to the opposite side of the road. When the dust cleared from the passing bus one detective lay on the roadside dying. He had been stabbed and the arrested man had disappeared. It was a tragic loss that could so easily have been avoided. The killer was eventually traced, convicted for his crime and hanged.

The African population commenced to form itself into various political parties and everyone, irrespective of race, was talking about Independence. This gave rise to some unusual incidents and, not surprisingly, the African 'con-men' had a field day with their very gullible cousins...

An Asian shopkeeper telephoned, stating that two Africans had entered his shop and insisted on checking his stock. Evidently they had given a large sum of money to a con-man, having believed him when he told them that the shop would be theirs the day after Independence.

Another trick was to accost 'country bumpkins' visiting town and engage them in conversation, asking if they would like to own a car?

Not surprisingly, the usual reply was "Yes please." But how could this be achieved?

They would be taken to a car park and told to wander around and choose a car. Reporting back to the 'seller', they were then sold a raffle ticket for ten shillings with the vehicle number on it and told to return the day after Independence to collect the car of their choice.

The most bizarre story I heard was from a European lady who worked in Nairobi. She made it known that she was returning to England. Later that day she was approached by one of the African clerks who told her, "You cannot go home... you are mine after Independence."

With the constant talk of independence for Kenya, various African political parties were formed and their candidates toured the Colony giving speeches about what they would do when in power. These meetings were normally held in football stadiums and our job was to keep a low profile but maintain law and order within the stadium. Outside would be a large Police Riot Squad, but inside perhaps just ten of us would be keeping an eye on the excited crowd containing elements from both supporting and opposition parties. It was a 'tinderbox' situation that could easily explode into violence. Again the only approach was humour. By using this, many incidents were averted and I was always thankful when each meeting was over. I recall Tom Mboya (who was later assassinated by a rival party) saying, "*Wakati ya uhuru, wazungu wata rudi yao, na wahindi wata shika mkia ya ngombe.*" (At the time of independence, the Europeans will return to their homeland and the Asians will grab the cow's tail.), the final few words being a typical African saying. Change was in the air.

9   Minus wig and gown

It was 9.15am. The telephone jangled on my desk. It was the Assistant Superintendent's secretary.

"You are wanted immediately."

"Is it good news, or bad news?"

"I have no idea, and don't delay."

What could it be? I tried to think if I had 'dropped any clangers'. Nothing came to mind. I entered the 'holy of holies'.

"Good morning Sir. You sent for me?"

"Yes, you can pack your bags. You are off to Nairobi. You have been selected to attend a training course for Court Prosecutors. The course starts on Monday."

"How long is the course Sir?"

"Months, and if you are any good, following the course you'll be in someone's chambers. So it could be many months. My secretary will give you the details."

I was dismissed. This had come like a 'bolt from the blue', a Prosecutor's course in Nairobi. I would be leaving all my friends and my current curvaceous blonde girlfriend Liz, not to mention the local trout fishing. The details stated that I was booked into the Police Mess in Nairobi for the duration of the course. I had already passed my Section One of the Kenya Police law exam, but this was just basic stuff, and I did not feel qualified to become a Court Prosecutor.

I knew from my brief court appearances as a police witness, that if I qualified I would be 'doing battle' with experienced Advocates (here we call them Barristers) in First Class Magistrates' Courts. It was a daunting prospect. I packed my bags and set off for Nairobi.

Maybe I was helped by my liking for history or my ability to remember historical dates, because I took to the Law 'like a duck to water'. I could remember section and even page numbers from *Archbold's Criminal Pleadings*, vital sections of *Indian Law* (Kenya's law was in the main based on the Indian Penal Code, and 'case law' was based on the British Courts.) There were daily lectures and I am sure that we developed writer's cramp from the daily recording of copious notes. Evening study was imperative, so there was very little time available for nights out in Nairobi. In addition to private study, some evenings we would quiz each other on certain aspects of the law and failure to agree on a specific point would send everyone scurrying to their rooms to trace in the law books the relevant section in dispute.

Unlike qualified Barristers who had to study Roman Law and Tort, we concentrated solely on Criminal Law. As a result of this concentration I was to discover later that sometimes my knowledge of this subject could exceed that of some of my 'learned friends', the nomenclature used in Court when referring to the defence.

As there were constant weekly tests, normally conducted on Fridays, it ensured that Thursday night was when everyone 'burned the mid-night oil'. As the weeks turned into months, we became more and more steeped in Kenya's Criminal Laws. The course ended with a lengthy final examination. When the results were announced, I was one of three selected to join a Crown Counsel (Government Barrister) in Chambers. A small part, but a very essential part of the course, was public speaking. During my period as a Prosecutor, and later when I finally returned to England, the skills so acquired 'stood me in very good stead'.

Once again I packed my bags and headed North to Nyeri and my new position as assistant to the local Crown Counsel. We had an instant rapport and Jeff Twelftree was an excellent tutor. I would be handed a police case file that had been forwarded for study prior to prosecution. My job was to read the file and then give an opinion on the following:

1. Was the police charge sheet correct in every detail?
2. Did the evidence support a 'case to answer'?

If the answer to the above two questions was 'yes', it meant that the Crown could justify the case being brought against the accused.

The next step was to ascertain if there were any weaknesses in the prosecution's case (what might the accused say to 'wriggle off the hook', etc) and, if so, to request the CID to seek more evidence on these points. This final step was, to my mind, the key to a successful prosecution. Perhaps unappreciated by the general public is the onus placed on the Prosecution, who have to prove 'beyond all reasonable doubt' that an accused person is 'guilty as charged' whereas the Defence has the easier task. All they have to do is to establish, no matter how tenuously, that an element of doubt exists.

Jeff would listen to my theories and findings and make constructive comments.

Prior to attending any Court cases with my tutor, my job was to study the case file and highlight any areas that could be subject to 'case law'. Case Law is when there has been a legal dispute which has been settled by the Law Lords. An example could be that someone had been found drunk in charge of a vehicle, but the vehicle could not be started. As it could not be driven on the road by the accused, was it a motor vehicle within the meaning of the Act? Therefore, assuming that the accused had been convicted, he could then lodge an appeal against the conviction. The Law Lords would subsequently give a ruling. This then becomes 'case law' to which every judge, magistrate and barrister can refer.

If Jeff Twelftree agreed with my findings, my next task was to consult the relevant law books and tag the appropriate section or sections. We always entered Court with a pile of law books with all applicable case law highlighted with paper tags. If the defence claimed that there was 'no case to answer' in that the prosecution had failed to prove its case (as in the above example), we were 'armed' and ready to quote the latest 'case law'. The most important lesson I absorbed from Jeff Twelftree was very detailed preparation.

I always enjoyed watching him in action. He never wasted any words, unlike some defence Counsels, who would drone on and on, particularly when they tried to counter our claim that there was a 'case to answer'. I often felt that this was their attempt to make their client feel that he was 'getting his money's worth'. It quickly became apparent that due to his preparation, Jeff could instantly quote sections of the law 'chapter and verse', much to the embarrassment of any Defence Counsel who had just asked for a brief adjournment to look up the section in dispute. I was personally to experience such a situation when I commenced prosecuting with Jeff sitting beside me.

Having been in Chambers for some time and having become more adept at my job, Jeff and I would have a small bet on each case's outcome; not only if a conviction would be obtained, but also the sentence. If we were not appearing in Court that day, the loser would pay for morning coffee and hot sausage rolls at the White Rhino Hotel, which was within easy walking distance of his chambers.

We continued to have an excellent rapport, and I continued to 'soak up' the law and Court procedures like a sponge. It was an interesting, absorbing and enjoyable time.

As the weeks went by I was very conscious that I was missing Liz, my girlfriend. We exchanged letters, but it was not like the real thing. As a result, although she was several hundred miles away, some weekends I drove back 'home', arriving at a about 1am and leaving on the Sunday night to be back in Nyeri by about 2am. These occasional weekend breaks, although tiring, provided a very welcome respite from the law.

The CID delivered a murder case file which, as part of the pre-Court analysis, I had to read. Despite the passage of years, the broad facts are still clear in my mind. Several Mau-Mau terrorists had been arrested and accused of butchering a number of their own people. The sole survivor of this savage attack was a young boy. The gang had entered his village and for no apparent reason seized several men and women and taken them deep into the forest. That night they had been bound with hands behind their backs and led in pairs to the edge of a deep cleft in the ground. There they were killed, their bodies falling down into the cleft.

Finally, it was the boy's turn. He was bound in the same manner together with a woman. They killed her first, but as her body fell she dragged the little boy (who was still alive) with her. He fell onto the pile of warm, blood-soaked bodies and, by the Grace of God, managed to free himself. Some members of the gang, realising that he was still alive, started searching for him. Trembling with fear, he hid in the shadows of the bank and they failed to find him. Hours later, he clawed his way out of the deep cleft and in the half moonlight made his way back to his village and reported the killings.

I was in the Supreme Court at Nyeri when Jeff Twelftree asked the boy if he could identify the people involved. From the Witness Box and without any hesitation he identified the killers. His testimony, supported by other evidence, secured a conviction against all the accused. I felt a deep sense of satisfaction when they were sentenced by the Judge to be hanged for their appalling crime.

Another case file I studied prior to prosecution involved a Kikuyu girl aged about eighteen. Her father had refused to take any Mau-Mau oaths and forbade his family to partake in any such ceremonies. His daughter ignored her father's wishes and attended an oathing ceremony. Later, she helped local Mau-Mau supporters kill her father. This was achieved by pinning his shoulders to the ground and holding his legs in the air. She then kept jumping very lightly on his chest until he was asphyxiated. She then helped carry her father's body, which was thrown down a pit latrine. It may amaze the reader that a daughter could do this to her own father, but the Mau-Mau oaths were designed to be so vile and binding that once having taken them, there was no going back, and the person so oathed had placed themselves 'beyond the pail'.

The opening of any Supreme Court Sessions was always a grand affair wherever it was held and Nyeri was no exception. The judge arrived in his red gown and long judge's wig to be watched by a large multi-racial crowd. The police always provided a guard of honour with fixed bayonets, led by a Chief Inspector wearing No.1 uniform, white gloves and carrying a sword. When giving the order "Present arms!" the officer, holding the sword vertically and at elbow's length in front of his body, would raise the hilt to just in front of his face, then rapidly, and in unison with the honour guard, 'drop' the sword point to the ground. At this juncture the judge would bow, the officer would give the order "shoulder arms!" and again in unison with the honour guard, he would quickly return the sword to its vertical position in front of his face, prior to resuming the original position. Evidently during a previous pre-Supreme Court ceremony the judge had been standing a little too close and was still bending as the sword point was raised. The Chief Inspector found himself facing a 'scalped' judge with the judge's wig impaled on the end if his sword! However, on this occasion at Nyeri the Judge's wig remained in place.

During this period the Russians launched a rocket into space with a dog on board. The world's media was crammed with details of this outstanding achievement. The dog was named 'Lemonchuk'. However, what goes up must come down. The following morning on our way to the 'White Rhino' for morning coffee, we passed a small dog with a placard around its neck, stating in English *"My name is 'Lemonchuk', anyone finding me should take me to the nearest Police Station without delay."* According to local insider sources, we later learned that a junior CID Officer was the culprit.

With Jeff Twelftree at my side I commenced my prosecution career. My first ever case was undefended (thank goodness) and despite its lack of complications, I read the file again and again. We secured a conviction, as we did with the second case. By the third case I was 'warming to my subject' and, with hindsight, became somewhat overconfident. The case was a straightforward assault involving two Africans. The complainant was taken to hospital and I had to establish what treatment he received. I addressed the African 'dresser' who had been called as a witness.

"When the complainant arrived at the hospital what treatment did he receive?"

"Two aspirins," came the reply.

The Magistrate intervened.

"I didn't quite catch that Mr Tompkins. What did he receive?"

"Two aspirins, your Honour, the cure for all ills."

There was the odd titter from the back of the Court. The Magistrate put his pen down.

"The Court will adjourn. I wish to see the Prosecutor in Chambers."

"You're in trouble!" Jeff said.

I knocked on the Magistrate's door and entered. He was not looking very happy. What had I done? I was about to find out!

"I want you to understand that I will not have my courtroom turned into a music hall! In future you will refrain from making glib remarks and act in a proper manner. Is that clear?"

"Yes your Honour, and I apologise for my bad behaviour."

I had learned a lesson.

As the months went by, from the initial minor cases I slowly progressed to more and more complicated cases and finally to a murder trial. It may surprise the reader that as a person unqualified in law I could represent the Crown in a murder trial, but the procedure is the same in this country. The Crown has to prove before a Lower Court that there is a 'case to answer'. Having established this, the accused will later appear before (in this country) the 'Quarter Sessions', or as we had in Kenya the 'Supreme Court'. The method of presenting the Crown's case in the Lower Courts (known as a First Class Magistrate's Court) is vital, as normally it is only this evidence that can be used by the prosecution when appearing before the Supreme Court to present its case. Therefore, the Prosecutor presenting the case for the Crown before the Lower Court, has to ensure that every scrap of evidence is produced in a logical sequence, and that any exhibits have a 'chain of evidence', and are produced and identified by the correct witnesses.

Just to explain the term 'chain of evidence'. From the moment an exhibit is handled, either by a member of the public or a police officer, it has to be identified in Court by that person. If during the investigation the exhibit is handed to someone else, for example, to test for bloodstains or fingerprints, then that person also has to appear before the Court to identify the exhibit, and state from whom it was received and to whom it was handed. This way, there can be no doubt that the exhibits are the actual ones collected at the scene, or later found during the course of the investigation, and now produced before the Court.

The murder case that I was about to prosecute was rather bizarre and, due to its complexity, had involved Jeff Twelftree and myself in some very prolonged and intensive preparation. It involved some African men driving two huge contracted tractors to plough a very large field. As it was being ploughed at night some of the farm labourers asked if they could 'have a go'. The contracted drivers were delighted as they could sleep in the cab and be paid for it! After several nights of driving these huge tractors in addition to working throughout the day, the involved farm labourers, due to lack of sleep, began to exhibit tempers that were easily aroused.

One night two farm labourers had a disagreement as to who was next in the driving seat. It culminated in one being hit over the head with a large steel towing pin and having his skull stove in. Now there was a state of panic. As both tractors were ploughing some distance behind one another and in parallel, the accused and the real driver dragged the body into the path of the oncoming second tractor and placed it into a small hollow, hoping that the body would not be picked out by the oncoming tractor's lights, and that as a result, the driver would think that he had run over the sleeping man and killed him, and that the severe head wound would be attributed to the 'accident'.

This is precisely what happened. The other tractor's 'crew' did not see the body until they had just passed over it. Naturally they were in a state of panic. What could they do? In the far distance they could see the headlights of the other oncoming tractor. Why not drag the body into its path, then they would think that *they* had run over him and killed him. Just like the others, they placed the body into a hollow directly in the other tractor's path.

Some fifteen minutes later, the actual murderer and his fellow accomplice had the 'shock of their lives'; their colleague hadn't been killed! Somehow he had crawled about twenty yards from where they had left him, and now, there he was, illuminated by the tractor's lights! They stopped the tractor and went to check. He was definitely dead.

Rather than bore the reader with even more bizarre details, the police were called, managed to sort out the mass of complications, and as a result, with Jeff sitting beside me, I was about to present my first ever murder case for the Crown.

As you would expect, the case was to be defended by a Barrister (remember in Kenya they were called Advocates.) As usual we entered the Court fully prepared and with a pile of law books, suitably tagged. Sitting to our left and at the same level was the defence, consisting of an Advocate and his Assistant. As this was in a First Class Magistrate's Court they wore the usual dress of black jacket, white shirt with a 'silvery' tie and black and grey finely striped trousers, plus (as you would expect) black shoes. The Magistrate entered the Court, we all rose and bowed. The Magistrate then bowed and took his seat on the Bench.

My first task was to give a very brief summary of the prosecution case and then, with the Court's permission, call the first and subsequent witnesses for the Crown. The prosecution case lasted several days until finally it was proven that there was a 'case to answer'. Now it was the turn of the defence to present their client's case. This was to involve the production of several documents, which were mainly sketches and plans. Documentary evidence is fairly complex, and the law is very clear as to what can and cannot be produced before the Court, the subject being covered by several chapters in *Archbold's Criminal Pleading*.

The defence Advocate rose to address the Court.

"With your Honour's permission I now wish to produce this document in evidence…"

But he had not mentioned under which section it was being submitted. Jeff tapped my foot with his shoe. Due to our preparation we realised that the defence case would almost certainly involve the production of documentary evidence. I knew what to do. I stood to address the Court.

"Your Honour, as my 'learned friend' is aware, there are several chapters covering the submission of documentary evidence. May I suggest that the Court be made aware under which section the defence proposes to submit this document."

The Magistrate agreed.

"Thank you Mr. Tompkins for your submission."

My 'learned friend' was looking flustered.

"It's the usual section, your Honour, dealing with documentary proof."

Jeff tapped my foot again. I again rose to my feet.

"Your Honour, I wish to stress yet again, the Court and the prosecution, need to be made aware of the relevant section."

My 'learned friend', who had obviously not 'done his homework', was looking even more flustered and virtually repeated his original submission.

"It's the usual section your Honour covering this type of document."

Jeff tapped my foot again. I again rose to my feet.

"With the Court's permission, may I direct my 'learned friend' to chapter (I quoted 'chapter and verse').

The Magistrate said, "Thank you Mr Tompkins for your information. The Court will now adjourn for ten minutes to give the Defence time to check under which section they wish to submit this document."

He rose, we all bowed and he exited the courtroom, and the press and the public were cleared. With the courtroom devoid of the public my 'learned friend' now 'exploded'.

"I have never been so humiliated in all my life! How dare you make me look a fool in front of this Court! You, you…"

He was lost for words.

Jeff was directly behind me saying in a low voice, "Demand an apology."

I cleared my throat.

"I am only doing my job and I demand an apology."

I was now facing a very irate 'learned friend'.

"Apologise to you? Never in a thousand years! I'll be damned if I will give you an apology!" He turned away and, with much heavy breathing, commenced talking to his legal colleague and hurriedly consulting his law books.

Some minutes later the Court reconvened, the public returned, the document was submitted under the correct section and the case continued. The following morning a messenger called at 'our' Chambers with a letter of apology addressed to me.

This example of thorough preparation is something that I never overlooked, and often I was to discover that despite being 'learned friends', who referred to me (as a person unqualified in law) as, 'my friend', very often they failed to 'do their homework' properly.

Soon after this incident Jeff felt satisfied that I could cope on my own and it was a sad day when we parted company. I had learned so much from him including the 'language of the court' but from now on I had 'to stand on my own two feet'. I returned to my previous posting and commenced my solo prosecution career...

I was asked by the Assistant Superintendent to withdraw a traffic case against a European. He stated the he had received a telephone call from one of the local Advocates, saying that in the event of the case going to Court, one of the investigating officers would be charged with perjury or, if this failed, for giving false information. I asked to see the case file. The broad details were: A four wheel drive vehicle going down an incline on a wet earth road had gone out of control and skidded approximately one hundred and fifty feet up the other side of the incline and struck an oncoming car, injuring the occupants. The call from the Advocate was based on two things. One, the driver of the other vehicle was the guilty party and could be in collusion with the police; and two, the distance that his client's vehicle was alleged to have skidded up the incline was impossible, in other words, the Police Officers were lying.

I read all the details, visited the scene with the investigating officer, and checked his note book for his sketches made when he first arrived at the scene. I also checked the statements of the people who were in the other vehicle. I could not see any reason for the police to withdraw their prosecution and I failed to see how any charges could be brought against the investigating officer concerned.

The Kenya Government produced a road safety leaflet (similar in content to the one issued here), which, amongst other things, gave average braking distances per speed of a vehicle. Armed with this information, plus the contents of the police file, I managed to convince my boss that we should proceed with the case. He very reluctantly agreed.

The case was defended, as you may have guessed, by the self-same Advocate who had made the phone call. In my final summing up, I submitted that there was a 'case to answer'. My 'learned friend' submitted otherwise. In summary, the Magistrate agreed with me. We had 'cleared the first hurdle'. The defence now called their client who swore under oath that he had not been driving dangerously on the wet, slippery road. Under my cross-examination he didn't 'budge an inch'. The defence now called their key witness. He produced the Government road safety leaflet. Being a Government publication it did not have to be 'proved', and I had no objection to it being submitted in evidence. The key witness was now asked by the defence to quote from this leaflet the average breaking distances at varying speeds. He did so. The defence now played their 'trump card'.

"Having visited the scene, and from the facts that you have stated from that leaflet, in your opinion, could my client's vehicle have skidded at least one hundred and fifty feet up the other side of the incline?"

As I expected the answer was "No."

Now it was my turn to cross examine this key witness and, thanks to Jeff Twelftree's training, I also had a copy of the self-same leaflet in front of me, which I had carefully studied.

I addressed the key witness.

"Can you please tell the Court if the facts that you have stated refer to what type of road surface? Can I direct your attention to the small print directly below the statistics."

The witness studied the leaflet.

"Tarmac."

"You have visited the scene of this accident with the accused, is that correct?"

"Yes."

"Will you now tell the Court what type of road surface did you see there?"

"It was an earth road your Honour." This was my first key point to shatter the defence's case.

Now for number two!

"I want you now to look at the small print at the end of the section referring to braking distances, it is the penultimate paragraph. Now will you please read out to the Court what it says."

"For dry earth roads, all the braking distances referred to above should be doubled."

I could see my 'learned friend' was 'tearing his hair out'!

Now for my next key point.

"Thank you. Now we have heard from the accused that his speed never exceeded forty five miles an hour. If we accept this as a fact, can you tell the Court the stopping distance on a dry earth road at this speed?" The witness consulted the leaflet again.

"Three hundred and fifty feet."

I was about to demolish the defence case.

"Now, both the accused and the police witnesses have stated that it was raining and the road was wet, have they not?"

"Yes."

"So the statistics for a dry earth road do not apply, do they?"

"No."

"The incline you referred to in your evidence was in your words 'shallow'. Is that correct?"

"Yes."

"Will you now read out to the Court the final paragraph that appears directly below the one referring to dry earth roads."

"For wet earth roads the above distances must be doubled."

"And double three hundred and fifty is, you will agree, seven hundred feet?"

"Yes."

I glanced at my 'learned friend'. His face was a picture of despair! I was enjoying every moment!

"The police evidence only alleges one hundred and fifty feet, a mere twenty one percent of the distance you have quoted?

"Yes."

"Faced with these new facts, plus your own observations, will you now agree with me that the police evidence regarding the length of the skid marks of the Accused's vehicle must be an accurate and true assessment?"

There was a long pause, he glanced at the defence Advocate and said in a soft voice, "Yes."

We had won!

The main reason for my exultation was not only winning my first solo defended case, but the fact that the defence had tried to 'browbeat' the police into having the case withdrawn. The Magistrate pronounced sentence and my 'learned friend' left the Court with a face like thunder.

I was often to 'do battle' with this local Advocate and every time it was very evident that I was not the 'flavour of the month'!

The cases that were placed onto my desk ranged from the petty right through to murder, so my work in Court was mainly routine but also included some very interesting cases, and from time to time some amusing incidents.

One day a case was being defended by a certain well known Asian Advocate. Suddenly he let out a very loud belch. The Magistrate looked up in annoyance and my 'learned friend' continued as if nothing had happened. A few moments later he belched again. The magistrate put his pen down.

"Mr Patel, I must object to the disgusting noises that you are making. Will you please desist."

Mr Patel looked quite surprised at the magistrate's comments, and said, "Your Honour must excuse me, but it is the hot gases rising from my stomach."

The next amusing incident was with another Advocate who had just qualified in England. He was cross-examining his witness and asked a leading question. What is a leading question? Let me give a brief hypothetical example. The defence or the prosecution cannot ask "Did you see the knife in the hand of the accused?" or even, "What was the accused holding in his hand?" Depending on the evidence, it may be possible to ask "Did you see anything in the hand of the accused?" to avoid any possibility of leading the witness into stating that the accused was holding anything at all, but perhaps the best question to be asked, is, "What was the accused doing?" This is a totally open question and therefore not 'leading' in any way.

To return to the newly qualified Advocate, I objected.

"This is a leading question your Honour."

"I agree Mr Tompkins." The Magistrate nodded to the defence to proceed. He again asked a leading question. Again I objected and the Magistrate agreed. My 'learned friend' tried a third time with the same result.

Eventually he turned to the Magistrate and asked, "Your Honour, what else can I say?"

Another basic case was that of a European farmer. He had been arrested and brought before the Court. When sentenced previously for some minor offence he had been fined and had asked for time to pay, which had been granted. The fourteen days had expired and soon after this he was arrested due to its non-payment. He stood in the dock and was asked by the Magistrate if he had the amount of the fine in his possession.

He was very flippant and said, "Good God no! On a Tuesday?"

The magistrate was not amused.

"Twenty eight days imprisonment in lieu of non-payment of fine. Take him away."

The farmer's flippancy melted in an instant.

"You can't do this to me, I refuse to go to prison!"

The Magistrate put his pen down.

"Unless you vacate the dock immediately, I will double your sentence for contempt of Court. Do you understand what I am saying to you?"

Without any more utterances the accused meekly left the dock under police escort to be taken to the local prison. His wife paid his fine that afternoon and he was released the same evening, a somewhat changed man.

During my time at this Court I was to experience another example of 'lack of homework'. It was a traffic case and part of the evidence hinged on the fact that the vehicle's steering was defective. I had proved that there was a 'case to answer' and now the defence Advocate proceeded to call his witnesses. One witness was placed before the Court as 'an expert witness'. Any witness so designated either by the prosecution, or the defence, can be subjected to cross-examination to establish whether or not the title of 'expert' is justified. As it was a defence witness I was about to carry out the cross-examination.

During his evidence this witness had constantly referred to vehicle mechanics as, "The rank and file of the motoring world."

I rose to my feet.

"Will you please tell the Court which University you attended."

"I didn't attend University."

"Then can you tell the Court which Technical College you attended?"

"I didn't attend any Technical College."

"I see. Surely you must possess some technical qualifications and if so what are they?"

"I do not possess any technical qualifications, but I have been in the trade for many years."

"But that is all you have to offer?"

"Well, yes."

"Based on the evidence you have just given, would it be fair to say that you are no better and no worse than, in your own words, "the rank and file of the motoring world?"

At this the 'expert' witness more than bridled!

"How dare you speak to me like this! I didn't come here to be insulted!"

The Magistrate intervened.

"Will you please answer the Prosecutor's question."

With a very flushed face the defence witness replied, "I have been in the motoring trade for years and I know what I'm talking about!"

We secured a conviction but I made another enemy.

Within the township we had a young Somali who was a rogue of the worst type. His basic *modus operandi* was the 'three card trick'. Anyone realising that they had been tricked and demanding their money back was threatened with assault and if they persisted were assaulted. He had a string of convictions and appeared before the Court on a regular basis. His father was well known for his 'bloody minded' attitude to any form of authority so I decided to 'kill two birds with one stone'. Following yet another conviction I applied to the Court to have the son bound over to keep the peace and for his father to stand as surety in the sum of two thousand shillings (£100), which in 1959 was no mean sum of money. The Court agreed with my request and the father and son left the Court, evidently cursing me in Somali. I later learned via the informer network that they had threatened to have me killed. Despite the alleged threats I remained unharmed and for the remainder of my time in the area the thought of having to forfeit two thousand shillings to the *Serkali* (Government) ensured that the father made his son 'toe the line'.

A case file arrived on my desk for perusal and comments. It concerned the theft of electrical power. The accused was Asian and the owner of the local grinding mill where the local farming community could have their maize ground into *posho* flour. It was a flourishing business as *posho* is a basic indigenous food. The local Electricity Company (flippantly known as 'East African Power & Darkness) could not understand how someone using a series of very powerful electric motors had monthly bills not much greater than a normal domestic bill. As a result they did a snap check whereupon they discovered that, situated on top of the electric meter was a very powerful magnet. The effect was alleged to slow down the disc that rotates inside the meter to record consumption. But the case had some loopholes. What had not been established was the exact effect this particular magnet would have on this particular electric meter, nor had a detailed check been made on past levels of consumption. The final item required was the record kept by the grinding company of their daily tonnage that the Court could compare with their alleged consumption of electricity.

Once I had these new facts I was satisfied that we should proceed to prosecution. The case was defended, but the story told by the accused was so utterly unconvincing and so easy to 'tear apart' that my task was made very easy as he almost convicted himself. The outcome to my mind was a foregone conclusion – we secured a conviction.

Following a reasonable period of time as a Prosecutor I was promoted and sent to take over a very large area that bordered Uganda. I was about to face another totally different environment and people.

10   When love is in the air

Before delving into cupid's activities under the East African sun, I wish to draw the attention of all male readers with daughters of marriageable age to a little known fact – namely that there is an African alternative to a matrimonial tradition which has existed in the UK for centuries. Indeed, no African father would countenance adopting the British tradition, even when 'blotto'!

Let us begin with the typically British scenario...

A couple marry and later produce a beautiful baby daughter. Over the ensuing years they nurture, clothe and feed her and ensure that she has the best possible education. We now enter the teenage years. The cost of clothing soars, not only as the young lady outgrows each item, but as fashion, that scourge of many a father's bank balance, takes its terrible toll. Now come the boyfriends and the trauma every parent experiences as they wait up at night for their daughter's safe return. If this is not enough, there are the failed love affairs and resultant tears!

Now we come to the crux of the matter. Over the years the cost of having this delightful daughter has been a small fortune. If you doubt this statement, I suggest you sit down with a calculator and a large brandy. The latter will be needed when the calculations are complete.

Now 'out of the blue' your daughter announces she has met 'Mr Right' and she is bringing him home to meet you and your wife.

Your first impressions are not very good.

"He's too smooth for my liking," you think to yourself, but with your wife all smiles and showering Mr Right with tea and home made cakes, progress towards the inevitable commences.

It's a slow build up, one advantage being that your wife is no longer worried when your daughter is late coming home... but beware, you are being softened up for 'the scalping'!

As expected, they announce their wish to marry. With a forced smile you agree, realising what you have agreed to. This daughter has cost you over the years thousands and thousands of pounds, not to mention the odd sleepless night, and here you are planning to give her away at enormous cost so that Mr Right can whisk off with her for free!

Post wedding, you (the father) sit down amidst the remains of the wedding breakfast, noting your wife's tears, not due to the fact that you are now several thousand pounds 'out of pocket', but to happiness.

Having read the foregoing, you must agree it's a crazy system!

In East Africa, however, fathers have it 'sussed'. It is called 'bride price' and the sooner we introduce this system into this country the better! This is how it works.

You, the ardent African male, spot a comely female. You note her broad shoulders, ideal for digging your vegetable patch, her sturdy child-bearing hips and furthermore it has not escaped your attention in passing by her village that she has been seen helping to prepare home made beer! On reflection you feel that she is just what you are looking for, so you approach her father and ask how much he wants to release his daughter. The haggling takes several weeks. The father says she's very good at tilling his small *shamba* (field), can wring a chicken's neck with ease, is very useful about the house… and how will he survive without someone to carry the water and the firewood? She is a 'jewel' that he is reluctant to let go. The would-be son-in-law states that he would really like her to be a bit fatter, but, providing the price is right he's willing to take a chance. Finally they settle on a 'bride price' and it's not cheap! At least ten cows, which the father will select himself from the young man's herd. Two 'drinks' of beer, not pints you understand, but two 44-gallon drums filled to the brim, plus several thousand shillings. They shake hands and the deal is done!

Any European father reading this page who already has a married daughter will appreciate immediately what he has missed out on! And any father with single daughters will find himself thinking what he might have in place of a future overdraft. Without any doubt African fathers have the right idea when it comes to marriage.

However, during the 1950s, for young unmarried European males, courtship in Kenya was not without its dangers, and I do not refer to terrorist activity or the criminal classes. I refer to 'situations'. Every summer, Swiss finishing schools would discharge hordes of young ladies to the four corners of the earth, a reasonable percentage of whom would be later found alighting at Nairobi airport. As a result there existed a smouldering situation, requiring only the slightest thing to set eager hearts thudding in youthful breasts. Young ladies who had been cooped up in Switzerland for months on end were about to meet up with bronzed, red-blooded colonial males; add to this smart uniforms, winning smiles and the heat of the African sun and anything could happen – and usually did!

A colleague of mine met one of these damsels and was 'swept off his feet'. She was young, vivacious, beautiful, kind – everything he had ever wanted. He took her out to dinners and dances; he was besotted. Her parents owned a large estate some miles out of town and were avid gardeners. They imported exotic plants, had scores of rose bushes and the house was surrounded by immaculate green lawns studded with frangipani, hibiscus, flame trees and jacaranda. Against this backdrop the house was approached by a wide sweeping gravelled drive. In order to maintain this floral haven they employed several gardeners. Viewed from the dirt road that fronted the property it was a sight to behold, the sun casting deep shadows onto the lawns and in the bright blue sky, big 'puff balls' of clouds passing lazily overhead. An idyllic scene, showing just what could be done with virgin African bush and British flair!

Tim had taken the 'love of his life' out to dinner and it started to rain – rain as only it can in East Africa during the wet season. Realising that his car was not going to be ideal on a wet and slippery dirt road, he decided (without authority) to use a police Land Rover. He drove with panache, handling the Land Rover with ease as from time to time it almost slithered out of control. They then entered the gravelled drive of her parents' home at speed. At this final moment the Land Rover did not respond as expected, but skidded sideways onto the wet lawn, scattering turf and mud in all directions. His girlfriend Diana made what was to prove a very prophetic announcement.

"Daddy will be very cross, you had better go." She ran through the rain towards the house, some twenty five yards away. The front door of the house crashed open. It was her father.

"You young bastard! You've ruined my lawn! I'm going to kill you!"

Moments later 'Daddy' reappeared with a shotgun and, before Tim could shout his apologies, opened fire with both barrels! Our ardent swain rapidly concluded that his beloved's father wasn't kidding and jumped headlong into the Land Rover, slamming it into gear and digging up even more lawn as he hurriedly reversed and sped down the drive, followed by the contents of two more barrels.

He arrived back at the Mess with a somewhat paler tan than at the time of his departure and was visibly shaken. On inspection, the Land Rover, had several small indentations made by the father's pellets. What a dilemma! Should he now arrest his sweetheart's father? There were two things that had to be done. One, telephone the father and negotiate a truce, and two, have the Land Rover fixed before the Superintendent found out. It is surprising what two bottles of 'Dimple Haig' can achieve.

Another colleague, James, had 'the hots' for a South African nurse. He was the anchor man for the tug-o'-war team and, upon reflection, it is a pity that unisex teams were not permitted, as she was rather large too, in every sense of the word.

James's libido was as yet 'untapped' and the love of his life decided that drastic action was needed. During a party at the Sisters' Mess, after most of the guests had departed, a somewhat-the-worse-for-wear James was seen ascending the stairs, carried on the shoulder of his strapping girlfriend, who was evidently intent on relieving him of his virginity.

She later described her father as 'a Boer of the old school'; honest, hard working, hospitable, and tough, a real man's man who had made a fortune from several business ventures.

James was invited to meet the parents and to stay for the weekend. Arriving at the twin metal gates they drove onto the large circular drive. When the car came to a halt, a succession of loud cracks could be heard emanating from the rear of the house. Could it be rifle fire?

Her mother greeted them on the steps, saying she would take her daughter to freshen up and that the African butler would take James to meet her husband, who was in the library.

James was duly shown into the library. The girl's father was sitting in a chair in front of the open French window and was shooting tick birds off the backs of the horses as they grazed in the paddock. A tick bird is about the size of a sparrow and these were some fifty yards away! Amazingly, the horses were not perturbed and were obviously used to this fusillade. Without even looking up he said in his guttural Afrikaans accent, "I trust, Sir, you will not try to interfere with my daughter."

James reported later that due to a very dry mouth he had great difficulty in replying, "It's never crossed my mind, Sir."

At one of my postings our local supply of female company was ensconced at the nearby European Hospital in the so-called 'Sisters Mess'. In the main the nurses were English, but there was also a smattering from Australia, New Zealand and as you now know, South

Africa. They lived under the 'eagle eye' of a matron who was well aware of some male intentions towards her flock. A friend of mine, Neil, (you will recall) owned a large old 1923 Rolls Royce. Due to its size, from time to time we would make use of this vehicle to take a contingent of off-duty nurses to the 'Jolly Farmer', an English-style pub some eight miles out of town, the road to which involved a constant climb of several thousand feet.

Arriving at the 'Sisters Mess' and having ascertained that matron was not on the prowl, a sofa was removed and placed into the rear of the 'Rolls'. Greatcoats would be distributed to the girls and when all six of us were aboard, 'Kiwi' would swing the brass starting handle, Neil would work the advance and retard levers, there would be a loud bang from one of the silencers and off we would go!

As previously mentioned, to reach the 'Jolly Farmer' involved a continuous climb and at an altitude of some seven thousand feet the engine would start to falter. At this stage Neil would call out, "Captain to engine room, we have trouble!" By now the car would be down to almost walking speed. 'Kiwi' would climb out onto the running board, open the four-foot toolbox, lift one side of the bonnet housing and insert a spanner. I have no idea what he tinkered with, but the engine revs would immediately pick up and with a cheer we would continue our journey.

At the 'Jolly Farmers' it was drinks all round and then we played the girls at darts for the next round. At closing time the starting procedure was exactly the same and we then coasted all eight miles down hill into town. Having sneaked the sofa back into the 'Sisters Mess', we all made our various secluded embracing farewells and roared off into the night with the odd backfire and its attendant tongue of flame accompanying our departure.

The local 'Ford' garage, wishing to attract more customers, organised a promotion: "FREE SERVICE – YOU ONLY PAY FOR THE OIL & PARTS." The 'Rolls' had not been serviced since being purchased and this promotion seemed too good an opportunity to miss, so it was duly booked in. Now normally it is the engine that contains the most oil. Had you seen underneath the bonnet of the 'Rolls' you would have instantly agreed as the engine appeared to be one normal sized car engine, with another of the same size directly behind it. This view was also taken by the 'Ford' garage. The mechanic commenced with the gearbox and held the usual small dish underneath as the oil drain plug was released. The bowl was soon filled to overflowing, with the balance cascading onto the floor of the inspection pit. As it was impossible to work paddling around in oil, quantities of sawdust were shovelled onto the pit floor and all work ceased until the resultant mess was cleared away. Now it was time for the engine to be drained. Having faced a deluge from the gearbox, a large empty oil drum was placed into the pit and the oil drain plug released. Only four pints emerged! Later that day Neil collected his 'Rolls' to be informed by the Service Manager that he would appreciate it if in future the 'Rolls' could be serviced elsewhere!

Despite its years, sometimes Neil would drive his 'Rolls' to Nairobi and it would 'bowl along' at a steady eighty, overtaking new cars such as the Ford 'Zephyr' with ease. Due to the height of the rear shooting compartment above ground level, plus one of the Mess sofas, the passengers would look down at these vehicles as they passed by.

They don't make them like that any more!

Neil was very much a practical joker and would phone the 'Sisters Mess' to offer our congratulations on the 'engagement' of some poor unsuspecting soul and any nurse he could name. The unsuspecting Police Officer would be walking along the main street when he would suddenly be greeted by a group of animated and excited off duty nurses offering their congratulations. All protestations were of no avail.

"Don't be shy," they would exclaim, "it's wonderful news!"

It would take at least two weeks for the atmosphere to return to normal.

As we were well known to the nursing staff, visiting hospitalised colleagues out of hours was never a problem. The key thing was not to be caught by Matron. One of our colleagues had accidentally sat on some sharp bamboo – the effect being to immediately curtail all thoughts of the opposite sex. Without going into fine detail, let it suffice to say that certain parts of his anatomy had swollen to such an extent that they now resided in a nest of cotton wool.

It was after midnight and we had just come off duty, so we decided to see how Bob was progressing. The nurses on night duty provided us with an update as to his condition, plus two cups of excellent coffee with cream. Bob, who was not asleep, greeted us warmly and we chatted in general terms.

Suddenly, one of the girls arrived, looking very flustered.

"Quick, you must hide. Matron's coming!"

To exit through the ward's swing doors would mean meeting Matron face to face. We had to do something and quickly! My colleague squeezed into the metal bedside locker, which was about four feet six inches in height, and I dived under the bed. I heard footsteps approaching and at the base of the bed appeared a pair of black shoes and two legs with black stockings.

"Mr Cooper, why aren't you asleep? If you are in any pain one of the night staff will arrange for the duty doctor to come and see you."

The shoes and legs now came around the bed and stopped no more than twelve inches from my face.

"Hmm, you don't looked flushed. Let me feel your pulse."

There was a pause.

"I'll ask one of the night staff to make you some Horlicks. Good night Mr Cooper."

We waited until we heard the ward's swing doors operate and the Matron's footsteps recede. I crawled from under the bed. Neil emerged from the locker looking like an old man with back trouble.

Our next problem was to 'escape' without bumping into Matron. One of the girls went ahead, stopping from time to time, then signalling to us to come on. By this method and involving several false alarms, we made our exit undetected.

As mentioned in a previous chapter, at the base of the escarpment on the road leading from Nairobi to Nakuru is an Italian church built by Italian prisoners during the Second World War. It is a masterpiece of devotion and ingenuity. During Mau-Mau times we received a report that it was to be desecrated and used for an oathing ceremony. Oathing was the method used by the Mau-Mau terrorists to recruit members and bind them to secrecy and this ceremony would be held at the dead of night. We were informed by Special Branch that a Ford car would arrive and park off the road on the dusty forecourt in front on the church. This would contain the gang leaders. The people to be oathed and the remainder of the gang would filter down the hillside at the back of the church. We planned to surprise them.

My companion, Jerry, was a South African and a Reserve Police Officer. We discussed tactics as to where we would position the ambush. We decided not to go near the place by road but to be dropped off just after dusk, then make our way through the lower edge of the escarpment to finish up on the opposite side of the road to the church. Heavily armed, our party of six achieved our objective then concealed ourselves in the grass, guns at the ready.

Before midnight the mosquitoes found us, to be joined by those horrible parasites, ticks. Ticks bite into your flesh, suck your blood and when bloated fall off; not very pleasant companions. Despite the fact that there was only starlight, we could see the church reasonably clearly. The hours ticked by. About 2am a small car arrived and stopped outside the church. We waited, tense and ready, but what we wanted was the whole gang, not just two or three. We continued to observe and to be devoured by insects.

I looked at my luminous watch. It was now nearly 4.00am and all we had observed so far were two figures leaving the front seats of the car and climbing into the rear. Due to the proximity of dawn and possible follow up by the security forces I decided that the gang would not be coming and that we should just capture this pair.

I tapped Jerry's arm. He eased himself very carefully towards me. I whispered my plan.

"We'll crawl very slowly across the road, keeping well spaced out in case they shoot at us. When outside the car I will wrench open the door, switch on my torch and you will have your machine carbine ready to open fire."

Jerry nodded in agreement. In whispers we told the remainder of the ambush party of our plan, stressing that they were not to open fire unless they had to rush to our aid, and only to do so if they could clearly identify the targets.

We crawled across the road like snails, inch by inch. Time was not important, the key thing was the element of surprise. There wasn't any traffic as this was Mau-Mau territory and it was not a good idea to be driving at night. We reached the side of the car; we had not been spotted. There were movements inside the car causing the bodywork to move slightly. We were in position. Ready?

I wrenched open the offside rear door, blinding one of the two occupants with my torch. The sight that met our eyes was the rear view of a semi-naked European male and the very frightened face of a European female, who quite unsurprisingly let out a scream. It was a courting couple *in flagrante delicto*!

It seemed pointless to ask "What are you doing here?"

No doubt due to the tenseness of the moment Jerry 'exploded'.

"You bloody idiots! We could have killed you! Don't you know this is Mau-Mau territory and a very dangerous area?"

They were both in a state of shock and it took some time before the girl could stem her sobs and they felt capable of driving off.

What if we had taken the safest approach and opened fire instead of crawling across the road or they had opened the car door as we were crawling across the road. How would we have reacted? It could so easily have been a fatal shooting.

As you will have guessed, from time to time 'the knot was tied' and the favourite place for a honeymoon was on the East African coast at Malindi, then a very small town that had some excellent hotels and a sandy corrugated road bisecting its length. There were palm trees, golden white sands and as yet no tourists from Europe; an idyllic spot.

At one particular wedding, due to guests booby-trapping the honeymooners' car with red and green smoke flares, their departure for the coast had been delayed. Add to this that some twenty miles outside Nairobi were dirt roads, very badly pitted and corrugated, it was going to be impossible to reach Malindi that night. In those days there was a typical old colonial hotel situated at about the half-way stage. The roof was corrugated iron painted with red lead, now very faded. It had a veranda and was, to say the least, somewhat primitive, but when you are tired, anything is better than nothing.

Having been booked in and shown to their room, the bridegroom noted that it contained two single beds. But this was his honeymoon; he wanted a double bed! No other room was available, however, the manager said that he would arrange to have the two singles removed and replaced. As you can imagine the new bride was very embarrassed as her husband made it very clear to the manager the reason for his request.

At long last they were alone, along with their double bed, but also in the room was a wardrobe of gigantic proportions, which dominated the room.

"My God it's big enough to sleep in!" exclaimed the expectant bridegroom, opening one of the doors and stepping inside. Unfortunately, what he had not noticed was that one of the front feet was loose. The wardrobe crashed to the floor with him inside!

It proved too heavy for his new wife to lift but before she could call for help the hotel manager started banging on the door demanding to know what was going on and what did honeymooners get up to these days!

The truth was soon revealed, staff were summoned and the amorous newlywed released, bruised but in one piece and suffering from mild concussion. Not a particularly auspicious start to married life!

A member of our Mess asked me to be his best man. I readily agreed and set about thinking of my speech. The only thing of note that I could recall about the bridegroom-to-be was that he could not sing in key! When he was in the bath it was excruciating. Even the Mess dog went into the garden!

One of the major duties of the best man was to hide and protect the newlywed's car from good-humoured sabotage such as switching the spark plug leads around or attaching smoke bombs (to mention but two methods popular with pranksters). As their luggage could also be at risk, it was decided that this would be kept in the boot of my car until the actual moment of departure.

The happy couple were duly married and I made a speech which I had planned to be witty. However, for reasons I could not understand, the guests laughed in all the wrong places. After the reception I drove the newlyweds to pick up their vehicle from its secret hiding place and they departed. I drove back to the Mess in a haze of champagne and it was not until two days later that I realised I still had their luggage in the boot of my car!

Let us now return to the indigenous population. A report came in that an African girl had been kidnapped and taken off in a car by two African males. My first ever kidnap case! We had the vehicle registration number, a good description of the occupants and the direction in which they were heading. Soon we had the eye witness, the mother who was wailing like a banshee and uttering the usual '*woy, woy, woy*' at the top of her lungs. The radio room contacted all stations in the direction the kidnappers were heading and we could only wait. An hour later a radio report came in; a car had been stopped, the occupants detained. They awaited our instructions. I was elated, the case was 'all wrapped up' in just over an hour.

The African Corporal asked if he could 'have a word in my ear'.

Did I realise this was the custom of this tribe? Single girls were taken 'by force' and the mother had to demonstrate how she would miss her departed daughter.

Could this be true? Where was this wailing mother? I questioned her closely in such a way as not to give her any leads. Yes it was true. It was the normal tribal custom.

"Then why in heaven's name did you still 'kick up such a fuss' in this Police Station?" I enquired.

"Well Bwana, she is my daughter and what would my people think if I hadn't made so much noise?"

With great reluctance I had to radio for the release of the ardent swain and his wife to be.

You will perhaps be surprised, having read the previous pages, to learn that serious courtship did exist, although sometimes this could cause disturbance to members of the Mess…

William was courting almost nightly and was obviously on the way to 'tying the knot'. The cause of our disturbance was his late arrival back at the Mess. Let me explain. Our rooms were in one long building with a door at one end and a long corridor down the centre. Over each doorway was a pane of glass to let in more light. At night the corridor was illuminated by a series of electric lights. Normally, if not on duty, we were all 'tucked up' before midnight and all lights would be out. William's room was right down at the end of the corridor on the right hand side. At about one o'clock nearly every morning he would arrive at the Mess, switch on the corridor lights and wake some of the snoring incumbents. This now almost routine disturbance had to stop! The plan was simple. Remove the electric light bulbs, and, as a final gesture, tie a condom filled (as late as possible) with ice cold water, to his door handle. We could hardly wait for his return!

At about one o'clock we heard his car stop outside. This was followed by two or three clicks of the light switch and some soft muttering. I was biting my bed sheet in order to stifle my laughter. He continued to fumble his way down the corridor, finally stopping outside his door. There was a pause.

"You bastards! You bastards!" These words were greeted with much hilarity as, using the light shed from his room, William rushed up and down the corridor, kicking all the doors!

They say that revenge is sweet. Within a few weeks it was Christmas. On Christmas morning at about 11am, those of us off duty gathered into one of the rooms for some pre-lunch 'snifters'. The rooms were fairly small and contained just enough space for a single bed, wardrobe and small chest of drawers. The room was packed. There were bodies on the bed, sitting on the chest of drawers and standing. The window was open, when suddenly a smoking object came through the open window and fell onto the floor. It was a thunderflash. (These were giant -sized army bangers used in field exercises and about ten inches long, powerful enough to blow someone's foot off.)There was pandemonium! Everyone tried to rush for the door at once. Glasses were broken and bottles knocked over! As I was sitting on the bed, I flung myself full length onto it, covering my ears with my hands and awaiting the ear shattering explosion...

Nothing happened. Was it a dud? A closer inspection revealed that some smouldering rag had been stuffed into the hollow 'safe' end.

William appeared outside the window laughing.

"Got you, you bastards!"

Sometimes even the best laid plans went astray. Stewart returned from home leave saying he had met the girl of his dreams and she was coming out to marry him. He decided to give her a pre-marriage present of a sea voyage via the Red Sea to Mombasa, where he would meet her and take her to Nairobi for their wedding. The big day arrived. He stood by the docking shed with a huge bunch of flowers with his heart thudding in his chest. There she was! He waved, she waved back and descended the gang plank with a European male helping her with her minor baggage. He greeted her with out-stretched arms, but they remained empty.

"Stewart, I hardly know how to say this, but this is my husband."

It had been a shipboard romance!

Another colleague had his fiancée travel by air. Having met her at Nairobi airport in his dilapidated Land Rover (without any doors) he sped into town. Negotiating the roundabout outside the New Stanley Hotel he turned to speak to his bride to be – but she wasn't there! He had had the three front seat squabs covered in Kongoni skin and the squab clips had been dispensed with. As a result she had slid sideways and luckily for her had fallen onto the road still sitting on the squab and had not been hit by a following vehicle. Despite this initial 'rejection' by her husband-to-be, they eventually married.

During one of my secondments I became friends with a fellow Police Officer who had a fiancée in (the then) Southern Rhodesia and she was planning to visit him for a week together with a chaperone. He asked me if I would I be willing to obtain a week's leave and join them? His idea was that my job would be to keep the chaperone at bay. Don't ask me why, but I agreed.

Using my car we met his fiancée and chaperone at Nairobi airport and later that day arrived at the Silverbeck Hotel in Nanyuki. Its claim to fame is that it has a brass strip on the floor of the bar. With just one step in either direction you can be North or South of the equator.

We booked into two twin-bedded bungalows, the girls in one and we chaps sharing the other. On day two we toured around the area. By day four I was becoming bored and, as I had farming friends not too far away, I had the day off, alone. I returned to the hotel at close to midnight, walked to our bungalow and opened the door. Inside was a European woman getting undressed! I hurriedly apologised and closed the door. I was positive it was No.10. My thoughts were interrupted by an irate male who from his manner was intent on speeding my departure from this planet.

"I'm terribly sorry... I thought it was No.10."

"This is No.10! What the bloody hell do you think you're up to!"

"There must be some mistake. I was booked in here with a friend..." My words were cut short.

"Well you're not now, so bugger off!" And with that, the door was slammed in my face.

I was stunned! What was going on?

I aroused the manager who appeared bleary-eyed and informed me that my friends had left.

"Where have they gone?" I demanded.

He had no idea, but said that the man had left a note for me.

It read:

> *"Dear Chips,*
> *I didn't like the lunch and complained to the hotel manager.*
> *As a result we had some words and have left. We are now at the*
> *Mawingo Hotel and will see you at the bar.*
> *Cheers,*
> *Arthur."*

Our new abode was several miles away so my arrival there was close to 1am. They were not at the bar and again I had to rouse a senior member of staff. Having traced our room I found Arthur fast asleep and snoring very loudly. I fell into my bed exhausted to be kept awake by deep rattling snores from the opposite side of the room. I could have 'throttled' him! I never did discover if my assistance helped in uniting the happy pair.

For a short while a member of the Police Mounted Section was staying in our Mess. According to his stories he had more girlfriends 'than you could shake a stick at'. He never stopped talking about girls. As thorn bushes can rip trousers to pieces in minutes, the Mounted Section wore cowboy-like chaps. 'Romeo's' were not ordinary chaps; down each leg of brown leather were six equally-spaced black hearts, and superimposed on these were six smaller red ones, with the centre of each red heart adorned with a small leather tassel. Evidently, each one represented a conquest, or was a reminder of some 'gorgeous' (his word) girl. Any visit to Nairobi resulted in stories of this blonde or that brunette and after a few weeks of this we had had enough!

On the radio each evening, there was a special programme for the security forces which featured the usual "I love you very much" messages, some of which were disguised digs at Senior Officers. For example, one officer wore a very small gold earring as (it was alleged) in his youth he had sailed around the Horn. Some wag sent him the dedication 'Golden Earrings' which had very sloppy lyrics. We decided to use this method to curb our amorous friend. Someone in the Mess had a girlfriend who worked for the Kenya Broadcasting Company who proved willing to obtain a sheet of their headed paper and an envelope. We composed and had mailed from Nairobi the following letter:

To Inspector Roberts,
Kenya Police Mounted Section,
c/o Divisional Police Headquarters xxxxxxxx.

A Very Special Request.

Dear Inspector Roberts,
We have received a request from a young lady who obviously loves you very much. As a result we are bringing forward her request and urge you to listen to the 'Security Forces Request Programme' this coming Friday evening.
Assuring you of our best attention at all times.
I remain,
xxxxxxxxxxxxxx
Director of Programmes.
Kenya Broadcasting Company

The letter duly arrived and our 'Romeo' was completely taken in. He showed it to everyone, giving his opinion as to which girl it could be. He, and we, could hardly wait for Friday evening! At the appointed hour we all sat around the radio and soon after the commencement of the programme, the announcer said:

"We now have a very special request for Inspector Roberts of the Kenya Police Mounted Section."

Romeo was beside himself!

"There is a very special message from Monica which reads: Darling, I miss you so very much and I am just dying for you to call me in order that we can be in each others arms once again. Call me tonight on 0873-4961."

This announcement was followed by a really sloppy love song.

Romeo rushed out of the door to use the Mess telephone. What he didn't realise was the telephone number was for the African Maternity Hospital in Nairobi. We waited for the outburst.

"You rotten bastards! What a rotten thing to do!"

He kicked open the swing door of the Mess and we all collapsed with laughter. The following Friday we sent him another request from 'Monica's husband'. It was a cowboy song: 'Cleaning my Rifle Thinking of You'.

It is amazing the variety of information that can be obtained by 'keeping one's ear to the ground'. For example, a local European of middling years was married to a young thirty-year-old. He was very keen on horses and had purchased a large panel van to convey all the usual tack and fodder. When not being used for this purpose it was the family's means of transport. Attending a party one night, his young wife 'fell' for a Colonial, also of some thirty years. With their mutual passions aroused they made their way to the parked van and climbed into its cavernous interior. Being panel-sided it provided complete privacy. Some ten minutes later, the husband noticed that his wife was missing and demanded to know where she was. Someone said that they thought she had been taken home. He decided to find out. He rushed out to the van and drove off at speed ... with the two lovers still entwined in each others arms in the back. Arriving home, he rushed into the house in search of his errant wife, whereupon she clambered out of the van undetected, leaving her ardent lover to disappear into the shrubbery before commencing a very long walk home...

Having been transferred 'up country', over a protracted period I was well settled into my new surroundings. One morning I had cause to visit Divisional Headquarters. On the steps was the Assistant Superintendent talking to a very attractive girl who had soft blonde curly hair and vivid blue eyes.

"Inspector Tompkins, do you have any work that this young lady can do?"

"All I have Sir are fourteen pairs of police socks that require darning."

I learned later that this glib comment was not well received!

The following weekend I decided to invite her to go trout fishing and she agreed. Evidently she was staying with friends and planned to return to England in about three months time.

The scenery in the forest was spectacular; the sun shining through the trees casting brilliant shafts of sunlight onto the undergrowth and when I stopped the car, the sound of the rushing water could be clearly heard. Birds chirped and sang in the treetops and from time to time there were distant sounds as colobus monkeys jumped from tree to tree. Taking the rods and our picnic we made our way down to the river's edge, passing trees that had visible signs of elephants having used the trunks as scratching pads.

At the river it was even more spectacular; the sunlight flashed onto the water as it bubbled and tumbled down mini-waterfalls into large natural pools. The noise of the falling water was so loud it made normal speech difficult. Just to add to the scene, fluttering around the edges of the pools were beautiful butterflies with iridescent coloured wings, some of them almost the size of your hand, and bright blue and green birds were flitting amongst the bushes and trees that bordered the riverbanks. We placed our bottle of white wine under a small rock to chill and it was time to fish.

As my new girlfriend hadn't fished before, I showed her how to tie the fly onto the line, how and where to cast to catch trout. As it was difficult for two people to fish one pool, having done this I scaled the rocks beside the mini-waterfall and went upstream.

Here it was 'wet' fly fishing and the flies had exotic names like 'Royal Coachman' or 'Watson's Fancy'. The method was to cast into the base of the waterfall and let the fly be washed into the pool like natural bait. Suddenly there would be a snatch on the line, the reel would 'scream' as the fish tore around the large pool, its sides flashing under the water as it caught the sunlight, then leaping into the air and crashing back into the water. The rod would be bending as the fish was played and brought closer and closer towards the bank. Finally tiring it would be reeled in, landed and 'donked' on the head. A beautiful two pound Rainbow Trout.

Apart from a break for our *al fresco* lunch, we continued to fish until late afternoon when we departed for home with eight good sized fish. From that moment the 'love of my life' was well and truly hooked! Well… on fishing, anyway!

I was not the only male who was interested in this new arrival from England. One Sunday morning I called at the house where she was staying and met my competition, who was dressed in a black golfing sweater and matching trousers, perhaps not the ideal colour for the East African sun. Her friend owned a playful black Labrador who was walking around furiously wagging his tail.

Patting my thigh I called out, "Come here Bruce, you ugly black beast!"

All conversation ceased. What had I said?

Evidently the other boyfriend was called Bruce and the dog was called Kim! I apologised, but it was accepted with ill grace.

My new girlfriend was an excellent golfer with a handicap of twelve and she invited me to spend a day with her at a golf club situated several miles out of town. Being a non-golfer I considered the game looked fairly simple. However, I would prove to be an even bigger handicap.

We arrived very early in the morning in order that I could avoid being a nuisance to other avid golfers. We were just about to 'tee off' when the club Captain appeared.

"Mind if I join you two young people for a quick round?" My heart sank. Of all people, the club Captain! My girlfriend really 'whacked it'. (Forgive my jargon; I'm a non-golfer). The club Captain now gestured to me to play. More by good luck than judgement I also 'whacked it'! I could see that our guest was impressed. However, it was at this stage that my golfing image 'fell apart'. Arriving at my ball I proceeded to dig a hole around it! Finally, after about ten attempts, my club connected. I will not mention how many strokes it took to get my ball onto the green, but I suggest that it was an all-time club 'record'.

We now arrived at the second tee. Well I 'whacked' it again! Instead of flying into the air the ball struck the concrete box that contained sand and water then ricocheted off, just missing the club captain's head by inches!

"Young man you are bloody dangerous!" he said, and stormed off back to the clubhouse! After nine holes completed by me in some two hundred strokes, we 'called it a day' and returned to the clubhouse for an excellent lunch.

There was a special rule at this club concerning baboons. At, I seem to recall, the fifth hole, the ground fell steeply away to the green and out of sight of the tee. Evidently it was not unknown for the baboon to chase the ball, pick it up and run off with it! This rule reminded me of seeing baboon stealing maize cobs from the fields of growing plants. No space was wasted. A maize cob under each armpit, one in each hand and one in the mouth, and could they run!

Despite my fiasco at the golf club (they say that love is blind) we continued to see each other and soon I was 'smitten'. Five weeks later I proposed and we planned to marry within the next three months. I now had to write to her parents requesting their permission. What could I say? I explained that I was in love with their daughter. I also stated that I was the owner of a Volkswagen which had two front seats with a handbrake in between. As a result, I now had the word 'Volkswagen' deeply stamped in reverse into my posterior and the only way that this unpleasant condition could be alleviated was for me to marry their daughter. I hoped they would give their consent. Some forty years on we are still happily married. I must have had an arresting manner. Incidentally, I have omitted something. Soon after our marriage, all my holed socks were burned.

Being newlyweds we were allocated a Government bungalow, but it was far from palatial. It was constructed entirely of wood but due to the passage of years and the fierce East African sun some of the wooden boards had warped to such an extent that it was possible to see inside through the gaps. From dusk onwards it presented an unusual picture with rays of light escaping into the night, attracting hordes of insects to each orifice. We were to discover that bees had nested in the wooden wall cavity and their nocturnal humming and buzzing provided a soothing background to our evening meals.

My wife was very keen to demonstrate her culinary skills. It will come as no surprise that our cooking appliance matched the age of our dwelling. It was an ancient wood-burning stove that emitted on start up a mass of smoke. The oven was to one side and had two small round discs on its top surface where extra fuel could be fed in, or with the discs removed, used to boil or fry. Our first ever home-cooked meal was roast chicken. It was cooked on one side, and semi-raw on the other! What with the heat, the smoke and the vagaries of this ancient appliance, my wife agreed that we needed to engage a cook! His name was Steven. In his earlier days he had been second chef in a large Nairobi hotel. Without any doubt he was a first class cook and despite our ancient appliance produced excellent meals.

With our 'jewel' in situ we commenced to invite friends for dinner. Our first experience was somewhat unusual. We invited some friends, who like us, had also been recently married. Our male guest made some general jest about mother-in-laws, then made the fatal error of bringing his wife's mother into the conversation. This resulted in a raging row across our dinner table as we sat back trying to look nonchalant. So this was what happened when mothers-in-law were discussed!

Having been in our new home for several months, and having converted the decor of our home from its original Public Works Department colour scheme of dark green and cream, our next assignment was the garden.

One day at the rear of the house I could hear a soft chirping noise. It wasn't birds, so what was it? As I turned the corner, facing me was a huge column of safari ants intent on entering our house! There must have been thousands and thousands of them. Once inside they devour everything edible and then leave. I grabbed some spare petrol from the car boot, poured it onto the column and ignited it. It went up with a whoosh! The survivors turned and headed away from the house.

However, it being sandy soil the petrol had soaked into the ground and was still alight, right beside the wooden rear wall and we were in the middle of the dry season! I was close to panic! Grabbing a broom I swept over the burning ground, noting that as I proceeded it had extinguished the flames. I paused at the other end triumphant... but within seconds the soil ignited! Again I rushed back down the line with the broom, and it ignited behind me! On the seventh sortie both the petrol and I were exhausted. It had been a close thing!

In town was a charming middle-aged European widow with a very ample bosom who went by the nickname of 'Lala'. It was her custom to give a gift from her home to newlyweds, accompanied by the remark "I'll see what I can find in Lala's chest." (Incidentally, we never did receive a present from the chest).

By this time we decided that it would be much nicer if we had our own furniture rather than the standard Public Works Department issue. In town there were several Asian carpenters so, calling upon my drawing office experience, I designed a suite of dining furniture, a desk, coffee table and some easy chairs. I drew the plans to scale and had all these items produced in solid East African mahogany. The dining furniture we still have to this day and it resides in our breakfast room. In time, despite the cracks in the walls and resident bees, our little Kenyan shack was starting to look more like a true home.

In order to acquire some capital for our next home leave, my wife joined Special Branch as a secretary. During a Royal visit she was called upon to go ahead of the Royal party using and trying everything that would be used by our prestigious visitor. Doors were opened, beds laid on, toilets sat on and flushed, windows opened and taps turned on and off. Following the testing of each site the site was 'sealed' then closely guarded. It was suggested later that we should apply to have our own family coat of arms, consisting of a toilet seat entwined with two chains surmounted by a steel helmet and in a scroll beneath the seat the motto *In Deo Fidemus.*

Eighteen months had passed since our marriage and now it was time for home leave. Our transport to Nairobi was to be somewhat unusual – a three ton Police truck loaded with redundant rifles and the wet season had just started! We sat in the front with an armed escort perched on the packing cases in the rear. Our driver was called Chebet and despite the adverse conditions he drove with panache! Many times the lorry started to crab sideways on the wet slippery earth road! With a great big grin on his face he remained in control remarking to my wife:

"Hakuna matata Memsahib, tuta fika Nairobi mbila shaka." (There aren't any problems Memsahib, we will arrive in Nairobi without fail).

And we did!

11   It could only happen in Kenya

Having arrived in England and met my new in-laws and family, plus visits to my own family and friends, I had ample time to muse over the dramatic changes that had occurred in my life since joining the Kenya Police. I had seen so many things; experienced so many things – and upon reflection, it was mainly people (some larger then life) that formed the basis of my recollections.

During my years in Kenya there had been numerous contacts with people of various races and incidents that were deeply embedded in my mind. Some were funny, others not so funny, with many being similar to those experienced by any Kenya Police Officer.

For example, language could be a problem for all races, either new arrivals from the UK attempting to speak Kiswahili or Asians and Africans attempting to speak English. As a result there could be amusing misinterpretations and misunderstandings.

Some of the following I experienced personally, whilst other incidents were common knowledge, but nevertheless could only have happened in Kenya...

Following the Second World War large numbers of ex-service people emigrated to Kenya, to be followed later by members of the civilian population. It was a land that offered promise and challenge. For a minority of people, the East African sun had a strange effect, as some of the following stories will illustrate. Before delving into the first tale, let me first explain to any non ex-service reader that in the Royal Navy, a Midshipman is known as a 'snotty'. The reason for this apparently innocuous piece of information will become apparent as the tale progresses.

A Rear Admiral was among those drawn to Kenya. Following his demobilisation he purchased a plot of land in the Kenya Highlands and commenced to create a farm. Having settled in, he had erected over the farm entrance that faced onto the main dirt road, the sign 'Admiral's End'. Two former midshipmen, not having the same funds as the

Admiral, had to combine what money they could raise and managed to purchase a smaller plot of land, again with the intention of creating a farm. It was almost opposite the Admiral's entrance. Here was an opportunity they considered too good to miss. They had a sign erected which read, 'Snotty's Bottom'.

The Admiral was incensed! As he could no longer 'pull rank' he sought recourse to the law, alas to no avail. The sign remained, much to the amusement of the local European farming community.

Within our area we had a former RAF bomber pilot who, with his long suffering wife, produced several children. He was very keen on a good Saturday night out, but sometimes his antics culminated in his being arrested for being drunk and disorderly. It became routine that virtually every Saturday evening, the beat patrols would keep an eye open for his pickup truck, and when spotted, would report which 'watering hole' was 'blessed' with his presence. Now it must be said that he was never violent and his disorderly behaviour was normally some schoolboy prank, for example, removing the glass dome from a petrol pump at the local petrol station to fill with beer. The cells at the Police Station (known as King George's Hotel) were normally filled to the brim on Saturday nights with drunken cases of a far more violent nature, therefore, from time to time, it was in our interests to avoid if possible arresting 'our reveller', providing he had not been involved in one of his pranks. The standard routine was to send a 999 car to the bar just before 'chucking out' time. By then, as you may well have guessed, he was 'well away'. His greeting was always a drunken but affable "I suppose you bastards have come to arrest me!" He would then be asked for his vehicle keys, which he always refused to hand over. This prompted the response, "Right, you are under arrest for being drunk in charge of a vehicle." And he knew that we were 'not kidding'. The keys would be produced and he would lurch towards the door, normally singing some lewd RAF ditty. He would then weave his way to the local hotel with the 999 car trailing him. Having ensured he was booked in for the night, his vehicle was placed into the Police Station compound.

From time to time he would travel to Uganda on business and book into one of the hotels normally frequented by civilian aircrew taking an enforced rest. This contingent always included a number of nubile air hostesses. Being a normal red-blooded male he was determined to impress. However, as usual he had been 'enjoying' himself. Having been to his room and donned his swimming trunks, he made his way to the pool and gave a very impressive shallow dive. Alas, he had failed to see the notice: 'SWIMMING POOL BEING CLEANED' and hit the base of the shallow end with a loud crunch! Rushed to hospital he had to have surgery and rumour had it, a metal plate inserted into his skull. From then on his Saturday nights were more subdued.

His mother-in-law, who was a charming old lady, one day appeared at the Police Station and placed a large .45 American automatic pistol on the charge office counter asking, "Can I have a tiny one that doesn't make quite such a loud bang." Adding, "You are not to give it to that terrible son-in-law of mine." The Duty Officer checked the automatic to find a full clip of ammunition and the safety catch was off!

Within an hour of her departure her son-in-law appeared, demanding to know "What had that old battle-axe of a mother-in-law wanted?"

I have mentioned Saturday nights. Every Saturday night the cells filled with African drunks and arrests for assaults and the odd stabbing. All drink related. Every month end was the worst as every employee was paid on a monthly basis. The Duty Officer on such a night was in for a rough time.

On this particular Saturday night a beat patrol arrived with a violent lunatic. The routine was, call the Government Doctor, who would assess the case and normally give an injection that 'knocked the person out', thus ensuring he, or she, was not a danger to either themselves or the night duty staff. Regular checks had to be made to ensure that the drugged lunatic was safe and well. This one was an exception! The injection had a marginal effect but the lunatic clung to bars of the cell door shouting "*woy woy woy*" at the top of his lungs and rattling the cell door. A call to the Government Doctor was of no avail as the level of injection could not be increased. As a result, everyone within earshot was not going to get any sleep. This included the local hotel just some seventy-five yards away. Within minutes the Scottish manager was on the phone complaining that his guests could not sleep for the noise and could it be stopped? The Duty Officer apologised and explained the situation. Three more calls were received during the night from the now very irate and frazzled hotel manager, who was 'getting stick' from virtually every guest. The Kenya Police were not very popular!

Now you will have noticed that the hotel manager was a Scot, a Scot living away from his native land and determined to remain loyal to his roots. During the war he had served in some famous Scottish Regiment and could play the bagpipes. The routine every Sunday morning was for him to appear in full regalia on the hotel steps, then puff up the pipes. At the same time an African member of staff would raise the Union Jack on the hotel flagpole. This Sunday morning, despite his lack of sleep, was to be no exception. The skirl of the pipes lifted into the cool morning air and descended onto the Police Station. You will recall that the Duty Officer had had one hell of a night. Lifting the phone he asked to speak to the hotel manager. The skirl of the pipes died away and the call was answered by the manager, dressed, you will recall in full regalia.

"Good morning Sir, this is the Duty Officer at the Police Station here. I wish to make a complaint. There is a dreadful noise coming from your hotel and my guests can't sleep."

I will leave the response to the reader's imagination! It was not seen as a joke and resulted in a series of complaints, including, or so we were led to believe, to the Colony's Governor.

The European female population also contained one or two 'different' people. One lady in question was titled. Earlier in the year she had purchased a new 'Ford' car and reported within days of its receipt that it was bucking and lurching. The local 'Ford' garage inspected it. They stripped down the fuel system, drained the fuel tank, checked the electric's, and could not find any fault. The next morning the lady returned with the same complaint. Again it was checked and road tested. No fault was found. She was there again the following morning to report the same problem and was met outside by the garage foreman. He spoke to her through the open driver's window and noticed that she had hung her handbag onto the spindle of the fully extended hand controlled choke!

Some weeks later a European Officer on traffic duty saw a 'Ford' car parked outside the bank with the engine running but no driver. He waited around and who should appear but a certain titled lady. She went to enter her car and he approached her.

"Madam, do you realise that it is an offence to leave a vehicle unattended with the engine running?"

"I refuse to speak to you!" was her reply.

"Madam, I am charging you with a Traffic Offence, leaving your vehicle unattended with the engine running. Can I please have your name and address?"

"I refuse!" she replied, in a slightly raised voice.

A small crowd started to gather.

"Madam, if you refuse to give me your name and address I have the right to arrest you until I can ascertain your true identity."

"You beast, you beast!" our titled lady screamed, hit the Traffic Officer with her handbag and burst into tears!

On the outskirts of the town was The Theatre. A slightly ramshackle building, but despite this, local European talent existed and gave full support to its various ventures. It was decided to try and hold a classical music evening. It was discovered that the local area could raise sufficient musical talent ranging from voice, tin whistles to violins and piano. After selecting the best talent, a task that even King Solomon would have found difficult, the date was set. Posters appeared about town, tickets were sold. It was to be a full house.

Just before the curtain went up it was realised that there was no one selected to play the National Anthem. Who better than the now retired lady concert pianist! The organiser approached the lady, who was suitably bedecked in a long black gown with the odd feather tucked into her special hair do, plus as much jewellery as she could show to her admiring public. The position was explained; would she appear on stage to play the National Anthem? The response was an emotionally charged, "No!"

"It's very simple, even a few opening bars will be OK."

"It is not simple and I refuse to play any piece of music that I haven't practised, and that's final! It's an insult to ask a person of my talent to do such a thing!"

Looking very haughty she left by the stage door and strode off into the African night. The organiser led the singing of the anthem and the programme was quickly rearranged.

On the edge of the township was a European residential club. Two of the longest staying guests were two ladies who were well into their seventies. Evidently they did not trust the African waiters whom they believed were 'interfering' with the breakfast cereals. As a result, each morning they would appear in the dining room clutching their own cornflake packet, and having sat down at separate tables, normally on opposite sides of the dining room, would proceed to discuss in very loud voices all the latest scandal and gossip.

One of the ladies owned a car. We received a telephone call from her stating that her car was being used by the club's African staff and she wanted it stopped! A colleague visited the club and interviewed the lady concerned. The vehicle was not garaged overnight, but was usually parked under a tree within the club's grounds. How did the lady know it was being used by the staff?

"Every morning the car has been moved. Not very much, but enough for me to realise it has been used."

Was the car locked each night?

"Yes, I always lock it and the key is kept in my room."

Has the key ever gone missing?

"No, and I can only assume somehow they have obtained a duplicate."

A close examination of the car did not reveal any signs of tampering either with the door lock or the rubber seals around the driver's door. A mystery.

After dark my colleague returned to the club. The car was parked under the tree and it was locked. Using chalk he marked with vertical lines the inside of the rear tyres and where the chalk line reached the ground, scratched two marks that married up with the chalk lines. Having done this, he wiped the window glass and door lock handles. Thus any new fingerprints would be revealed.

The following morning he returned to the club and, before checking to see if the vehicle had been moved, contacted the lady owner. Together they went to inspect the vehicle.

"Officer, it has been moved, I can see that it has. And, very cleverly, they have tried to return it to the same position." My colleague checked the marks on the inside of the rear tyres. They lined up perfectly with the marks on the ground.

"I can assure you that the vehicle has not been moved" he said, and explained what he had done the previous night. The lady bridled!

"You may believe that it hasn't been used, but I know better! From now on I will deal with this matter myself"!

A visit to the club the following morning revealed the lady's car secured to the tree with a chain that was threaded through the driver's and the offside door handles, with a padlock that would not have been out of place in a bank vault. From then on all complaints from the car's owner ceased.

Within a few miles of town was a very pleasant hotel with a very congenial owner. From time to time we would go there for an evening meal and on arrival approach the bar to be greeted by 'mine host'.

"Have you ever tried a drink called 'snakebite'? If not let me show you how its done. You need a shallow salver like this, a spoon and some rum." Turning around he took a bottle of 'Navy' rum from the shelf.

"Now watch this. Pour into the salver two double rums. Add a spoonful of brown sugar. Damn where did I put it? Ah, here it is. Now here's the clever bit. Take a spoonful of rum from the salver and heat the spoon until the rum ignites. Look, I've got my hands full, use these matches and make sure the rum's on fire." I struck the match and held it under the bowl of the spoon. Nothing happened.

"You'll need to do it again." With my second match the rum ignited.

"Now watch this. I carefully pour the flaming rum into the salver… like this. Careful, careful. Yes, now all the rum's alight. Now I stir gently to mix in the brown sugar and continue until the colour of the flame changes… there it goes! Blow it out like this… quickly pour it into two very thin glasses and there we are. He handed us the two very thin glasses of hot rum. Tell me what you think." The hot rum and dissolved sugar tasted very potent and I could understand why it was called 'snakebite'.

"Pow! That's some powerful brew, how much do we owe you?"

"Well as you were very willing testers – nothing. It's 'on the house'."

"Are you sure?"

"Yes of course."

Following dinner and coffee I was presented with the bill by his wife. On it, and underlined, were two 'snakebites'.

"I think there is some mistake, your husband said they were 'on the house'."

"He may have said that they were 'on the house', but I'm in charge and we have to make a profit."

We paid up and vowed never to accept his 'free' drinks in the future.

Kenya had all sorts of interesting people, with the majority of these being ex-service types. One evening, my wife and I were invited out to dinner at a local farm. The meal was excellent and served on plates, each and every one bearing the family crest, as did the table silver. Like several of the 'up country' farmhouses, it was constructed of mud and wattle and the walls had been whitewashed. The ceilings were not panelled, but showed the adzed cross beams and roof supports made from local 'blue gum' trees. The roof was thatched native style. The furniture was all antique and on the walls were several oil paintings. The most outstanding feature of the house was its latest addition, a new bathroom. It was vast and completely covered in maroon tiles. In the centre was a goldfish pond complete with fountain. All the taps and fittings were gold plated and the water was fed into the maroon coloured bath via a gargoyle's head. The windows were 'Norman' style, tall and slim with pointed arched tops, they were not glazed but instead had the most exquisite wrought iron work, and there were no curtains. It was in complete contrast to the rest of their single story dwelling.

There was a very unassuming person who owned a farm within the Division. In the thirties he was the only Englishman ever to get his sweetheart out of Russia. Even before the 'Cold War' the Russian borders were closed to all but the very few. During the late thirties he had visited Russia, fallen in love with a Russian girl, and wanted to marry her. However, the NKVD (Secret Police) refused to give her an exit visa. He left without her, promising that he would return and take her to England where they would marry. He hired a light aircraft and flew from England into Russia but, due to head winds and lack of fuel, he had to land far short of his illegal destination and was arrested by the dreaded NKVD. At first they did not believe his story that this incursion was to rescue his sweetheart, surely he was an English spy? He adhered to his story, and finally they believed him, saying "Only the mad English would do such a thing!" Not only did they release him, but granted the girl an exit visa. Upon their arrival in England they were married and later emigrated to Kenya. Their story was featured many years later in the 'Readers Digest'.

Another interesting pair were two European debtors, both ex-service types. A warrant had been issued for their arrest and they were due to appear before a Civil Court hearing in Nairobi. I was delegated to act as their escort. As they were both 'locals' and known to me, there was no question of any trouble on route, so rather than go by train, I chose to use my car. Not surprisingly they were keen to know about their personal arrangements.

"What happens when we arrive in Nairobi this evening?"

"I book you into the Police Station near the Court and you'll spend the night in custody."

"Where will you be staying?"

"I've booked into the 'Norfolk Hotel' for the night. I'll collect you in the morning and produce you before the Court."

"Why can't we stay in the 'Norfolk?"

"Because you are under arrest and the police do not provide hotel accommodation."

"But what if we pay for it out of our own pockets?"

"For two reasons. One, I repeat you are in my custody, and two, I doubt very much if, in the circumstances you can afford it."

"Look, what if we stay at the 'Norfolk' and share a room. You can have our room key and lock us in when we arrive, let us out for dinner, then lock us inside again for the night?"

Now Police Station cells are not the best of places, and after all they were not criminals. Also, every hotel window was covered in a thief proof security mesh, so even if they did escape, there was no where to 'run' to. I was beginning to 'soften'.

"How much do you have between you?"

"We calculate that we are about three hundred shillings short (£15), can you lend it to us? We promise to repay it the day after we get back home."

As they both lived within our police area, why not?

"On one condition, it has to be cash."

"Done!"

As agreed, I saw them to their room and locked them in. We had dinner together, and I locked them in for the night, then presented them at Court next day. They were not detained and upon our return they kept their promise and duly delivered three hundred shillings in cash.

Even those born and bred in England can become confused at the vagaries of the English language, so it will come as no surprise to read that both African and Asian attempts to master it could lead to some strange situations. However, before we smile at the stumbling attempts of non-English speakers, it would be as well to point out that new arrivals from the UK were equally prone to make fools of themselves. In particular, two words in Kiswahili were regularly confused with each other. One word was for a 'table fork' and the other for a very delicate part of the female anatomy. New male arrivals from the UK were easily spotted by their red and peeling noses, white knees and their propensity to try to speak *Kiswahili*. The usual venues for these attempts were hotel restaurants.

The normal scene was to see a new arrival call over the waiter and (unknowingly) ask for the delicate part of the female anatomy. The waiters had heard it all before and the standard reply was "Effendi, *you* want a fork, *I* want (the Kiswahili word for the delicate part of the female anatomy!)".

African Constables were encouraged to learn English and, once qualified, became known as 'Literates'. From various sources outside the normal run of Queen's English they would acquire additional words not to be found in the English dictionary. One day an African female reported to the Constable behind the Charge Office desk that she had been sexually assaulted. The standard procedure was to record details of the complaint, complete a brief description of the nature of the injury/attack on a special form, then send it and the complainant (under escort) to the Government Doctor. On this occasion the Constable excelled himself. In the description section of the form stating the nature of the assault, he penned the letters '*f-a-i-c-k-e-d*'.

It was framed and placed on the Charge Office wall!

How the four-letter word was picked up, sometimes defied belief. A Mission Station asked the local European Police Officer if he could take on a young African called Francis. Francis was about fourteen and according to the Mission mad keen to improve his English as, when of age, he wanted to join the Kenya Police Force. Philip, the son of a UK vicar was not keen, but said all he could do was to offer Francis a position in the household assisting the cook and later serving at table.

Philip, being of clergy stock, never used bad language and made it well known that he did not approve of some of his more forthright colleagues. Francis soon fitted into the household and Philip, time permitting, helped Francis to improve his linguistic ability.

From time to time Philip and his wife entertained the local *boma* (administrative area) Europeans. Their invitations were always well received. They had an excellent cook and under the watchful eye of the lady of the house they always produced a memorable meal.

Francis by this time was regularly serving at table, looking very smart in his long starched *kanzu* (a long, white one-piece garment), white gloves, red cummerbund and red tarbush hat. On this night the first course was cleared away and the guests waited with expectation for the main course. Francis served the meat and then commenced to serve the vegetables. Whilst doing so he dropped one of the serving spoons onto the floor and in a soft voice said "f*** it."

There was a stunned silence. The ladies looked at their plates and the men tried to look nonchalant.

Philip, deeply embarrassed, said "Francis, I want to see you outside, now!"

When outside he said, "Francis you have used a terrible word and upset my guests."

Francis looked nonplussed and asked innocently "Which word was it?"

Philip, with some difficulty, repeated the word.

Francis, still looking nonplussed, asked "What does it mean?"

After a long pause Philip replied, "It means going to bed with a woman."

The reply, based on African logic, was, "But there's nothing wrong with that Sir!"

From time to time we would receive letters from Asian mechanics seeking work in the Police workshops. One priceless one read:

> *Dear Sir,*
> *I live just five miles from your Police Station as the cock crows and I badly need the work as I have five little stomachs hanging round my neck and I cannot make their ends meet.*

A very common letter was:

Dear Sir,
I wish to be a spanner in your works.

We may laugh, but could we do as well in Hindi or Urdu?

Sometimes complainants would come to the Police Station and report in a mixture of English and Kiswahili. I well recall an old Sikh rushing in and shouting, "Sahib, Sahib, rascal buggers broke into backside of *duka* (shop) *usiku* (at night). Real rascal buggers Sahib!"

As in the example above, some older Asians used the word 'backside' to express the rear of anything, which always amused me. Such a use of this word may have seemed logical to them, but it always sounded strange to me to receive a response to a question such as "where is so-and-so?" with the answer "He's round the backside."

Another linguistic curiosity I well recall was a local Scottish Mission Station which had its telephone manned by an African who had picked up a strong Scottish accent so pure he could have come from Glasgow!

Most Europeans were given (often without their knowledge) an African name. The name tended to refer to some aspect of that person that anyone could easily identify. For example, a fat man would be called Bwana Tumbo (Mr Stomach), someone who shouted a lot Bwana Kelele (Mr Noisy), someone with a moustache Bwana Msharubu (Mr Moustache), someone who kept lots of chickens Bwana Kuku (Mr Chicken) etc, etc. I was discussing this with an old European farmer, who told me that at one time a fat man lived on top of a nearby hill and was therefore known as Bwana Tumbo Juu (Mr Fat Up). Much lower down the hill was another fat man, who was called Bwana Tumbo Chini (Mr Fat Down). He told me that one day he called at the small local post office as the incoming mail was being sorted and was very amused to hear the two African postal clerks saying as they placed their mail into respective piles.

"Bwana Tumbo Chini"
"Bwana Tumbo Juu."
"Bwana Tumbo Chini."
"Bwana Tumbo Juu."

Some farming friends travelled to South Africa by car. The amount of tarmac road from Kenya, until arriving at the South African border, is close to zero. In order to obtain some form of drainage, some of the roads have a high point in the centre. However, this does have a disadvantage, because as the rainwater runs off it causes corrugations to form across the surface of the road which cause terrible vibrations within any vehicle that travels along it. The best method to combat this is to drive as fast as possible, which makes for a slightly smoother journey. Very few cars, if any, in the 1950s were designed to take this kind of punishment for several thousand miles. As a result, when they arrived within South Africa the silencer of their exhaust system had usually either fractured or fallen off.

This fate had befallen my friends, who were stopped by a South African police officer of Boer extraction and asked in a strong Afrikaans accent, "Where is your quietess?"

The next Police Division had a large Afrikaans population and one particular family did not like the British and was always in trouble with the police. The father would be in a bar and a British person would enter and order a drink. The father would then go over and introduce himself and say in his guttural Afrikaans, "Before you leave 'ere, you will say 'ello to me in my own language." Failure to comply with this request, or even worse to use the Kiswahili word 'Jambo', resulted in an assault. His other approach was to introduce himself and say "'Ave a drink with me my friend." To respond that you had your own drink resulted in the same outcome.

During a temporary secondment, a filling in one of my teeth became loose. Enquiries revealed that the nearest dentist was in Nairobi, some hundred miles away, so what was I to do? Someone at the District Commissioner's office said that there was a dentist at the nearby Mission Station. My colleague said that he also needed treatment, so we decided to go together. As the Mission did not have a telephone we simply arrived. It was run by Italian nuns. Having made our wishes known to the Mother Superior, we were introduced to a nun no more than five feet tall with spectacles like jam jar ends. This was the dentist! With reluctance I opted to go first.

The surgery consisted of an old-fashioned dentist's chair and beside it an even older treadle-operated dentist's drilling machine. My courage started to wane. She spoke to me in Italian, which I could not comprehend. I tried my schoolboy French; she couldn't comprehend. I then asked her in Kiswahili "Una fahamu Kiswahili?" (do you understand Kiswahili?)

She said that she did and then asked in Kiswahili (which translated means) "Can you hold up?" I understood from this comment that she was not able to give me an anaesthetic and would this be OK? As the tooth needed fixing I replied with great reluctance, "Yes." but quailed at the thought of having my tooth drilled using an antiquated treadle machine *and* without any anaesthetic. She then went to a wall cabinet and poured some clear liquid into a glass and told me to drink it. It was orange liqueur! I then had an injection and, using her foot 'like a fiddler's elbow', she proceeded to drill my tooth and then fill the cavity. I went outside to wait for my colleague.

"I bet you didn't expect an orange liqueur," I said to him as we drove back together.

"What orange liqueur?" he said, "she didn't give *me* any."

"Oh..." I replied. "She asked me could I hold up and I said 'yes'. What did *you* say?"

"Well... I thought she meant could I manage without an injection and so I said 'no'."

That nun's equipment may have been old fashioned, but her filling lasted for nearly twenty years.

It was easy to overlook things we Europeans took as normal, but to African eyes appeared abnormal. The questions could come at any time. Sometimes when resting during a patrol, or from the driver when on a routine visit to Headquarters.

The questions were always phrased in a similar way. Here are a few typical examples:

"Effendi... Why do Europeans blow their nose and then put it into their pocket?"

"Effendi... Why do European men allow other men to see their wives bodies?" This in reference to European ladies wearing a bathing costume, or worse still, to African eyes, a 'bikini'.

"Effendi... You have the best grass in your garden that is ideal for sheep and cattle but you don't allow them to graze there. Why not?"

"Effendi… Why does the local Mission have one God, and the Mission twenty miles away have another?" This referred to C of E and Catholic Missions.

These 'out of the blue' questions always brought to mind that old saying, "If only we could see ourselves as others see us."

12   Rissoles, toothbrushes and PT

Our six months home leave had now expired and we were on our way back to Kenya, but not just the two us, my wife was expecting our first child and experiencing very severe morning sickness. They say that pregnant women bloom, with us it was just the opposite. She had lost weight and looked quite drawn.

Our flight was uneventful and upon arrival in Nairobi we checked into the New Stanley Hotel. As we were both feeling the effects of the usual twenty-eight hour flight, we had a light meal and 'fell' into bed.

Next morning I reported to Police Headquarters to receive details of my next posting and was directed to report to the Provincial Headquarters where I had first joined Crime Branch.

During our home leave we had purchased a new 'Ford' car which we had returned to 'Ford's' export department some weeks prior to our departure, and on arrival we collected it from the main 'Ford' dealer in Nairobi. Thus armed with independent transport we set off on a leisurely but lengthy drive. It was the 'dry season', so I had no qualms about being stuck in thick mud on the side of the road with my wife in her current condition.

On route we passed many familiar land marks. During our descent of the escarpment, we had had wonderful views across the Kedong Valley to Mount Suswa and ahead of us in the far distance, Mount Longenot. At the base of the escarpment on our right was the Italian Church, the scene of our night ambush some years before, then past the Kijabe crossroads and, to our left, the dirt road to Narok and Akira Ranch. These initial sights recalled very many pleasant memories.

Arriving at Provincial Headquarters, to our surprise and delight, we were informed that we were to return to our previous posting.

It had been a long drive, with at least half the distance on dirt roads, but now we were almost 'home'. Entering the township's outskirts we were onto a tarmac road again, first passing the Country Club and then the theatre where the lady pianist had refused to play 'God Save The Queen'. We stopped outside the Police Station. I alighted to be greeted by one of the Constables. He saluted and shook my hand.

"Jambo Effendi, ngosi yako ni sawasawa rangi ya mziwa!" (Hello Sir, your skin is like the colour of milk). My previous Kenya tan had faded, although I wasn't aware that it had faded that much!

At Divisional Headquarters I learned that I had been posted to take charge of a Police Station situated in the heart of the European farming community. Its claim to fame was that during the time of *Dini ya Msambwa* (a violent quasi-religious sect) it had been attacked; most of the buildings were burned to the ground and some of the Police officers killed. However, that was many years ago and *Dini ya Msambwa* no longer existed, so we could sleep soundly in our beds.

Our Government bungalow was part of the Police Station main building and, by walking through a door from our lounge I was immediately in the Charge Office. We did not have a bathroom or any running water. Our toilet was a 'long drop' situated some twenty yards away against our boundary fence. Beyond this was Africa. Water was brought in daily by donkey. The ration per day was the same for all ranks, four gallons per person. This was not only for cooking, but for washing clothes and personal hygiene. As a result, the only 'bath' that we could have was in a canvas folding 'safari bath', about thirty inches square and some twelve inches deep. The only possibility was to have a daily sponge down using as little water as possible.

Within weeks of our arrival we were being invited out for dinner by members of the European farming community. Our hosts, realising our water situation, would normally ask if we would care to have a bath before dining? We never refused, and it was utter bliss to soak in a lovely hot, normal bath and not be averse to using masses of water (although to this day we both hate to see water wasted).

During our leave I had maintained contact with Steven our cook, so when our final destination was known, I wrote to him and he appeared within days, greeting us with a big smile and asking how *Ulaya* (England) had been and had we seen our mothers and fathers and were they well? With Steven in situ, we knew that despite the obvious shortcomings, at least we would eat well!

Not every household was blessed with a good cook. Within the area nominally under the 'control' of 'my' Police Station was a bachelor farmer who was very proud of his cook's ability to produce his favourite main course, rissoles. He waxed lyrical about their texture, just sufficient onion to create the right flavour and the shape, so uniform, with a slight mound in the centre.

Now let us dwell for a brief moment on the perfect rissole shape. How might it be achieved? Perhaps the raw ingredients were cupped between two palms to produce the required shape? Alas no. Purely by chance our gourmet friend entered his kitchen, which was not far removed from the type the army must have used in the Crimea, to find his cook wreathed in a cloud of wood smoke and producing, yes you've guessed it, his favourite main dish. So how was the unusual shape produced? In a special mould? Well almost. The cook was using a mould given to him by nature. His left armpit! But the story does not end there. It was later discovered that the cook had impetigo!

In the light of the foregoing information I was very thankful that I had never been invited there to lunch!

When the term 'colonial' is used, many people imagine a group of Europeans living a life of indolence supported by a host of coloured servants. However, in our experience, nothing could have been further from the truth.

Some farmer friends of ours had come to Kenya soon after the war. Both had been in the RAF, had met, married and arrived in Kenya with just two suitcases and very little money. For three years they worked for a European farmer for no pay – just their keep and a small, grass-thatched African-type hut in which to live. They kept chickens, sold both the meat and the eggs and later moved to a paid position. Now with a degree of security they commenced to have a family. Some years later, due to diligence and careful husbandry of their money, they had a small farm of their own and, by this time, two children aged six and eight. Now being more affluent, they also had a cook, who, under Bea's guidance, produced excellent, wholesome meals. However, not all was domestic bliss. The problem was toothbrushes.

The toothbrushes owned by the parents mysteriously became useless within a few weeks, the bristles all splayed back. They were discarded and replaced by new brushes, but only to be reduced to the same condition in a very short space of time. The children were suspected of tom-foolery, and given that imported toothbrushes were not cheap they were told in no uncertain terms that this abuse of their parents' toothbrushes had to stop! All protests of innocence were rejected. It was naughty to tell lies and if it continued the imprint of father's hand would be left on their bottoms!

One night when the family were engrossed in eating their dinner, during a brief period of silence a sound of soft scrubbing could be heard. Peter tiptoed down the passage. The noise was coming from the bathroom. There, deeply engrossed, brush in hand with toothpaste all over his mouth and teeth was the cook! He'd been sharing their toothbrushes for weeks!

Peter and Bea were a very enterprising couple, and as their farm progressed and consequently produced more income, they decided to make extensive improvements. All the required bricks and roof tiles would be moulded and baked on the farm. The basic idea was to add extra rooms and extend others. However, an initial period of demolition isolated the bathroom in an area that was planned to form an internal courtyard, resulting in a situation whereby, in the interests of privacy, baths could only be taken after the staff had retired. Furthermore, as this pro-tem 'bathroom' had no ceiling or electric lighting, moonlit nights were preferred as bath nights, as a paraffin 'hurricane' lantern would attract all the *dudus* (insects) in East Africa.

With my wife's pregnancy advancing by the day I was concerned regarding our distance from the hospital in town and I had mentioned this when at Divisional Headquarters. I was assured that closer to the event we would be transferred back into town. The morning sickness was still bad and my wife was advised by the European lady doctor in town, who was in private practice, to take a new 'wonder drug' 'thalidomide' which would alleviate her condition. My wife declined, saying she did not normally take any form of medication and was not keen to take any drugs that might affect the baby. Thank God she refused! Within less than six months babies were being born in Europe and America with deformed limbs and 'thalidomide' was withdrawn. It had been a very close call.

Having taken over the Police Station from the out-going incumbent and settled in, I could sense that morale needed a boost. It was evident in the attitude of all ranks and I had a pretty shrewd idea what was needed. I called the Sergeant Major.

"Every Wednesday morning at 7am we will have physical training. Every Friday morning at the same time we will have a drill parade, followed by inspection of the 'lines', the Police Station and finally our Land Rover and three-tonner. The only people excused will be the night duty staff, and the staff who relieved them."

"Ndiyo Effendi."

"And Sergeant Major, I do not want to find any dirt, dust or litter anywhere, including over our perimeter fence. Is that clear?"

"Ndiyo Effendi."

He saluted and left the office.

The following Wednesday it was time for P.T. Like the *askaris* I was dressed in shorts and a short-sleeved vest. Having done some simple exercises we went for a run for about a mile. Following more simple exercises we tried press-ups. As I normally did these most mornings my muscles were well toned and ten press-ups were a 'doddle'. I faced the men and I did each press-up very slowly. By five, over fifty percent of my new team had collapsed onto the ground. The remaining percentage had not collapsed, but at every press-up their arms were quivering with the effort.

"Come on we're men not women, get off the ground!" I exhorted.

Only about ten percent managed ten. It was my oblique way of proving to them that I led from the front and it gained their respect.

For the next exercise I split them into two teams with one team forming a large circle and the other in the centre. I then produced a football, explaining that the team forming the circle had to try and hit those within the circle below the knee. Anyone so hit joined the outer circle and would try to eliminate their former team mates. I joined those within the circle. They loved it! There was lots of laughter, shouted instructions to one another, with lots of "Ah la's!" – a typical African expression. I was in the last three to be eliminated and there were shouts of delight when I was 'clobbered' with a well aimed ball. The teams now changed sides.

This broad pattern was repeated every Wednesday. Sometimes when unobserved, I was amused to note some of the men in the 'lines' practising press-ups prior to our Wednesday morning P.T. session.

These Wednesday mornings became so popular, that the Sergeant Major would take them for a run before 7am then knock on my window at about 6.55am saying they were back and all ready for P.T. Both the press-ups and the morale improved.

I could still muster up my 'parade ground voice', developed at the Police Training School, Kiganjo, so, armed with this, plus attention to even small details, it was noticeable that the men took pride (*heshima*) in their turnout, plus their joint ability when performing drill on our small parade ground. Morale was soon back to normal.

Something I had quickly learned during my first tour was to lead your team from the front, be firm, be fair, be human, have a sense of humour, and your men would follow you 'to hell and back'. When I finally returned to the UK I encountered many so called 'managers', (including several in the American company that I joined), who had yet to learn and apply these very simple rules.

During our stay nothing major happened. There was the occasional assault, normally drink related, plus some minor traffic offences. Due to the distance into town, all these minor offences were dealt with by a local Magistrate, the Court being held within the 'all ranks' canteen.

We often carried out routine raids for illegal brewing.

To explain the system, drink was the cause of most assaults and murders. In order to keep drinking within reasonable limits, Africans working on European farms had to apply to their employer for permission to brew beer. The limit of four gallons of home brew per person was quite generous. Within the Reserves there was no limit, unless this was imposed by the local Chief or Headman.

On one occasion my wife and I had been away for the day and upon our return, as I passed by our dustbin, there was a distinct smell of beer! Lifting the lid the smell was more than potent! I called Steven. He appeared 'glassy eyed' and had difficulty with words.

"Steven, have you been brewing illegal beer?"

He looked down at the ground.

"Ndiyo Effendi."

"And you know this is an offence don't you?"

"Ndiyo Effendi."

"Steven I will have to charge you, if I do not do so, others will see that you are being favoured."

"Na fahamu Effendi." (I understand Sir).

The next Court day, Steven greeted the Magistrate at the entrance to the Court and handed him a twenty shilling note! I had to quickly explain to the surprised Magistrate that this was not a bribe, but that Steven was simply unaware of Court procedure. Steven was later fined fifteen shillings, which he thought very fair as he received five shillings change, and he promised not to break the law again.

With my wife's pregnancy nearing full-term, as promised we were transferred back into town and allocated a very pleasant bungalow of stone construction with a large garden, which was situated not so very far from our original wooden shack.

Within three months of our son Michael's birth, and following a change of Officer i/c Divisional Police Headquarters, we were transferred within the same Division and I was to take on increased responsibility.

13 Africa as far as the eye can see

Having been transferred back into Divisional Headquarters prior to the birth of our son I had been employed once again as a Court Prosecutor, a position I thoroughly enjoyed. We had a very pleasant home, an excellent social life, and, as Steven was still with us, excellent food. However, being offered increased responsibility in a new area was something I couldn't resist.

So we were on the move again. I was being posted within the same Division but taking charge of an area not so dissimilar to Masai. I had a much larger staff and with this, in addition to the main Police Station, three Police Posts under the control of African NCOs. There were no European farms, just one huge native Reserve that stretched to the Uganda border. Although there were European farms along one of the boundaries, the local natives, unlike the Masai, never stole their cattle, this they reserved for their own kind and only stole from each other which, based on my previous experience, was quite a novel twist.

Taking over a Police Station was a reasonably complicated affair. There were files to be checked and signed for, including secret files such as the 'informers file' and attendant cash. Then every firearm had to have its number checked against the inventory and every round of ammunition had to be accounted for. Last but not least was the cell register, as no prisoner could be held in custody for more than 24 hours (excluding weekends) before being charged in Court. In addition, there were 'handing over notes' in which the out-going officer detailed anything of importance, together with observations on members of staff who were good or who needed watching. Once the handing over document was signed and countersigned everything became the incoming officer's responsibility.

Having completed the above procedures and duly taken over my new Police Station in the north west of Kenya, I was quietly confident that everything was under control.

One day later, Corporal Joram, a member of the Investigation Section, asked what I was going to do about the body.

"Body? What body?"

"The body that was reported three days ago Effendi."

"I don't know about any body. Where is it?"

"In the hills about twenty miles away Effendi"

"Did the Chief Inspector know about this?"

"Oh yes Effendi, I gave him the report two days ago."

It was immediately apparent what had happened. Home leaves to UK took place only about every three to three and a half years, depending on whether you were working in a healthy or unhealthy climate and were therefore very precious. However, anyone becoming involved in a criminal case could not go on leave until the Court case, or Supreme Court case was finalised, hence the departing Chief Inspector's 'omission' to avoid becoming involved.

It turned out to be a simple case, though somewhat gruesome. The deceased had come home drunk and commenced beating his wife and children. When he was asleep she had chopped his head off. We investigated the case, recovered the decapitated body plus the head, obtained first class statements from various witnesses and arrested the wife. Later she appeared before the Supreme Court and received a reasonably light sentence due to extreme provocation.

There was very little violent crime, the most common being assault due to drink, with the 'odd' murder once a year, when a wife (as I had so quickly discovered) decapitated a violent and drunken husband, or, again due to drink, a male was accused of murder. These murders involved very little investigation in the true sense of the word. The local Headman normally arrested the accused and produced her and sometimes him at the Police Station. The accused normally pleaded "guilty", so apart from visiting the scene of the crime, taking statements from witnesses to uncover the facts, recovering the body for an autopsy and placing the accused before the Court, there were never any complications as far as domestic violence was concerned.

When taking over a Police Station, irrespective of its size, it was always rewarding to make an immediate improvement. This was not usually very difficult, as an incoming officer sees everything 'with new eyes'. However, on this occasion perhaps the term 'new nose' would be more appropriate. The Officer concerned inspected the cell block and decided that the prisoners' long-drop (a pit toilet; this was up country and water-borne sanitation wasn't available) was, to say the least, odorous and needed some form of action. Apart from this, he was well pleased with everything else. But how does one cleanse a pit latrine some twenty feet deep? Having considered every possibility he decided that the obvious solution was fire. For safety reasons he cleared the cell block and then had four gallons of petrol poured down the pit with a trail of petrol leading from it to some ten yards away. He placed a match to the trail, ignited it and… there was an enormous explosion which demolished the prisoners' toilet block, scattering 'night soil' in every direction and placed the Inspector in hospital for 24 hours. The reason? Not only the petrol but also the methane gas generated by the latrine had added to the explosion.

Exertions now urgently required but not previously considered, included a massive clean-up of the entire Police Station building, including the roof!

At my new posting my wife and I were allocated a very pleasant stone built bungalow with a large surrounding garden of such proportions, that it was possible to 'chip' a golf ball within its confines using a No. 7 golf club. The immediate surrounding area was very green with numerous tall trees, so unlike the arid conditions of Masai. The *boma* that contained all the European housing, plus the administrative buildings associated with the District Commissioner's Office, the Police Station and the hospital, was at some eight thousand feet above sea level. This made for an ideal climate with gentle warm days and, perhaps difficult to believe, as this was Africa, frosty nights. Following dinner, we would enter the lounge where there was a crackling log fire, then sit beside its warmth, feeling the heat on our faces, listening to the wet wood hissing and spitting as we consumed our coffee. There was no electricity, so we had a series of paraffin pressure lamps that emitted a soft hissing sound, giving a circle of bright light and casting deep dark shadows into the corners of the room. The firelight would dance on the walls and the ceiling, superimposed with our own shadows. As I pen these words remembering our then new home and those fireside nights, two words immediately come to mind, 'cosy' and 'contentment'.

Having consumed our after-dinner coffee, Steven would come to collect our empty cups and bid us goodnight.

"*Kwa heri Effendi. Kwa heri Memsahib.*"

We would then read for a while, sitting close to a pressure lamp. Then feeling tired, would retire for the night, taking one pressure lamp into the bedroom. As I carried the lamp, I would be conscious of its heat rising towards my face, plus the soft hissing of the pressure burner, with the bright light cutting into the shadows ahead and leaving darkness in our wake. At this height there were no mosquitoes, so at first it was strange sleeping without a net over our bed, or our son's tiny cot.

However, there were two aspects connected with living at this altitude which I had overlooked but having taken Physics at school I should have been aware of. Firstly, it was impossible to have a decent cup of tea, because water's boiling point is lower at eight thousand feet. The other problem was that the altitude affected a car's carburation with a loss of some three percent efficiency per thousand feet. My Volkswagen still performed, but whereas second gear would normally be adequate for very steep climbs, I now had to use first. Later, Volkswagen produced a special carburettor which contained a small sphere that was affected by atmospheric pressure and adjusted the flow of fuel to the engine. It proved to be very effective. I suppose that I should add a third. A little whisky 'went a very long way'. Any visitor newly arrived from England would begin to look 'cross-eyed' after two tots of 'Scotland's best'.

Within the *boma* we had an excellent tennis court which was well frequented and, due to the number of European families, there was also a small club house. There was always something going on organised by the ladies, with our trips into Divisional Headquarters always providing a welcome diversion. It would prove to be a very pleasant and enjoyable posting.

It was at this posting that we acquired 'Judy', a gambolling Golden Retriever pup. She was an utter delight, a ball of playful golden fur. Perhaps it was because she was female, as without any training over time she developed a natural instinct to guard our baby son. Normally she was docile unless any stranger approached our son's pram, then her hackles rose and her teeth were bared. When we finally departed to England, 'Judy' was also flown home into quarantine and six months later re-joined our family. It was a very sad day when some years later she died of a kidney complaint.

My three Police Posts were distinctly diverse. One was situated on the river that was our border between Kenya and Uganda. Another was on the border of the Reserve and the European farming area. Its prime function, as this was a Native Reserve and a closed area, was to prevent illegal entry, so it could only be entered by obtaining a permit from the District Commissioner The third, was a full day's journey away which normally involved an overnight stop and staying with the local District Officer. The climate there was very different from that of the boma. It was below sea level and therefore very hot and very humid.

Some evenings my wife and I would walk up the track from the *boma*, enjoying the cool evening air, then from a vantage point look in the direction of this far-flung Post. The mountains stretched away to the horizon, the far peaks appearing almost a deep purple at that late hour of the day, with the remotest peaks fading into a pale mauve. Soon the sun would start to sink low in the sky, staining the clouds a deep orange red, then finally, it would appear right on the horizon as a bright golden orange ball that was almost too bright to look at. At this juncture, with the sun rapidly sinking below the horizon and with the light now fading, we would make our way home with the pram gently bumping over the rough, stony earth track and with Judy, who was now about four months old, walking alongside, wagging her tail.

At this stage of their development, the local native population would be best described as being 'wild and woolly'. Several years before, some of them had been recruited into a quasi-religious organisation that was led by one of their own people who told them he could converse with God. He did so using an empty tin (about the size of a can of baked beans) talking into the open end, and then placing his ear to the opening to listen to 'God's response'. Some of the people believed him, and as a result he started to amass quite a following. Now this in itself did not project any threat, however, the sect called itself *Dini ya Msambwa*. The word *dini* means religion and they became militant. This culminated in a small Police Station being attacked, some policemen killed and buildings set alight.

Something had to be done. A small armed police party under the command of a European police officer and accompanied by a District Officer went into the Reserve to arrest the ringleader. Having de-bussed several hundred yards from a large group of some two hundred armed members of *Dini ya Msambwa*, the Police Officer formed his men into a line and told them to load their rifles and be ready to open fire, but only to do so on his order. The natives started to advance on the police party and they were told to halt or the police would open fire. The District Officer assured him that they were not posing a threat but merely performing a 'dance of welcome', but as the armed natives continued to 'dance' closer and closer, the Police Officer again called upon them to halt or the police would open fire.

This was ignored and still they came on.

By now the distance was under fifty yards. The order to fire was given, but was immediately countermanded by the District Officer. The distance was now very, very close. Again the order to open fire was given, and again the order was countermanded by the District Officer.

It turned out to be a fatal error. The police party was attacked and very few survived, ironically, one of the few being the District Officer, who managed to reach the police truck with just a few police askaris. Some years later at another posting I met one of the surviving askaris. He told me the story and afterwards declared, "Effendi, if ever you feel that we may be killed, never hesitate to give the order to open fire!"

Following this tragic incident, the Enquiry stated that, should there in the future be a valid and legal reason to use firearms, only the Police had the ultimate authority to issue the order to open fire, an order which could not be countermanded by anyone in the Civil Administration. A stone memorial was erected at the site of the massacre to commemorate this needless loss of life.

Christmas (known as *sikuku*) was seized upon by the locals as an opportunity to make some money. The method was for them to appear in all their native finery, including shields, spears, rattles around knees or ankles, war paint, and with many in the 'war party' having the skin of a leopard draped around their shoulders or heads adorned with ostrich feathers. Thus attired they would perform 'war dances' on the lawn of each house. As each party consisted of at least fifty individuals, to have given a small sum such as one might give to a bunch of English carol singers was out of the question – the sum required was more like one hundred shillings (£5), a not inconsiderable sum in those days. With hindsight, perhaps the spears and shields provided more than an oblique encouragement to be generous in the amount of each donation!

On route to my farthest Post, which (as you now know) was a whole day's drive away over many miles on a very rough stone and earth 'road' (which, incidentally, was always dotted with piles of elephant dung) there was a Catholic Mission run by nuns and overseen by a Catholic priest of advanced years. I was to learn that the Mother Superior was a rugby fanatic and always wanted to know how the Irish team was faring and that the Father was not allowed to have any alcohol unless it was first offered to a guest. Consequently, after greeting me his next words hardly ever differed.

"Would you be fancying a cold beer?"

As it was always very hot when I called and I was one of the very few Europeans that he ever saw, I never refused. Being a Mission they always received plenty of local information so, by calling, it allowed me to pick up the latest gossip and to 'keep my finger on the local pulse'.

Whenever I called I normally sat on a wooden chair, however, during one particular call the Father offered me a seat in a large, over-stuffed armchair. Having been bounced around in a Land Rover for many score miles I gladly accepted. I sank into it and grasped the cool glass of beer he handed to me, enjoying the feel of the cool condensation on the outside of the glass. We raised our glasses to each other and I took a long, thirst-quenching draught. Nectar! We discussed many things; he was an excellent raconteur and I always enjoyed my brief visits. Having drained our glasses and politely refusing his offer of another, we said our goodbyes and I set off for the long, rough journey back to base.

Some days later my back began to feel uncomfortable. Two days after that, a series of small bumps on my back were starting to feel sore. That night following dinner, I asked my wife to look at my back.

"It looks as if you've been bitten by something," she told me. "You have about thirty small boil-like lumps on your back. I'll put some 'Savlon' on them."

Sleep was difficult and by morning, although the redness had reduced, the lumps had increased in size and were very uncomfortable.

The following day I worked at my desk but by the evening I had gained the distinct impression that the lumps had movement. Surely this was not possible? That evening by the light of a pressure lamp my wife again examined my back.

"Your lumps look like boils. Let me take a closer look."

She used a small magnifying glass.

"You won't believe this," she exclaimed, "but the heads of the boils are moving!"

This I couldn't believe!

"Are you sure?"

"Yes. Oh my goodness, look at this one! I can see it moving!"

She squeezed the lump – it hurt like hell! Out popped a small wriggling maggot! I could hardly believe my eyes – and I had thirty of them! During the next few evenings I suffered as the numbers were slowly but surely reduced. I realised what the cause must be – the 'tumbo fly'. They normally lay their eggs in the soil and if any washing is placed on the grass to dry, the eggs hatch and the maggots, which are finer than a human hair, enter into the cloth. When the clothes are worn, the heat of the body attracts these minuscule maggots which burrow into the flesh and commence to feed and grow. I questioned our 'house boy' but he was adamant that all our washing was dried on the clothes line. My back soon healed and the incident was forgotten.

Some weeks later, I received information that a group of American anthropologists had received permission to enter the area for a month in order to carry out some research. We invited the group for dinner and they explained their plans and intentions. The leader was a Dr Francis Conant from the University of San Francisco. One of his colleagues stated it was his intention to apply the 'Rauch Test'. This test consists of a blob of ink being placed into the fold of a sheet of paper, the paper is then folded and opened to reveal a specific shape. The person taking the test is then asked what the shape represents to them.

"Where you are going they will not even know it is ink," I told him.

I don't think he believed me.

Some weeks later we had them to dinner again and I could not resist asking, "Well…? How did the ink test go?"

"Hell, you were right!" he exclaimed, "they didn't even know it was goddam ink!" We all collapsed with laughter.

Francis Conant stayed on to complete his research and suffered a chain of disasters. I had warned him about flash floods. Our area could be enjoying a normal pleasant climate. However, it being a vast mountainous region, many miles away it might be raining very heavily, creating a 'wall of water' that would rush down a dry river bed for mile after mile, carrying all before it. On my arrival I had been warned about this. Even when there was no rain, the standard procedure before crossing a dry river bed was to stop the vehicle, get out and listen. If you couldn't hear any roaring, it was safe to cross.

Francis must have ignored my warnings. On one occasion, his Land Rover was hit by a flash flood and swept about two miles downstream. He was very lucky not to lose his life. He arrived at our bungalow in a very distressed state looking like a survivor from the 'Titanic'. The Land

Rover was later recovered and the engine stripped to remove every vestige of grit and soil. When the bodywork had been repaired, it looked as good as new.

His second disaster was that he too developed lumps on his back from the dreaded tumbo fly. Just like mine, they developed and became very sore. For several nights he sat in our bathroom, fortified by whisky and muttering "Oh my God!" as – by the light of a pressure lantern – I squeezed out the maggots from his back. I knew from personal experience just how painful this 'operation' could be, so I was not surprised by his constant exclamations to the Almighty, each one followed by a tot of whisky!

Some days later we were comparing notes as to when and how we had managed to pick up these tiny pests. The only common factor was to sit in the Father's over-stuffed chair at the Mission. I sent a message to him explaining that I had reason to believe his cosy chair was the cause of our mutual discomfort. It was duly examined and found to be crawling with these pests and had to be burned.

We enjoyed Francis Conant's company and his ability on the tennis court, so it was a sad day when he finally had to return to the United States.

By now our son was ten months old and had not yet been Christened. As a result, when passing, I called upon the Reverend Totty at the C of E Mission and arranged a suitable day. Steven, our cook, produced a special cake and Annette Totty said it was the first time she had ever seen a child eat some of its own christening cake! The Totty's became firm friends and ever since those far off days we have remained in touch.

The Totty's, who were now into their sixties, were the first missionaries into the area and over the years had created many converts. Several years later Annette Totty translated the Bible into the local language and, as with most Europeans, was given an African name, 'Chepaipai'. It means the Smiling One.

Life as a Police Officer was never dull. One morning I received a radio message from a Police Post which was many miles beyond the Catholic Mission Station; a man had been shot with a poisoned arrow by some cattle thieves who had crossed from Uganda. I loaded our medical kit and with a driver plus two askaris, we set off for the long and very rough drive to the Post.

The native poisons were usually grass based and were quite capable of killing an elephant, therefore, I did not think that we would find this man alive. But we did. He had saved his own life. The barbed arrow had penetrated his side, just below the rib cage. Realising that he would be dead in minutes, using his knife he cut around the arrow and deep into the muscle, removing the arrow with a lump of his bleeding flesh attached. He had then staggered for several miles to obtain help from the Police Post. When we arrived he had lost a lot of blood and was very weak and unable to speak. Would we be able to save his life? The deep hole he had cut into his side would almost have accommodated my fist. Using our biggest wound dressing I bound the wound as tightly as possible, but even before we set off on the return journey, the blood was already soaking through it. It was incredible that he had survived so far. The 'road' on the return journey – rough track would be a better description – must have caused him agony. I decided to stop en route at the Mission in order to check if they could administer some morphine, but also to give the poor man some respite from being bounced around on the floor of the Land Rover.

The Sisters were marvellous and gave him the much needed injection, but like me, doubted if he could survive the journey. We had a dilemma. We needed to get him to hospital as fast as possible, but if we drove at speed over this very rough track he would not survive. We chose a middle course of action and he was still alive when we arrived at the hospital some hours later. By now it was close to 1am; had he been a European, I feel sure that shock alone would have resulted in death.

Next morning I made enquiries at the hospital. He had survived the night but was still very weak. To my surprise, two weeks later, although not fully recovered, he came into my office and through our interpreter gave a statement about the attack and the theft of his cattle. As the thieves came from Uganda where we had no jurisdiction, I did not believe, that despite our efforts, they would ever be brought to justice, which eventually proved to be the outcome.

In Kenya, when one was responsible for a Police Post or a Police Station, irrespective of size, anything could happen at any time….

It was close to midnight; my wife and I were fast asleep when I was awoken by Judy barking and someone banging on our door, and with shouting, "Effendi, Effendi! *Kuna matata!*" (Sir, Sir, there is trouble.)

I was instantly fully awake and opened the door; it was one of the night duty staff.

"Effendi, we have just received a radio message from our Post by the river. There is a big fight taking place on the Uganda side of the river and people are being killed!"

"Right, I want a driver and four men, all armed. Radio the Post and tell them we are leaving now and we will be there in just over an hour. Inform the Sergeant to issue rifles and ammunition to six of his best men and to have a medical kit ready. When we arrive I intend to cross over into Uganda and put a stop to the fighting. Next, send a radio message to Headquarters telling them what we are going to do and tell them to contact the Uganda Police."

"Ndiyo Effendi!"

We set off at speed. This earth road was much smoother than most, but despite this we were being bounced around as we travelled in excess of sixty five miles an hour. It reminded me of our 'call outs' during the Mau-Mau times. The headlights cut into the darkness, the Land Rover leaving a heavy dust trail in its wake. As we sped along I realised that we had no legal right to cross the river and 'invade' Uganda. However, if people were being killed and the Uganda Police were not in the vicinity, then I would face the 'flak', if and when it came. Uganda, like Kenya was still a Crown Colony, so it was not as if we were a foreign power.

We arrived at the Post in a cloud of dust. The Sergeant and his men were ready and we packed as many as possible onto the Land Rover, including on the front wings and bonnet, then roared across the river's bridge. As we drew closer even above the noise of the vehicle we could hear the yells and screams. A few hundred yards ahead, and turning left off the road, the headlights illuminated a number of African huts. We could see a score of bodies on the ground and people running away. We de-bussed and I restated my order to the men.

"No one will open fire unless they believe that they will be killed. Do not aim for the body, aim for the legs. (I did not want to escalate the situation by adding to the body count and I could well imagine how it would look if the Kenya Police shot and killed Uganda citizens).

"Try and stay together." I shouted at the people that we were many police and that all fighting must stop at once! As if by a miracle all sound ceased. It went deadly quiet. We advanced cautiously, ready for any eventuality. The village was almost deserted apart from the scattered bodies.

Upon investigation the 'bodies' turned out to be injured people and no one had been killed; the basic cause of the incident was, once again, drink. Evidently many people had attended a 'big brew', then following some minor argument, the people from the visiting village had started a fight. When we approached the uninjured from both villages had fled into the bush. We spent the next few hours patching up the wounded and, as no one was at 'death's door', having ensured that all was quiet we re-crossed the river into Kenya.

The following day The Kenya Broadcasting Company news stated:

> "Following a report of fighting just over the Kenya border, a party of Kenya Police crossed the border into Uganda, put a stop to the fighting and gave first aid to the injured. No one in the Kenya Police party was injured during this incident."

As I had 'gone out on a limb' I expected at least a "well done", if not from Kenya Police Headquarters, then a "thank you" from Uganda, but all I received was silence.

The 'rains' had arrived and it poured down day after day as if someone 'up there' had left the tap on. Soon floods became a problem and we received a call from the same Police Post on the Uganda border that the river was in full flood and on the Uganda side people were in danger of being swept away. Despite having four-wheel drive and a low ratio gearbox our driver found it difficult to keep the Land Rover on the now very slippery, water-logged dirt road, and where the 'road' was level it was more like being in a boat as the Land Rover surged through the deep flood water. From time to time the vehicle almost turned sideways as the road's camber caused the rear end to slide round. A journey that normally took about an hour, took over two.

When we arrived, the river was a raging torrent with trees, dead cattle and even a crocodile being swept downstream. Normally the river was some fifty feet wide at this point but now it was close to a hundred and fifty. Across on the Uganda side we could see some native huts flooded by the rising tide of water with several people sitting up in the trees, clinging to the branches and waving in our direction. Being in the trees they were out of immediate danger, but obviously needed rescuing. We had brought a long rope, but even with this tied around the waist, plunging into this torrent of water with its attendant mass of debris meant instant injury, if not death.

A Constable called out "Effendi!"

I quickly turned around. Corporal Joel had plunged into the torrent and was striking out for the opposite bank and being rapidly swept down river. By the Grace of God he was not hit by any of the debris and waded ashore some one hundred yards downstream. It was a very, very brave act. He checked on the people sheltering in the trees and shouted towards us, his voice being drowned by the roaring noise of the raging river. We tried to convey to him by hand signals not to try and return and by his gestures he apparently understood.

I opened up our VHF radio, reported our situation and requested, if possible, the assistance of a helicopter. About forty minutes later the District Commissioner arrived, quickly followed by several European female Missionaries. Amazingly, even within this short period, the flood water had subsided and the river, although still in rapid flow, was almost half its previous width. As a result I cancelled the helicopter. The 'DC', now wearing only his 'birthday suit', waded into the river up to his waist and headed for the opposite bank – causing the Mission ladies to do a very sharp about turn to look the other way! He soon crossed and from his hand signals I deduced that everything was OK. Even within this short time the river had subsided even more and at this rate it would soon return to its normal width. Corporal Joel and the DC now returned and as no one had been drowned and everyone was safe, we made our slippery journey back to base.

I congratulated Corporal Joel on his bravery and said I would inform Divisional Head Quarters about what he had done. I verbally applied that he be awarded the 'Colonial Police Medal' for gallantry, or failing that, at least a commendation. He received neither. When I questioned this, I was told that as I had not ordered him to swim across, the award or commendation could not be made. I could not believe it! The situation was so dangerous I could not have asked him to risk his life, nor would I have done so.

The floods had been very bad and, as a result, news of this in the English press had resulted in various charities sending 'aid' to our area. I was shown a typical aid package. It consisted of a plastic wash bag containing a tube of toothpaste, a toothbrush, a bar of soap, a tiny 'Matchbox' model car, and the only viable item, a blanket made up of numerous knitted squares. I imagined the effort and enthusiasm that must have gone into putting these aid packages together, by well meaning people who had no understanding of how the people of our area lived. The only items that were used, were the soap and the blanket. Even the soap was not universally used due to its perfume, which was strange to the nostrils of the locals. The other items they had never seen before and as a result were discarded.

By now the floods had totally subsided and our duties were back to normal. As the area was so vast I decided to 'go off the beaten track' to explore areas that I had not seen before and 'show the flag' to the locals. For the initial patrol I chose a point equidistant from the Catholic Mission Station and our furthest Police Post. There were no maps, so we set off across bush country. The 'bush' had large areas of exposed red ochre earth, thorn bushes, almost semi-dry grasslands and masses of termite mounds, some of which were over four to five feet high. As the terrain was almost flat it was not difficult to keep 'pushing ahead' with the Land Rover. We then came to a river about fifteen feet wide. As we were 'off road' we needed to test its depth. I alighted from the Land Rover and walked down the river bank to the water's edge with the intention of wading across.

As usual there was brilliant, hot sunlight and as I looked down at the water's edge where it lapped the bank, I could see in either direction where the sandy soil was wet, tiny flakes of gold. It was everywhere! There was alluvial gold in the Reserve, but it had never been reported in this remote area. I bent down and scooped up a handful of wet sand. Using my fingernail I was able to pick out tiny flakes of gold. What a discovery! I could not benefit, but a discovery of this magnitude would most certainly assist the locals. Using my handkerchief, I placed two handfuls of this gold encrusted sand into its centre and secured it by knotting the corners together. We forded the river and continued with our patrol. During the whole day we only encountered about twenty of the locals so, with the sun now settling low in the sky and leaving our usual trail of red dust in our wake, we headed for the Catholic Mission.

As usual I was greeted warmly by the Father and, having settled into a wooden chair, was offered his usual hospitality. It had been a long hot day – how could I refuse? I now produced my handkerchief of gold and told him about my find.

His opening statement was "Holy Mary, we'll build a cathedral!"

I told him that I would have it analysed by the local Government Geologist and if it was gold, then I would have to submit a report to the District Commissioner. It was then up to him to progress my discovery.

The following day I contacted the Government Geologist and arranged to have my sample analysed. Arriving at his office he analysed my find using the old method of a wash pan. The sample is placed into a metal dish, almost like a wok and about the size of a large dinner plate. A small quantity of water is added and the total contents are swirled round and round. Gravity then starts to separate the various minerals. Gold being the heaviest always settles on the outer edge. I watched as the sample commenced to separate with clear lines between the various minerals. Alas, my 'gold' did not finish up on the outer edge. It was identified as iron pyrites, which, I was informed, was known as 'fool's gold'. I could easily understand how in the past many people had been persuaded to part with a fortune for a 'gold' mine containing nothing but this stuff. The mere fact that it was possible to pick out the tiny flakes from the sand had certainly fooled me! I sent a message to the Father stating that his Mission Station would be remaining in its current state.

Posho flour, which is ground maize, is one of the basic foodstuffs of the African population and it was not uncommon to see lorries carrying sacks from the grinding mills for distribution. Each sack weighed 200lbs and often these lorries were grossly overloaded, and as a result, were an obvious 'target' for traffic offences. The danger of having a grossly over-laden lorry was not so much that the springs would fail, but that the centre of gravity would become too high, causing the lorry to overturn. On one occasion, this is exactly what happened, and to add to this disaster, the rear of the lorry was enclosed. Travelling on top of this unstable load was an Asian family, consisting of a young boy aged about eight, his slightly older sister and their Mother and Father. When negotiating a bend the lorry overturned and the passengers were crushed to death under the sheer weight of the load. We 'toiled like beavers' to free them, realising that there was little hope, but we had to try. As we placed their bodies on the side of the road the family looked as if they were asleep – as we had arrived within less than thirty minutes of the accident, *rigor mortis* had not set in. The driver was only slightly injured but was later charged in Court.

Posho was an African staple food, rather like potatoes are to us, and it was not unknown for some shopkeepers (usually Asian) to 'rig' their scales and thus give short measure. We received one such complaint and as a result took the suspect bag to the Government Inspector of Measures. It should have weighed fourteen pounds but weighed just over twelve. A visit to the shop with the Inspector showed how it was done. He unscrewed the back of the scales; inside was an additional spring that came into play at around twelve pounds. The front of the scale, as seen by the African customers, registered fourteen. The shopkeeper was taken to Court, heavily fined and the scales ordered to be destroyed.

In the northern part of Kenya, just across the border, lived a tribe well known for their banditry, who from time to time would send a well armed raiding party into the Colony, intent on murder and pillage. They were always well armed, normally with Italian weapons obtained during the Second World War. They were tough and skilled fighters who would not hesitate to engage any police unit. We received an urgent radio message that one such raiding party was heading our way and we were requested to intercept them. It could not have come at a worse time. My one and only Land Rover was giving trouble! As a result I requested to borrow the District Commissioner's brand-new long-wheelbase model. Armed to the teeth, plus water and rations, we set off at top speed. Our route would take us over the Kerinyang River. From there we would proceed over rough bush country until we established contact with the raiders. It was during the dry season, so fording the river should not pose a major problem.

When we arrived at the riverbank the flow level was low and without difficulty I waded the thirty-odd yards across to the other bank and signalled for the Land Rover to come across. As the water had only reached just above my knees the driver would have no problems... or so I thought. As usual I had sent one askari upstream to ensure that we would not be hit by a flash flood.

Half way across the Land Rover keeled over to the driver's side and water started gushing in through the open window, then it stalled. As I waded back towards it I could see that it was keeling over even more!

We were miles from both base and the enemy and stuck in the middle of a river! What a 'pickle' to be in!

We had some pangas (machetes) on board, so I had half of our party cut down some slim trees to use as levers while the other half used the thin branches to weave into mats. I planned to place these mats under the wheels to prevent further subsidence, then to use the levers to raise the vehicle before placing more mats and large rocks on top of the originals to bring it onto an even keel. Finally, by using more mats, I hoped to extricate the vehicle from this very soft bed of sand. We all set to work. I made sure the man up-river stayed alert and said that he was to blow his whistle then run 'like the wind' to warn us of any approaching flash flood.

In just over an hour we had five mats and six levers ready. Working up to our necks in water, the levers were placed underneath the Land Rover onto the firmer sand with the ends resting on the mats. Now it was time to heave! The vehicle lifted just about three inches, but it was sufficient for me to be able to force our mats under the sunken offside wheels. We needed more mats! I was hoping and praying that we would not be hit by a flash flood. Little by little we continued to raise the vehicle. Everyone was sodden and despite the water, very hot. At long last it was on the level. As the radio was not water damaged I called up base to be informed that the raiders had been turned around and were being pursued by security forces towards the border. So, after several hours of hard work we could now try to reverse out of the river – if the Land Rover would start. It did! Using the mats, and again up to our necks in water, the driver, accompanied by much shouting to keep stopping as the mats were continually moved, slowly made his way onto dry land. It had taken just over four hours of non-stop work to extricate the District Commissioner's brand new Land Rover. Now dripping wet but very happy, we headed back to base.

Some weeks later I learned that three months before a three ton lorry had sunk in exactly the same place. It had been hit by a flash flood and was found some two miles downstream and an absolute wreck. Obviously we had been very lucky.

I continued to lead exploratory patrols into areas that perhaps had never seen the Kenya Police before. It was during one such patrol into a long deep valley that we encountered a large herd of cattle. This in itself was not unusual, but based on my Masai experience, I noticed that the markings (usually cuts into the ears) were not common. Unless they had been purchased, or obtained by 'bride price', it was highly likely that they were stolen. Questioning the two herdsmen produced conflicting stories. I decided to arrest them and drive the cattle back to base. We set off with the two prisoners and arranged for a follow-up party to take over the droving. It took over three days to get them to the boma. We now had twenty-two Boran cattle to look after and they had to be marked for identification should the two accused plead "not guilty". This would prove to be no easy task, but more of this later.

Via the District Commissioner's office we made it known that we had recovered suspected stolen cattle. The two accused were sent before the Court next morning, pleaded "not guilty" and were placed on remand. I sincerely hoped that we could trace some of the owners as I was merely acting on a 'hunch', which was partly supported by their conflicting stories.

I decided to mark each cow with paint. However, the cows had other ideas and each 'painting' involved galloping cows with galloping askaris in hot pursuit. It caused much merriment particularly when one of the men, who was holding onto a cow's tail, fell over and was towed along behind a large cow intent on escape! At long last every cow was marked, the herding and guarding being arranged by the local District Officer.

Nature was about to 'upset the apple cart'. What I had not realised was, that a cow's hide contains a certain amount of natural oil, so the paint started to rub off. This time we had learned by our past mistakes, so we constructed a small corral; the herd was driven inside and the 'paint job' was completed in under an hour.

We had the cows in safe custody for nearly two weeks before the first witness identified some of the cattle as his own. Careful questions were asked prior to exposing the stolen stock as I did not want to hand over cattle from one thief to another. Finally, after three weeks every cow had been identified and the two accused, having pleaded not guilty the day after their arrest, now changed their minds and were convicted of stock theft and sentenced to three years imprisonment. Following the hearing one old man came to thank me for recovering his cattle and said he wished to give me a bull as a present. I thanked him, but explained that as a Police Officer I could not accept gifts. Would I like a chicken? Again I explained that I was not allowed to accept anything.

"Bwana, you must have something. My cattle were stolen months ago and I am so pleased. You must have something."

Grazing in our special boma was one of his bulls. Around its neck was a typical African cow bell.

"Can I have the bell off your bull's neck?" His eyes glowed with pleasure. Running into the field he grabbed and hung onto the bull's tail until it stopped trying to run away. Using his knife, he cut the leather thong and, holding the bell aloft, came running back and handed it to me. It now hangs on a small hook in my hall. Each time I look at it, I picture this old man hanging onto the bull's tail, running down the field, and the pleasure in his eyes when he handed me his gift. The cow bell is just as he handed it to me, with the leather thong clearly showing the cut mark from his knife. It never fails to give me pleasure, particularly when I shake it from side to side and it emits that familiar sound so evocative of the Kenya that tourists never see.

We had really enjoyed this posting, but now it was time to move on. This time to a large town very close to the Uganda border where, several years before, I had been invited to an alfresco breakfast on the shores of Lake Victoria. Where we were going was at a much lower altitude, so I knew the days would be hot and frosty nights would soon become a distant memory.

14 My final posting

Having been living at close to eight thousand feet with its pleasant climate of sunny days and frosty nights, the prospect of the heat and humidity at what would prove to be our final posting caused us some misgivings, the main reason being our baby son and the effect it might have on him, plus the fact we were once again back into a mosquito infested area.

The Police Station was the second largest in Kenya and on arrival I was informed that I was to head the town's Crime Branch Section, but before commencing my duties I was given two days leave to settle into our new abode.

We were allocated the usual Government bungalow which had double French doors opening from the lounge onto the front garden. The interior was spacious and cool, thanks to the angled shades over the windows and the polished stone floor. At the entrance to the drive was a large flame tree that (we were to discover) housed a lizard about three feet long. The lizard was to become Judy's daily 'target'. It would often scamper down the tree onto the drive to sunbathe. Judy, with hackles raised, head lowered and eyes 'locked' onto the lizard, would move very, very slowly towards it until, when only a few yards away, she would rush at it, stopping in a cloud of dust, as yet again the lizard made good its escape!

The Lake frontage was within walking distance and the township had a reasonable shopping centre. Initially we found the heat during the day oppressive and the nights not much better; all we had for covering under the mosquito net was a bed sheet. On a positive note, at 6.30am the early mornings were cool, and as we sat in bed drinking our morning tea with sunshine flooding the bedroom with light, there was always a delicious smell of the earth mixed with the scent of frangipani coming through the security mesh of the open bedroom window.

The decor of the bungalow was a typical 'Public Works Department' colour scheme – cream and green. We decided that all the interior woodwork should be painted white and the walls changed to a soft pastel grey. However, our main objective was to settle in, make our new abode more like home and engage some servants, and in particular a cook. Decorating could follow later.

We had arrived without our superb cook, Steven. He did not like the tribe that lived in this new area and, despite our offer of increased salary, we very sadly parted company.

Africa works in mysterious ways. We did not broadcast our arrival, yet within hours we had a queue of Africans at the door offering their services as cooks, gardeners, house servants and nursemaids. Being a Police Officer who could be better placed than I to choose the servants? With my experience, naturally I could spot a villain 'a mile away'. We were not impressed with African nursemaids who, at that time, had very doubtful standards of hygiene, but someone to replace Steven was a No.1 priority. I studied each one carefully. Yes, he definitely looked shifty. The next one, I doubted if he had ever cooked and he did not have any references. No, too risky. The fifth one had excellent references and a very engaging personality. We agreed his monthly salary and terms... and we had a cook!

His first morning at work was not exactly what we had expected, but he had to settle in. For dinner that night my wife requested carrot soup (Steven's was always excellent), some grilled chops and some form of sweet. We sat down expectantly at 7.30pm. The 'soup' was duly delivered. I looked down at my soup plate which was filled with very hot water and floating in the middle was a large carrot!

"What is this supposed to be?"

"Carrot soup Effendi!" our beaming new cook replied.

This announcement was made in such a way as to indicate surprise that I could not recognise carrot soup when I saw it.

The rest of the meal was equally disastrous. The chops were so burned that the meat had shrunk to the size of a ten pence piece and as a result each semi-cremated bone had curled and was pointing towards the ceiling. The vegetables defied belief! He would have to go!

The following morning I commenced my duties at Police Head-quarters. It was standard practice for new arrivals to view the local 'rogues gallery' – a file containing photographs and information on all the 'regular offenders' in the area. I studied each picture in turn, trying to memorise each face and description. I came to page five. There staring back at me was my new cook! He had 'umpteen' charges for theft by servant! He must have shown me references stolen from a genuine cook. I drove home at speed! Having now discovered that I was a Police Officer he had also departed at speed, taking with him one of my wife's silk scarves and two pairs of my socks, never to be seen again.

So much for my ability to 'spot a bad un'.

Despite the heat, our new 'home' proved to be very pleasant. During the day my wife would take our infant son to the local Country Club swimming pool and on evenings when I was not on duty, with Judy 'riding shotgun' on the pushchair, we would walk beside the Lake to take advantage of the cool breeze coming off the water and admire another incredible sunset. The only 'downside' was that the house did not have a telephone, or even a telephone connected to the Police Station. This would often prove to be a problem. If I was 'on call' the only method of communication was to send a Police vehicle to collect me. Within a week or so, I became attuned to the noise of the approaching vehicle and I would normally be wide awake before Judy barked or someone banged on the door.

An unusual feature of our new posting was the presence of a large herd of Impala which roamed freely around the European quarter in and out of gardens, and during the rutting season it was possible to see and hear the males doing battle for control of the females. During this time they completely disregarded humans. It was a case of head down, charge at your opponent, lock horns and push! Then unlock horns and charge again!

Having found someone who had genuine references and could cook, we commenced with our redecorations. Being off duty, I was applying white paint to the bathroom door and being watched by our tiny son Michael who by now was at the crawling stage. I went to find the white spirit and I could not have been gone for more than a minute. When I returned Michael had the paint brush in his mouth with white paint running down his chin! I just about 'froze on the spot'. Thoughts of lead poisoning ran through my mind. I picked him up and held him upside down, at the same time calling to my wife to come quickly. Michael, due to his sudden inversion, was screaming his head off as his mother started to wipe out his mouth with a cloth soaked in cooking oil. I had arrived just in time to avert disaster. Following a rapid visit to the hospital he did not have any after effects. Thank goodness!

During our redecorations, behind the cooker in the kitchen, my wife discovered some tiny snakes – they were baby black mambas which are just about one of the most deadly snakes in Africa! Having eliminated this threat we began an intensive search for the mother, she had to be somewhere. We failed to find her and perhaps coming across her slaughtered brood in the garden, our 'home loving' snake decided to go elsewhere. Following this incident during daylight hours our son was never out of his mother's sight.

It was during the early part of this posting that I had a very strange experience. It was late afternoon and I was at the house of a colleague when I suddenly had the feeling that I must go home. It was so strong it could not be ignored. I made my apologies and left. I met my wife in our driveway holding our infant son; she was distraught. He was limp in her arms and only the whites of his eyes were showing. My blood 'froze in my veins'. We rushed him to hospital. His temperature was one hundred and five degrees and heading to one hundred and six. The hospital was staffed by nuns who were so calm, comforting and serene. As soon as we arrived they stripped him and commenced to tepid sponge him. Within ten minutes his temperature slowly began to fall. First to one hundred and five, then one hundred and four.

The doctor took me to one side.

"I must warn you that with such a high temperature your son could have suffered brain damage."

I cannot describe my feelings, but fear was most certainly one of them. We stayed beside his bed all night as the tepid sponging continued.

I must have dozed off and it was now dawn. My wife was slumped in a chair by Michael's cot fast asleep. I looked at our infant son. He was sitting up playing with one of his favourite toys. I could not believe it! I could not contain my pent up emotions, I just held his tiny hand and wept, thanking God for coming to his aid.

What made me feel that I had to go home that day? I cannot offer any explanation. I have never had a feeling like it before, or since.

The doctor later confirmed that Michael had made a complete recovery and had not been affected by his ordeal. Evidently, despite my wife's attention to hygiene, he had contracted one of the many viruses that abound in Africa. Very few people realise how dangerous Africa can be. Some years previously some friends had taken their infant son on holiday to the coast where he contracted a virus that blinded him for life. Like us they had taken every possible precaution.

Another feature at this posting was the likelihood of electrical storms of unusual ferocity. Every time we had a storm people were killed by lightning. Normally it was cyclists, but the worst case I ever had involved five people sheltering in a hut. During one of these storms a small tree just beside our French window was struck. There was as sizzling crashing sound, followed in a millisecond by an enormous explosion! Everything in the house that could rattle and shake did so; I even felt the actual structure move! Later we found that the tree had been split completely in two and was charred and shrivelled. On another occasion we witnessed a metal pylon situated opposite our bungalow being struck. Again, a blinding blue sizzling light combined with an enormous explosion! Until this point in time, even as a child, electrical storms had never concerned me. Now when these fierce storms were raging, I, like other sensible people, stayed under cover.

I found the morale of the Crime Branch staff to be below par. The main reason was that there was a lot of crime but very few arrests. The two major crimes were thefts of bicycles and shop breaking. We needed some successes. I have always been a believer in the following:
"If you want to achieve unusual results, then you have to apply unusual methods."
It was now time to put theory into practice.
The bicycle carries anything and everything in Kenya and was a No.1 target for thieves. The worst place for theft was at the African Hospital, where scores of people arrived every day. The thieves knew that anyone arriving by bicycle would be there for at least an hour, which gave them ample time to select their targets and make their getaway. Things were about to change. From the hospital I obtained on loan, some crutches, slings and large bandages; the walking sticks I obtained from other sources. I now briefed my new anti-crime team.
In Crime Branch we always wore plain clothes so it was not difficult to blend in with the locals. I briefed my new team to position themselves around the hospital disguised as injured people, using the

crutches, slings, etc. The crutches and sticks could be used to thrust into the wheels of the stolen bicycles and would assist them in making an arrest. In addition, each man would be supplied with a newspaper with a medium-sized hole cut into every page. At a distance, to the casual observer, the hole would not be noticed. However, through this hole they would be able to observe a very large area, and when turning the pages, as if killing time waiting to be seen by a doctor, it would add to their authenticity. I demonstrated this.

There was much hilarity when they commenced to try out their various disguises, plus experiencing just how much they could observe using the 'doctored' newspapers. From their reactions I could see that they were very keen to try out this new approach to bicycle thefts.

The next morning our 'cripples' took up their positions around the hospital. Within less than thirty minutes we had our first arrest. Having seen the owner park his bicycle, the thief removed it and set off in a leisurely manner. The next thing he was 'flying through the air' landing on the path with a heavy thump and whilst still dazed was being handcuffed. During that first day we had five arrests. Things were looking up! Africans have a great sense of humour and my new team were 'falling about' when describing the various arrests.

"Effendi, you should have seen the expression on his face! He went up into the air like this and landed like this!" The arrest was mimed, followed by more laughter.

However, with police work nothing is static, so when the thefts switched to another area, we had to change tactics.

The next item to be tackled was shop breaking, which was rife. Nearly every night one of the Asian shops was broken into and ransacked. I organised 'prowler patrols', often joining in myself. We wore plain clothes, soft shoes and stayed in the shadows, keeping 'our ears open'. Sound carries very easily at night, so we needed to keep stopping and listening. The patrols consisted of four or five men dressed in 'scruffy' clothes and armed with police nightsticks (a truncheon about eighteen inches long and ideal for attack or defence).

Another crime was breaking into locked cars, which occurred normally at night when vehicles were parked outside peoples' houses. No one was immune and several cars in our road had damaged doors due to the leverage caused by large screwdrivers. As a result, I devised a car alarm that was simplicity itself. It consisted of three thin brass bolts affixed to a small piece of wood some four and a half inches by two inches. One bolt was affixed to the top of the wooden oblong, and the other two bolts positioned about three inches below, set side by side and one inch apart. From the top bolt a bare copper wire was suspended between the two lower bolts and the lower end weighted. The wooden oblong was screwed (underneath the bonnet) onto the car's external bulkhead, in such a manner that it could be twisted from side to side, with the vehicle's horn being connected to the top brass bolt. By twisting the wooden oblong it was possible to position the bare copper wire very close to either of the lower brass bolts. By trial and error the setting could be so fine that the ground vibration of a passing vehicle could set off the alarm. A senior officer tested my second prototype and on the first night was alerted by an intruder who had merely tried the vehicle's door.

We also needed to improve our informer network, so by letting 'the girls' (prostitutes) know that we would pay good money for information that achieved an arrest, our activity had a major impact on crime. Within a few months our informer network became so effective that we knew when any 'bad hats' had arrived in town intent on shop breaking. On one occasion, acting on information received, we picked up two would-be shop-breakers who were so shocked to learn that we knew why they were in town, one pleaded guilty to intent and was jailed.

The key to any successful shop or house break-in is silence; essential if you are to stand any chance of carrying out the crime without being seen and walk away with the 'loot' undetected. The local villains' *modus operandi* was to use a carpenter's brace and bit (hand operated wood drill). Arriving late at night they would make a series of large inter-connecting holes around the lock/locks, remove the complete section, then enter the premises. What could be easier? Even a heavy safe presented very little problem; placed onto a mat, a safe could be moved across a shiny office floor to where it could be 'attacked', or even removed. However, very few of the better quality safes were ever opened. The main targets were shops selling materials. Stolen cloth was difficult to identify and there was always a ready market for it at a 'knockdown price'.

In order to make our activities more effective, at the Crime Branch office we had a map of the town on the wall. Each type of crime for which we were responsible to solve or eradicate, was denoted by a different coloured pin. In addition, we had a circular chart divided into twenty-four sections. If we could ascertain the approximate time each type of crime was committed, then a corresponding coloured pin was inserted into 'the twenty-four hour clock' chart. This way we could (hopefully) be in the right place at the right time. Also this information could be passed on to the Officer responsible for the Constables on beat duty and to the Dog Patrol Section. This pre-planning of our mainly nocturnal activities had a marked effect on reducing both house and shop break-ins.

The method of 'dressing up' (disguise) that had proved such a success in combating bicycle thefts I employed many times and the Crime Brach staff, as always, could hardly wait to become involved. One evening an automatic pistol plus two clips of ammunition was stolen from a locked car which was parked outside the local hotel. Now there is a very important supporting 'staff' that any Police Officer needs – good informers. The best sources as already stated (and based on my experience) were the local prostitutes, the reason being, that when a criminal had 'had a tickle' (a rewarding theft), he then wanted two things; drink and women, and in that order. The only information that I ever paid for was when we had an arrest and a subsequent recovery of stolen goods. For such a tip-off I always paid well, meeting the prostitute very late at night and always accompanied by a police-woman and carrying a police issue revolver, just in case I was being set up by criminals intent on eradicating the opposition.

By 10.00am next morning my phone rang. It was 'one of the girls'. She told me that the person holding the gun was a real 'bad hat' and had only recently been released from prison. Yes, she had seen the gun which was under the pillow on his bed. She gave me the address. Now the last thing we wanted was a 'shoot out', so I had to devise a method of gaining entry to the house without arousing the thief's suspicions.

I contacted the manager of the local Water Board and explained the reason for wanting to borrow one of the company vans, an 'ear trumpet' that they used for tracing leaks, some surveying poles and chain, plus some of their overalls…

The police party, suitably disguised and armed, drove to the road where the house was located. Having positioned a small group near the rear of the house with surveying poles and chain as 'cover', the main party proceeded to make a great show outside each house of listening to the ground with the 'trumpet', then knocking on each house door to ask if they had any leaks?

Curiosity is a very powerful thing. As the police party drew closer to the 'target' the villain was seen observing from his window. Soon it was his turn. Following the knock on the door by the 'Water Board' he opened the door, whereupon he was immediately 'flattened' and handcuffed. Sure enough, under his pillow was the automatic and two clips of ammunition.

I purchased a case of 'Tusker' beer for the 'hit team' to celebrate. Later that night, I met the 'lady' concerned and paid out a reasonable sum of money, perhaps more than she could earn in a week.

The next morning both the owner of the automatic and the thief were in Court, the latter being remanded pending sentence.

Often seen wandering around town was a bearded African, who always clutched a Bible and professed to be very religious and keen to ingratiate himself with the police. I had cause to speak to him several times and formed the opinion that he was 'too good to be true'. One night at about 1am a beat patrol surprised two shop breakers who were pursued but got away. However, one of the Constables recognised one of them as 'Holy Joe'. A 999 car was rushed to his address to find him in bed, apparently asleep. He stated that he had not been out that night. However, his shoes were beside his bed and on being checked were still warm inside! He was arrested and charged.

It was during this time that we had a Constable fresh from Police Training School posted to the Police Station. One night when on beat duty he had helped to chase and catch some thieves. The arrest had been secured with the assistance of one of our dog patrols. The Sergeant Major called at my office the following morning saying this new Constable wished to see me to lodge a complaint.

"What's it all about Sergeant Major."

"It's about the police dog Effendi, it grabbed him and not the thief."

The Constable duly visited my office and after giving a very smart salute stated his complaint.

"Effendi, when I saw the thieves running away I drew my truncheon and gave chase. However, the first person the police dog 'arrested' was me! Why can't police dogs be made to recognise a policeman in uniform?"

How was I to answer this one? The standard procedure was this: When the dog was released to secure an arrest, the dog handler should shout "Stand Still!" The reason for this is that the dog will tackle anyone running away. The procedure had been followed, but in his enthusiasm our new recruit had continued 'hot foot' after the criminal, only to be brought to an abrupt halt by the police dog hanging on to the rear of his Police greatcoat!

One day I arrived home for lunch and entered the lounge to switch on our portable radio to listen to the one o'clock news. It was missing! Neither my wife or the 'houseboy' had removed it. My wife had just returned to the house with Michael and Judy so I could only assume that someone had entered our home via the open French window and stolen the radio. After lunch I returned to the Police Station; there in the Crime Branch office was my missing radio! A Ugandan African had been spotted by two members of Crime Branch with the radio under his arm. He had been arrested as being in possession of suspected stolen property. When searched at the time of his arrest, tucked into his belt was a large knife! Thank goodness he had not been disturbed by my wife or our 'houseboy'.

The current Officer in Charge of the Police Station was posted to another area and I was promoted and replaced him. I was to discover that being in charge of a large multi-racial staff was my forte. Our total strength was listed as one hundred and thirty-two, however, our actual numbers (all ranks) when checked against the Duty Roster, was one hundred and twenty-seven. During this posting I was fortunate to have the support of two excellent No.2 i/c's. The first was Frank Cornwell, and when he went home on leave he was replaced by John Smith.

During my first week as O i/c we held the usual Friday morning parade. Only some twenty staff appeared. The following Friday we appeared with the Duty Roster and checked who was missing. This resulted in some forty members of staff being on a 'maktab' (charge) for skiving off duty. The excuses had to be heard to be believed. They ranged from wives being sick to, "I couldn't find my hat Effendi." There were very few genuine excuses and I imposed a standard fine of five shillings per offender. From then on the numbers on parade swelled and as always, the routine was the same, names checked against the Duty Roster.

Following the Friday morning parade, the first item on the agenda was the inspection of the police lines (quarters) and the latrines, followed by our fleet of vehicles, then finally the Police Station itself. Slackness of any kind was not tolerated, and within weeks there was a total change of atmosphere.

It was during this initial period that some Constables on night patrol had been found asleep, so they also appeared on 'maktab', were fined and issued with warnings. I briefed the beat NCOs to be very vigilant and to increase the rate of their checks on night duty staff. I now pondered how the whole beat system could be 'tightened up'?

This was my solution. In order to ensure that both the NCOs and night patrol staff were 'on their toes' I devised a method of issuing 'beat tags'. Each man going on night duty was issued with six small metal discs stamped with the number of his patrol area. On the charge office wall was a board with hooks and the beat numbers. As the NCOs checked their men, they would collect one of their tags. On returning to the Police Station the beat NCOs would place the collected tags onto the board. Therefore, at a glance, it was possible to see who, and how many times each Constable had been checked. In addition, with my own snap checks on the night patrol staff, we could quickly ascertain how many tags each man had and if this 'tied in' with the board. Initially some 'idle lumps' decided it was not for them and threw their tags away, stating they had 'lost' them. They were charged by their respective NCOs and appeared before me on 'maktab'. This resulted in more fines and warnings. Within three months of taking over I had three men dismissed from the force. In each instance they had received a nominal fine, followed by two more fines and recorded warnings. Not one of them said they wished to appeal against dismissal.

Morale is always eroded when 'skivers' are seen to 'get away with it' and no doubt scoff at those who do their job to the best of their ability. People often use the term 'discipline' and confuse it with being 'hard', or 'tough'. Constantly 'bawling people out' only achieves resentment. I have always found the following guideline the best option.

"Praise in public, discipline in private, do so with justice." Then you have discipline.

When conducting a 'maktab' and assuming the accused was found guilty, I normally asked them the following question:

"If you were the Officer in Charge of this Police Station and someone came before you charged with this offence, and having heard the Sergeant's evidence, how would you feel?"

The normal reply was "I'd be very cross Effendi."

"That is exactly how I feel. Now how would you deal with this person?"

Surprisingly, sometimes they would suggest a fine way in excess of what I had in mind.

Every Wednesday we held riot drill in full view of the 'locals'. Near the bus station was a favourite venue. I would request 'Traffic' to block off some road or other and the riot squad would appear in full 'regalia'. Steel helmets, riot shields and riot battens. At the rear would be the armed party and right at the rear the first aid party. These jobs were rotated every week in order to give everyone a wide experience of riot training. In order to add authenticity, a small number would be dressed in civilian clothes to throw stones and shout abuse. By this method the riot squad had to use their shields to protect themselves and continue to do so when ordered to advance on the 'crowd'.

In order to give the reader some idea of how the riot control system operates, think of a long column of fifty five men marching in pairs. At the head of every fifth pair is an NCO. At the rear of the column is the Riot Commander with a loud hailer, plus the armed party (three men with rifles) and first aid party. On the order "extend" each pair of five double to the left and right of their respective NCO. On the order "stand at ease" the shield is placed across the front of the body and the riot batten rested on the right shoulder. There are now five parallel lines of men spaced some ten yards apart, and at least thirty yards from the crowd. The Riot Commander now reads the 'Riot Act', telling the crowd to disperse. Failure to disperse leads to Action No.1 'tear gas'. If this fails to disperse the rioters, then use of the batten is employed. The Riot Squad must stay intact. Each wave of eleven men attack the crowd for no more than thirty seconds, holding their ground for the second wave to pass through their ranks and take over, and then the third wave etc, until the first wave are at the front again. This way the crowd is pushed slowly but surely back. If, and only if, life is under threat, then the Riot Commander can sanction the use of armed force. The crowd must be warned that if they persist live bullets will be used. Following a second warning, the Riot Commander directs his armed party to fire one round per man, to kill one specific identified rioter. If this fails the crowd are warned again and a second rioter shot. You will note that there is total control, no random shooting and the response by the riot squad is only escalated in a series of steps, and each escalation is only taken as a last resort. Only once did we ever have to call out the riot squad. At the sight of this disciplined body marching towards them, the crowd 'melted away' – no doubt due to our constant weekly exposure of the riot squad in 'action'.

Having just taken over I was in my office re-reading the previous O i/c's handing over notes. What intrigued me was a section under 'Action Required'. It stated that there was a European serving a long sentence in the local prison and to date all efforts to take his fingerprints had failed. This was a challenge that I could not resist! I 'phoned the Senior Prison Officer and told him of my intentions and arranged an appointment.

"You'll be wasting your time, many have tried and failed."

"Don't put your money on it, we will be arriving in force." I told my No.2 to find the four biggest and 'beefiest' men and to equip them with ratchet handcuffs and some cord. Within the bounds of the law I intended to obtain these elusive fingerprints!

We duly arrived at the prison and were shown into an interview room. I was expecting to hear sounds of an approaching struggle, but all was quiet. Just how big and strong would this man be? If everyone else had failed I realised that we were in for a rough time! My team were well briefed and we had even carried out a couple of 'dummy runs' with one of the team acting the part of the struggling prisoner. There was a knock at the door. Accompanied by an escort was a European male, grey haired, aged about sixty and no more that five feet six inches tall. This couldn't be him, there must be some mistake?

"Good afternoon Sir, I understand that you want to take my fingerprints?" He was smiling and held out his hands, palms uppermost. I looked at the fingertips – all the ridges were smooth!

"Well Sir, do you wish to proceed?" He stood there smiling.

"How many years have you been in here?"

"Four Sir, I was convicted for forgery and still have several years to go."

"So why have you done this to your finger tips, what's the point?"

"That's my secret Sir. Can I go now?"

After he had been led away, the Senior Prison Officer who had been present at the interview said "I told you that you would fail. Every day he spends hours just rubbing his finger tips on the stone walls." I had to admit that I had never seen this method used before.

"It is an offence to refuse to have your fingerprints taken."

"Yes, but he's not refusing, just making life difficult. Anyway, what would be the point?" I had to agree. It seemed a very odd thing to do. Had he been involved in some very serious crime, perhaps murder, and by daily eradicating the ridges on his fingers he would avoid detection?

We were never to discover the answer.

It is worth noting that it is impossible to completely eradicate the ridges on ones fingers. Even with our European forger, given time the ridges will always return. It was the first and only time that I encountered someone so determined to ensure that his fingerprints never appeared in police files. It also transpired that his finger tips were in the same condition at the time of his arrest. To this day, I cannot believe that this was done just because he was a forger.

An area of great activity within the township was the Bus Station. Do not have any mental pictures of smart buildings and sleek well maintained buses. It consisted of a large, dusty earthen square with equally dusty, battered, single-decker buses constantly arriving and leaving, crammed 'to the gunnels' with humanity, bags, large baskets containing live chickens, bicycles and every form of human impedimenta. And, it will come as no surprise, scores and scores of people sitting around waiting for their bus to arrive. On the edges of the square were sellers of various items and foodstuffs. During daylight hours it was always a frenetic and colourful scene.

The phone rang in my office; it was the duty Sergeant.

"Effendi, about one hundred people are about to commit suicide at the bus station."

This was something new, even within my experience! Jumping into one of our 999 cars we arrived at the scene within minutes. Forcing my way through the crowd of onlookers, I could see a large group of people all trying to throttle themselves and making the attendant throttling noises! What was going on? A witness who had been traced by the beat

Constable on duty there, reported that a young African boy had been selling 'sweetmeats' to the crowd. These are normally made from spiced beef or lamb (and look rather like a beefburger). However, a rumour had spread that the meat was pork. As many of the crowd belonged to a religion that believed to eat pork was a deadly sin, they had decided to kill themselves by strangulation – and all these people were affected! Where was the African boy? Evidently he had just managed to escape, otherwise they would have killed him!

Now, to be faced with a large group of people all intent on death is quite an awe-inspiring sight! However, I was aware that it was impossible by using the hands alone to commit self-strangulation because as soon as the person becomes unconscious they let go of their throat.

By now, just to add to the scene, some of the zealots were writhing on the ground and making the most hideous sounds. I sent the 999 car off to do two things: one, return with the local religious leader and two, try and find the boy.

The 'crew' soon returned with the 'leader' and I informed him that I needed his help to placate his people. He was by now aware of the problem and his reply was the last thing that I wanted to hear.

"It's a terrible sin to eat pig meat. If it's true, then yes, they must die!"

This was all I needed! Luckily the boy was found together with his supplier, who informed the 'leader' and his people that the 'sweet-meats' were made with lamb. This announcement was greeted with relief and much back slapping by the 'suicide squad', and still talking excitedly about their experience they dispersed.

Life as a Kenya Police Officer was never dull!

It was just before 8.00am and as I drove into the car park at the rear of the Police Station I saw an African roll underneath a parked Land Rover. What was going on? Within seconds Constables were dashing all over the place – it was an escape! Walking as quietly as possible I grabbed the man's ankles and pulled. Before he could roll over I applied finger pressure just behind one of his ears saying *"Usi jaribu ku toroka rafiki"* (Don't try to run away friend). I blew my whistle, help soon arrived and he was placed back into cells. The officer responsible for allowing the escape appeared before me on 'maktab' the following morning.

A very important function for anyone in charge of a Police Station was checking the Cell Register. Apart from weekends, every prisoner had to appear before the Court within twenty-four hours of being arrested. Failure to ensure this procedure was adhered to could result in the Police Officer being charged in Court with illegal detention. Into the Cell Register would be entered the name, sex, age, address, reason for arrest, date and time and if possible the case file number. It was a daily ritual that you never, ever failed to carry out.

One morning I saw a French-sounding name entered against an African male prisoner. He was charged with being a vagrant (no money, no visible means of support or employment). He had been found by the beat patrol sleeping 'rough'. About two weeks later I was checking the Cell Register again. There was the same name and the same charge again, but with a different case file number. I spoke to the Duty Sergeant.

"This man here (pointing to the register). Is it the same man who was in here about two weeks ago?"

"Ndiyo Effendi, he was found sleeping rough again and he hasn't any work or money."

"Bring him here and let me speak to him."

"He doesn't speak Kiswahili Effendi, we can't understand him."

The prisoner appeared and I greeted him in Kiswahili. To my surprise he replied in French! Recalling with difficulty my schoolboy French I managed to obtain his story. In the Congo there was anarchy and in order to avoid the bloodshed and chaos, he had come from there by lake steamer. On arrival at the port he had been 'mugged' and his money, watch and passport had been stolen. He had slept in shop doorways and some people had given him food. He was asleep when the policeman arrested him. I asked if he was a Catholic?

"Mais oui, je suis un Catholique."

The reason for my question was that I knew that every priest had a small fund to help Catholics in distress.

The local European 'Father' questioned the man in French, which was somewhat superior to my own. As a result, he parted with sufficient funds for a steamer ticket, food for the journey, plus a little pocket money. The next major problem was a passport. At this time the Congo was in chaos and only anarchy existed. *Simbas* (a terrorist group) were on the rampage, killing, raping, looting and burning. The chance of obtaining a passport was zero. I made out a letter on Police headed paper in English, with the expiry date in both French and English, 'giving him the right of passage' to the Congo. I then stamped it with our official seal and signed it. I handed him his ticket, letter and money. He thanked me over and over again. He was escorted to the steamer and I hope that he arrived home safely.

This was not the end of the story. Some weeks later I had a signal from the Immigration Department in Nairobi asking for the whereabouts of one Congolese illegal immigrant? I responded in writing setting out the facts and the action that I had taken, plus the fact that due to the situation in the Congo it was impossible to have obtained a passport. I received a lengthy reply which in summary stated, that whilst I had solved an insoluble problem, I was not to use my initiative in a similar manner in the future. I 'had been slapped on the wrist'.

At this stage of the Colony's history the indigenous population was starting to 'feel its feet' and politics were being thrust into everyone's face. This was to cause us many problems. To some, politics meant that for them, law and order didn't exist. One of the local political parties had a member killed in Nairobi by a rival faction. They let it be known that they were bringing the body home and it would be placed on display in the township's square. I visited their offices and spelled out the law, break it and they were under arrest. Their attitude was hostile and almost contemptuous. However, they realised I wasn't 'kidding'. The body was transported back into town, but buried in the normal manner.

On another occasion a local political figure, surrounded by his acolytes, was ranting and raving at the Duty Sergeant about someone's arrest. Hearing the noise I went into the Charge Office. He continued to rant and rave. I warned him that it was an offence to cause a disturbance in a Police Station, therefore, he could make his complaint in the normal manner. He gave me a sneering look and recommenced his tirade. I'd had enough.

"Sergeant this man is under arrest for causing a disturbance in a Police Station. Charge him and place him in cells."

"Ndiyo Effendi!"

"You can't do this to me, I'm in politics," our local political figure shouted, but his acolytes fled!

Later that day he was released on bail, appeared in Court next day with his lawyer and pleaded "not guilty." No doubt on advice from his lawyer, he later changed this plea and was fined.

Our next political situation was the arrival of Jomo Kenyatta, complete with his motorcade and bodyguards dressed in brown 'boiler suits' and armed with pick-axe handles. The cavalcade was stopped and the bodyguards disarmed by Inspector John Smith. It was important to let not just the politicians, but also the 'locals' know, that law and order still existed. That evening Jomo Kenyatta was booked into the local hotel. We received a call that things were getting out of hand. On our arrival it was obvious drink was the problem. Sitting quietly at one of the tables was Tom Mboya and at that time he was a leading Kenyan political figure. (Following Independence he was assassinated in Nairobi by political rivals). As there were (unarmed) 'brown boiler suits' on the stairway, I assumed that Jomo Kenyatta was upstairs in his room.

It was past closing time so I went up to the bar and said in a loud voice. "This bar is now closed!"

There was much muttering and judging by some of their looks they had unpleasant thoughts aimed in my direction. I waited until the bar shutters were secured and left. I arranged for a 999 car to frequently pass by the hotel. For the remainder of the night all was quiet.

It was now time to start thinking about home leave. Our son had been born after we returned from our last home leave and we were sure that his grandparents were dying to see their grandson. We discussed possible holiday plans and started to become excited at the thought of seeing our families again. Our departure date drew closer and closer.

One morning the Sergeant Major requested a personal interview. I wondered what could be the problem? He entered my office resplendent with his red sash across his chest, immaculate uniform and glistening boots. He saluted.

"Effendi, very soon you will be going home to England and perhaps when you return you will be posted a long way from here. In the 'lines' we have been having some discussion and we would like to invite you, your wife and tiny son to a farewell party. Will you come?"

I hadn't been expecting this!

"Sergeant Major, of course we will come and please thank everyone for this very kind invitation."

Some days later I received a written invitation and we went to the party. Constable Francis, who was a member of the Crime Branch team, was the 'master of ceremonies'. We were led to a large settee which was placed at one end of their bar/recreation room. The place was packed with all the off duty personnel, plus their wives and children. Francis made an announcement, first in English, then in Kiswahili.

"We will start with some dancing and games. Then we will have tea. Later we will have beer."

This last announcement was greeted with great enthusiasm!

It was obvious that they had gone to great trouble and had arranged for a series of African dances, each one performed by a different tribe. The first one commenced. A large board was carried in by four women. In the centre of the board was a 'bird' formed from white sheets. It was placed on the floor before us and the dancers sang and chanted as they circled the 'bird', calling to it in a native tongue that I did not recognise. As they did so, they threw corn onto the board just under the 'bird's' head. To my utter amazement the 'bird' started to peck at the corn. There was someone who must be very tiny under the sheet! Upon completion of the dance the girl under the sheet appeared to wild applause! Each dance was different, enjoyable and something that I had never seen before. During the last performance (before tea) I was invited to join in. I readily agreed and there was much clapping and laughter at my attempt to copy my female partner. I sat down to more wild applause! Francis made his next announcement.

"There has been a change to the programme. We will not be having tea, we will now be serving beer! Even more wild applause! My wife and I were handed pint bottles of 'Tusker' beer and our small son, now twenty-two months old, a bottle of 'Coca Cola'. The dancing now started in earnest! Everybody was on the floor and again I was approached by one of the wives to join in. Again it was a native dance and I did my best to follow the incredible pulsating rhythm and bodily contortions, which again caused much mirth and clapping. It was all very enjoyable.

When the party ended the Sergeant Major gave a speech, saying how they had enjoyed my leadership and they hoped I would return when my leave was over. I was deeply touched, not only by the party, but by these sincere words. I thanked them all for the party and for their support, saying "With the Kenya Police, irrespective of race or colour, we were all in the same tribe. We worked together, laughed together, and sometimes cried together." I wished them well for the future. This was greeted with prolonged applause, and before leaving I must have shaken everyone's hand, some twice.

It was time to go home.

The next morning Corporal Abikar who had been on duty during the party asked to see me. He handed me his farewell gift, a signed photograph of himself taken when he was stationed in the Northern Frontier District. I still have this photograph. It shows him wearing a kepi with his highly polished bandolier across his chest, and wearing an immaculate starched tunic. Wherever he is I wish him well.

All our personal effects had been crated and delivered to the Government Storage Depot in Nairobi. We were on our way home! The aircraft landed at Entebbe to take on more passengers and extra fuel. There was now a new aircraft on this route, the 'Britannia', which had four turbo-prop engines and was known as 'The Whispering Giant'. Evidently it was now possible to fly from Entebbe to England in 'one hop'.

Within the aircraft and sitting on the opposite side of the aisle was a Yorkshireman. He tapped me on the shoulder.

"Have you seen the amount of baggage we've taken on board? And the fuel. I bet we're overloaded."

I replied that I was sure the pilot knew what he was doing.

His constant comments were causing disquiet with some of the passengers. He was approached by a stewardess.

"Can I help you Sir?"

"I've just been saying to my friend here, we'll be lucky if we get off the ground with this load!"

She gave a sweet smile.

"I can assure you Sir that the Captain is very experienced and he will ensure that everything is in order before he consents to take off.

Despite this assurance he still continued his mutterings.

"It's all right for her, she has to say that, I'm telling you, this aircraft is overloaded."

With the cabin doors closed, and having taxied onto the runway, the engines were given full boost. As the aircraft started to accelerate he leaned across to me and shouted.

"They're giving it everything they've got! If I shout now and we haven't left the ground, we are straight into Lake Victoria!"

As expected the aircraft took off. He leaned across to me again.

"Bye, that was a close thing. I thought we were going right into the drink!"

On our arrival in London, as our new 'Vauxhall Victor' would not be available for another week, we hired a car and set off in a Northerly direction. As we were suffering from jet-lag after the long flight, at about 4.00pm we decided to stop for the night and came across a very pleasant hotel situated in its own grounds. We booked in and having been allocated a room on the second floor, we asked for someone to assist with our large amount of luggage. An old man who must have been close to sixty five appeared. He was no more than five feet six inches tall and I wondered if he could manage on his own? Being an old hotel there was no lift and we had a pile of luggage. He kept appearing at our door puffing and panting as yet another suitcase was brought into the room. At last he had finished. I gave him a handsome tip and he departed.

At this juncture, as the room seemed stuffy, I decided to open the large sash window to let in some air. As I did so, a complete pane of glass detached itself and I watched in horror as it plummeted to earth two floors below, striking the ground with a splintering crash! There was a pounding of feet outside our door. It was our aged porter puffing and panting wanting to know what had happened.

As another room was not available we stayed where we were. We both felt very tired and once again we settled down to obtain some rest before dinner, but where would our tiny son sleep? We needed a cot. I dialled reception. Yet again our aged porter appeared puffing and panting returning some minutes later with a cot. Somehow I felt that he would be overjoyed to see our departure!

Having arrived home and done the 'rounds' of the family I received a letter from Kenya Police Headquarters stating that Independence was about to take place. I had two options. One, to stay in England and receive a sum of money (spread over five years) for loss of career or two, return to Kenya. If I chose the second option it would have to be for a minimum period of two years and after this there was no guarantee of an extension.

It was a very difficult decision. I really enjoyed my job and the life in Kenya. Before we had left there had been lots of rumours regarding what might happen after Independence. Should I risk my wife and tiny son returning to a possible 'bloodbath'? Some of these rumours appeared in the British press saying anything could happen. With a heavy heart I chose the first option.

I now had to commence job hunting, daily reading the 'Situations Vacant' in the *Daily Telegraph* and the *Times*. One of my applications for a trainee manager resulted in an interview with a very well known high street store group. The first part of the interview took place at the local store. It was conducted by the manager and I was shown around the store and also behind the scenes, then asked to make comments regarding possible improvements. I must have 'made all the right noises' as I was later invited to attend a final interview at their head office in Manchester. This store was considered to be their 'flagship'.

It was now late Autumn and almost daily I was missing the Kenyan climate. The smell of the earth in the mornings, the brilliant blue sky, the large 'puff balls' of clouds, and last but not least, the life and the people that I had discarded for dull skies and a feeling of being 'trapped' within what was now an almost alien land.

In England I found the people very class conscious and often 'small minded'. The difference in attitude between most people in the UK and the average colonial was remarkable.

It was raining and as the train drew closer and closer to the city centre we passed mile after mile of dowdy, soot-blackened, back-to-back housing. At the station I took a taxi and as we proceeded we passed dull overpowering buildings, litter, people hunched against the rain and dressed in drab-coloured clothing. The thought crossed my mind... "I could never live like this. I would die of claustrophobia."

I now sat facing five men who were seated at a long table, each one dressed in a black jacket, grey striped trousers, immaculate white shirts and 'silver' ties. Five pairs of eyes surveyed me through five pairs of horn-rimmed spectacles. The interview began.

"Now Mr. Tompkins, we note that you are thirty-two years of age, somewhat older than we are accustomed to. If we engage you it will mean us 'pulling out all the stops', I'm sure that you understand our position."

I replied, "I do not view it in that light, this has to be a two-way thing. Basically, we are both making an investment. I must be able to offer your company something of value and your company must be in a position to do the same for me."

They glanced at each other; this was not the reply they had been expecting. The man in the centre now asked a question.

"Tell me, what do you think about Manchester?"

"I assume that you want the truth?"

"Yes of course."

"Based on my observations this morning, it is the filthiest place I have ever seen in my life."

They all glanced at each other. I intervened.

"You said that you wanted the truth."

My interviewer said, "Yes… yes, of course."

I was now questioned by one of his colleagues.

"Tell me, what do you know about merchandising?"

What a ridiculous question!

"With respect, I have been a Police Officer for ten years. You have my CV in front of you, which I assume you have read. Your question is rather like me asking you what you know about *Archbold's Criminal Pleadings*."

It will come as no surprise that I received a "no thank you" letter!

At this time the 'Crown Agents' were sending out circulars advising about vacancies within the marketplace, stating what types of employment had been secured, and finally: "There have been numerous reports from would-be employers that very often they are encountering a marked cavalier attitude in ex-colonial candidates."

I must admit that I found many British companies 'very stuffy' and they often gave the impression that I was almost standing before them with a begging bowl.

Some weeks later I was interviewed by, and joined, an American company. They told me that I was the oldest person (I was aged thirty-two) that they had ever engaged! But their attitude was entirely different. Everyone joining had to start 'at the bottom of the ladder', and "if you are any good, you'll make it."

On the first day with my new employer, my induction trainer, 'Chippy' McConnell-Wood, who must have been following some set of guidelines, said, "This is the most important job that you will ever do in your life."

I looked at him and said, "Chippy, you must be kidding!"

~ END ~

PHOTOGRAPHS

A typical young Masai Moran.

Masai Elder (note short-bladed spear).

A Masai husband and wife at a man yatta.

~ 293 ~

A married Kikuyu woman in typical attire.
(Note the slit ears and shaven head.)

Kikuyu elder with goatskin
cape and horn for tobacco.

A typical random patrol in the Masai Reserve.

Patrol Country.

Kenya Police Land Rover on patrol.

The Kedong Valley.

Mrs Stephens' farm in the Kedong Valley (see page 60).

Hand-drawn ferry on the way to Malindi (see page 49)

A member of the Police Mounted Section – the 'Kenya Cowboys' (see page 76).

The church built by Italian POWs in WW2 (see pages 36 & 58).

My tracker, Kipkoske (see page 65).

Our first home.

My wife and son enjoy the African sun.

Neil's Rolls Royce shooting brake (see page 147).

The author in highly impractical Morgan roadster (see page 146).

*Corporal Abikar presented me with this picture of himself – in the uniform of a
Kenya Police askari – as a leaving present (see page 288).*

Pauline at the Equator.